CONTEMPORARY AMERICAN POETRY:
A Checklist

Second Series, 1973-1983

by Lloyd Davis

The Scarecrow Press, Inc.
Metuchen, N.J., and London
1985

Library of Congress Cataloging in Publication Data

Davis, Lloyd M.
   Contemporary American poetry.

   1. American poetry--20th century--Bibliography.
I. Title.
Z1231.P7D38 1985   [PS323.5]   016.811'54   85-11815
ISBN 0-8108-1829-9

PREFACE

This addition to the first Contemporary American Poetry: A Checklist, which Robert Irwin and I compiled for Scarecrow Press (1975), follows the original purpose of presenting an accessible guide to poetry published by Americans in mid-twentieth century. The Second Series covers the period from 1973 through 1983 inclusively, and includes titles of books published by Americans born after 1900.

As with the first edition, I have eliminated publication by vanity presses, works of joint authorship, anthologies, translations, broadsides, postcards, poemcards, poemcomics, and very small publications of fewer than about ten pages. I have also eliminated compendiums of poems combined with other literary forms such as short stories, but works with illustrations have been included. Since most of the material found on audiotape recordings can also be traced to published books, I have not listed tapes.

As it was impossible to examine firsthand all of the more than 5,000 volumes listed herein, I apologize in advance for inevitable errors and omissions.

Among countless individuals who have given generously of their time and encouragement, I would like to single out the following for grateful acknowledgment: Elaine K. Ginsberg, former chairwoman of the West Virginia University English Department, who generously granted reassigned time from my teaching schedule to allow for the completion of this project; S. B. Gribble, friend, colleague, and Associate Dean of Library Services at West Virginia University, who helped to solve many problems, scholarly, technical, and human; Clifford Hamrick, Head Reference Librarian at West Virginia University, for his knowledge and for his kind and friendly help; John S. and Phyllis Morris, for invaluable editorial services far beyond the call of friendship; and, finally, Robert Irwin, friend and former collaborator, without whose enthusiasm and persistent good humor this checklist would be another unrealized idea.

Morgantown, W. Va.   L. D.

October 18, 1984

THE CHECKLIST

AAL, Kathryn Machan
1. The raccoon book. Ithaca, NY: McBooks, 1982

AARON, Howard
2. What the worms ignore, the birds are wild about. Waldron Island, WA: Jawbone, 1979

AARON, Jonathan
3. Second sight. New York: Harper & Row, 1982

ABBOTT, Keith
4. Red lettuce. Fremont, CA: The Fault, 1974
5. What you know with no name for it. Berkeley: Blue Wind, 1976
6. The book of Rimbaud. St. Paul: New Rivers, 1977
7. Erase words. Berkeley: Blue Wind, 1977

ABBOTT, Lee K.
8. Cowboy. Cleveland: Bits, 1981

ABBOTT, Stephen
9. Transmuting gold. San Francisco: Androgyne, 1978
10. Stretching the agape bra. San Francisco: Androgyne, 1980

ABBOTT, Steve
11. Wrecked hearts. San Francisco: Dancing Rock, 1978

ABERG, W. M.
12. The lark and the emperor. Cleveland: Bits, 1980

ABSHER, Tom
13. Forms of praise. Columbus: Ohio University Press, 1981

ACCONCI, Vito
14. Kay Price and Stella Pajunas. New York: Out of London, 1977

ACHTENBERG, Anya
15. I know what the small girl knew. Minneapolis: Holy Cow, 1983

1

ACKER, Kathy
    16. Hello, I'm Erica Jong. New York: Contact II, 1981

ACKERMAN, Diane
    17. The Planets. New York: Morrow, 1976
    18. Wife of light. New York: Morrow, 1978
    19. Lady Faustus. New York: Morrow, 1983

ACKERSON, Duane
    20. Weathering. Reno, NV: West Coast Poetry Review, 1973
    21. I am an eagle. Eugene, OR: Dragonfly, 1974
    22. The lost refrigerator. Eugene, OR: Dragonfly, 1974
    23. The eggplant and other absurdities. Lewistown, ID: Confluence, 1978

ADAM, Helen
    24. Selected poems and ballads. New York: Helikon, 1974
    25. Ghosts and grinning shadows. Brooklyn: Hanging Loose, 1977
    26. Turn again to me, and other poems. New York: Kulchur Foundation, 1977
    27. Gone sailing. West Branch, IA: Toothpaste, 1980

ADAMO, Ralph
    28. Sadness at the private university. Fayetteville, AR: Lost Roads, 1977
    29. The end of the world. Fayetteville, AR: Lost Roads, 1979

ADAMS, Anna
    30. The ratio of one to a stone. New York: First East Coast Theatre, 1982

ADAMS, Betsy
    31. Face at the bottom of the world. Eau Claire, WI: Rhiannon, 1980

ADAMS, David
    32. Another place. Menemsha, MA: Stone Country, 1980

ADAMS, Glenda
    33. Lies and stories. New York: Inwood, 1976

ADCOCK, Betty
    34. Walking out. Baton Rouge: Louisiana State University Press, 1975
    35. Nettles. Baton Rouge: Louisiana State University Press, 1983

ADLER, Anthony
    36. Love poem: the vestments of the dance. Chicago: Ommation, 1978

ADLER, Carol
   37. Arioso. Milwaukee: Pentagram, 1975

ADOFF, Arnold
   38. Today we are brother and sister. New York: Lothrop,
      Lee & Shepard, 1981

AGEE, Jonis
   39. Houses. Carrboro, NC: Truck, 1976

AGOSTIN, Ann Lerew
   40. Aegis. Mount Vernon, NY: Peter Pauper, 1975

AGUERO, Kathleen
   41. Thirsty day. Cambridge, MA: Alice James, 1977

AGUILA, Pancho
   42. Dark smoke. San Francisco: Second Coming, 1977
   43. Clash. San Francisco: Poetry for the People, 1980

AHERN, Tom
   44. The sinister pinafore. Providence: Burning Deck, 1975
   45. Superbounce. Providence: Burning Deck, 1983

AI
   46. Cruelty. Boston: Houghton Mifflin, 1973
   47. Killing floor. Boston: Houghton Mifflin, 1979

AISENBERG, Nadya see ALSENBERG, Nadya
   48. [No entry]

AJAY, Stephen
   49. Abracadabra. New York: New Rivers, 1978

AKILLIAN, Michael
   50. The eating of names. New York: Ashod, 1983

AKIN, Katy
   51. Impassioned cows by moonlight. Brooklyn: Hanging
      Loose, 1974

ALAKOYE, Adesanya
   52. Tell me how willing slaves be. DeRidder, LA: Energy
      BlackSouth, 1976

ALBERT, Harvey
   53. Blue. Dennis, MA: Salt-Works, 1973
   54. Ox. Dennis, MA: Salt-Works, 1976
   55. Wits end. Dennis, MA: Salt-Works, 1976
   56. In (is) out. Dennis, MA: Salt-Works, 1978
   57. The is that is. Dennis, MA: Salt-Works, 1980

ALBERT, Sam
   58. As is. Green Harbor, MA: Wampeter, 1983

ALCOSSER, Sandra
  59. Every bone a prayer. Baltimore: Charles Street, 1982

ALDAN, Daisy
  60. Stones. New York: Folder, 1974
  61. Verses for the zodiac. New York: Folder, 1975
  62. Between high tides. New York: Folder, 1978

ALDRICH, Jonathan
  63. Croquet lover at the dinner table. Columbia: University
       of Missouri Press, 1977

ALDRIDGE, Richard
  64. The wild white rose. Ogunquit, ME: Crow Hill, 1974
  65. Red Pine, black ash. Thorndike, ME: Thorndike, 1980

ALENIER, Karren La Londe
  66. Wandering on the outside. Washington: Word Works,
       1975

ALESHIRE, Joan
  67. Cloud train. Lubbock: Texas Tech University Press,
       1982

ALEXANDER, Floyce
  68. Bottom falling out of the dream. Amherst, MA: Lynx
       House, 1976
  69. Red deer. Seattle: L'Epervier, 1982

ALGARÍN, Miguel
  70. Mongo affair. Houston: Arte Publico, 1978
  71. On call. Houston: Arte Publico, 1980
  72. Body bee calling from the 21st century. Houston: Arte
       Publico, 1982

ALICIA
  73. Psychic poetry from the French quarter. New Orleans:
       Persons, 1980

ALIESAN, Jody
  74. Soul claiming. Northampton, MA: Mulch, 1975
  75. As if it will matter. Seattle: Seal, 1978

ALLARDT, Linda
  76. The names of the survivors. Ithaca, NY: Ithaca House,
       1979
  77. Seeing for you. Pittsford, NY: State Street, 1981

ALLEN, Dick
  78. Regions with no proper names. New York: St. Martin's,
       1975

ALLEN, Gilbert
  79. In everything. Detroit: Lotus, 1982

ALLEN, Mark
80. Seeds to the wind. Berkeley: Whatever, 1979

ALLEN, Michael
81. Offerings. Medina, OH: Jump River, 1980

ALLEN, Paula Gunn
82. The blind lion. Berkeley: Thorp Springs, 1974
83. Coyote's daylight trip. Albuquerque: La Confluencia,
     1978
84. A cannon between my knees. New York: Strawberry,
     1981
85. Star child. Marvin, SD: Blue Cloud Quarterly, 1981

ALLEN, Robert
86. Blues & ballads. Ithaca, NY: Ithaca House, 1974

ALLGOOD, Steve
87. Dis/courses. Laurinburg, NC: St. Andrews, 1979

ALLISON, Dorothy
88. The women who hate me. Brooklyn: Long Haul, 1983

ALLMAN, John
89. Walking four ways in the wind. Princeton, NJ: Princeton
     University Press, 1979

ALLSCHWANG, David
90. From a serpent's scroll. Milwaukee: Peacock, 1975

ALMON, Bert
91. Taking possession. San Luis Obispo, CA: Solo, 1976
92. Poems for the nuclear family. Los Cerrillos, NM: San
     Marcos, 1979
93. Blue sunrise. Saskatoon, SK: Thistledown, 1980

ALOFF, Mindy
94. Night lights. Portland: Prescot Street, 1979

ALON, Susan
95. Bells & clappers. Clinton, CT: Ashford, 1978

ALONSO, Ricardo
96. Cimarron. Middletown, CT: Wesleyan University Press,
     1979

ALPAR, Murat
97. Memet. Willimantic, CT: Curbstone, 1980

ALPERT, Michael
98. Die Winterreise. Dennis, MA: Salt-Works, 1976
99. Darkwood. Orono, ME: Puckerbrush, 1982

ALSENBERG, Nadya
100. Invincible summer. Mason, TX: Timberline, 1980

ALSPAUGH, John
101. Everything dark is a doorway. Richmond, VA: Palimpsest, 1980

ALTA
102. I am not a practicing angel. Trumansburg, NY: Crossing, 1975
103. Momma. New York: Times Change, 1975
104. Theme & variations. Berkeley: Aldebaran, 1975
105. Letters to women. Berkeley: Shameless Hussy, 1976

ALTREUTER, Gregory
106. The death collection. Ann Arbor, MI: Neither-Nor, 1982

ALURISTA
107. Timespace Huracan. San Diego: Maize, 1976
108. A'nque. San Diego: Maize, 1979
109. Spik in glyph? Houston: Arte Publico, 1981
110. Return; poems collected and new. Ypsilanti, MI: Bilingual, 1982

AMEZQUITA, Richard Mario
111. Eating stones. Springfield, IL: Sangamon, 1977

AMMONS, A. R.
112. Sphere: the form of a motion. New York: Norton, 1974
113. Diversification. New York: Norton, 1975
114. Highgate Road. Ithaca, NY: Inkling, 1977
115. The selected poems, 1951-1977. New York: Norton, 1977
116. The snow poems. New York: Norton, 1977
117. Six-piece suite. Ithaca, NY: Palaemon, 1979
118. Selected longer poems. New York: Norton, 1980
119. A coast of trees. New York: Norton, 1981
120. Worldly hopes. New York: Norton, 1982
121. Lake effect country. New York: Norton, 1983

AMOROSI, Ray
122. A generous wall. Amherst, MA: Lynx House, 1976
123. Flim Flam. Amherst, MS: Lynx House, 1980

ANANIA, Michael
124. Set/sorts. Chicago: Wine, 1974
125. Riversongs. Urbana: University of Illinois Press, 1978

ANBIAN, Robert
126. Bohemian airs & other kefs. San Francisco: Night Horn, 1982

ANDERSDATTER, Karla Margaret
127. I don't know whether to laugh or cry 'cause I lost the
     map to where I was going. San Francisco: Second
     Coming, 1978

ANDERSON, Barbara
128. Ordinary days. Bisbee, AZ: Porch, 1981

ANDERSON, David
129. The spade in the sensorium. Bolinas, CA: Big Sky,
     1974

ANDERSON, Doug
130. The one real poem is life. New York: Braziller, 1973

ANDERSON, Elbridge
131. We come around the years. Hollywood, CA: Pygmalion,
     1975

ANDERSON, Gene
132. Coyote space. Whitehorn, CA: Holmgangers, 1983

ANDERSON, Jack
133. City joys. Brooklyn: Release, 1975
134. Toward the liberation of the left hand. Pittsburgh:
     University of Pittsburgh Press, 1977
135. The clouds of that country. Brooklyn: Hanging Loose,
     1982
136. Selected poems. Brooklyn: Release, 1983

ANDERSON, Jon
137. Counting the days. Lisbon, IA: Penumbra, 1974
138. In sepia. Pittsburgh: University of Pittsburgh Press,
     1974
139. The Milky Way: poems, 1967-1982. New York: Ecco,
     1983

ANDERSON, Maggie
140. The great horned owl. Riderwood, MD: Icarus, 1979
141. Years that answer. New York: Harper & Row, 1980

ANDERSON, Mark
142. The broken boat. Ithaca, NY: Ithaca House, 1978

ANDERSON, Teresa
143. Speaking in sign. Minneapolis: West End, 1979

ANDRÉ, Michael
144. My regrets. Milwaukee: Pentagram, 1977
145. Studying the ground for holes. Brooklyn: Release, 1978
146. Letters home. Flushing, NY: Cross Country, 1979

ANDREJCAK, Dawna Maydak
147. Because the death of a rose. Miami: Earthwise, 1983

ANDREWS, Bruce
148. A cappella. Lansing, MI: Ghost Dance, 1973
149. Corona. Providence: Burning Deck, 1973
150. Edge. Washington: Some of Us, 1973
151. Vowels. New York: O Press, 1976
152. Film noir. Providence: Burning Deck, 1978
153. Praxis. Berkeley: Tuumba, 1978
154. Sonnets (memento mori). Berkeley: This, 1980
155. Excommunicate. Elmwood, CT: Potes & Poets, 1982

ANDREWS, Jenne
156. In pursuit of the family. St. Peter, MN: Minnesota
      Writers', 1974
157. Reunion. Amherst, MA: Lynx House, 1983

ANDREWS, Margaret
158. Defying gravity. Manchester, MA: Cricket, 1977

ANGELL, Barbara
159. Games and puzzles. Cleveland: Cleveland State Univer-
      sity Poetry Center, 1978

ANGELOU, Maya
160. Oh pray my wings are gonna fit me well. New York:
      Random House, 1975

ANGLESLEY, Zoe
161. Something more than force: poems for Guatemala, 1971-
      1982. Easthampton, MA: Adastra, 1983

ANGLUND, Joan Walsh
162. Goodbye, yesterday. New York: Atheneum, 1974
163. Almost a rainbow. New York: Random House, 1980
164. The circle of the spirit. New York: Random House,
      1983

ANSON, Joan
165. Before the trees turn gray. Belfast, ME: Wings, 1981

ANTHONY, George
166. The road to Deadman Cove. Columbia, MO: Open
      Places, 1978

ANTIN, David
167. After the war (a long novel with few words). Los
      Angeles: Black Sparrow, 1973
168. Talking at the boundaries. New York: New Directions,
      1976
169. Who's listening out there. College Park, MD: Sun &
      Moon, 1979

ANTLER
170. Factory. San Francisco: City Lights, 1980

APLON, Roger
171. Stiletto. San Francisco: Dryad, 1976
172. By dawn's early light at 120 miles per hour. San Fran-
      cisco: Dryad, 1983

APPEL, Allan
173. New listings. New York: Inwood, 1974
174. Not so much love of flowers. West Branch, IA: Tooth-
      paste, 1975

APPLEMAN, Philip
175. Open doorways. New York: Norton, 1976

APPLETON, Sarah
176. Ladder of the world's joy. Garden City, NY: Double-
      day, 1977

APPLEWHITE, James
177. Statues of the grass. Athens: University of Georgia
      Press, 1975
178. Following gravity. Charlottesville: University Press of
      Virginia, 1980
179. Foreseeing the journey. Baton Rouge: Louisiana State
      University Press, 1983

APRILL, Arnold
180. More never again. Chicago: Ommation, 1976

ARENAS, Rosa Maria
181. She said yes. Highland Park, MI: Fallen Angel, 1981

ARGIROFF, Louis
182. Seed of milkweed, spun of steel. Belfast, ME: Wings,
      1981

ARGUELLES, Ivan
183. Captive of the vision of paradise. Brooklyn: Downtown
      Poets, 1978

ARKIN, Rose G.
184. Journey into awareness. Mount Vernon, NY: Peter
      Pauper, 1976

ARMANTROUT, Rae
185. Extremities. Berkeley: The Figures, 1978
186. The invention of hunger. Berkeley: Tuumba, 1979

ARNETT, Carroll
187. Come. New Rochelle, NY: Elizabeth, 1973
188. Tsalagi. New Rochelle, NY: Elizabeth, 1976

ARNOLD, Bob
189. Thread. Markesan, WI: Pentagram, 1980

ARNOLD, Lois
190. Time, pieces. Milwaukee: Peacock, 1974

ARNOTT, Ann Louise
191. From one to another. Corte Madera, CA: Anthelion, 1976

ASHBERY, John
192. Self-portrait in a convex mirror. New York: Viking, 1975
193. The Vermont notebook. Los Angeles: Black Sparrow, 1975
194. The double dream of spring. New York: Ecco, 1976
195. Houseboat days. New York: Viking, 1977
196. Some trees. New York: Ecco, 1978
197. As we know. New York: Viking, 1979
198. Shadow train. New York: Viking, 1981

ASHLEY, Franklin
199. Hard shadows. Davenport, WA: Peaceweed, 1975

ASTOR, Susan
200. Dame. Athens: University of Georgia Press, 1980

ATCHITY, Kenneth John
201. Sleeping with an elephant. St. Petersburg, FL: Valkyrie, 1978

ATKINS, Russell
202. Here in the. Cleveland: Cleveland State University Poetry Center, 1976

ATNARKO, Susan
203. Mountain talk. Milwaukee: Thunder, 1979

AUBERT, Alvin
204. Feeling through. Greenfield Center, NY: Greenfield Review, 1975

AUER, Eric
205. Splinters of the light. University Center, MI: Green River, 1977

AUGUSTINE, Jane
206. Lit by the Earth's dark blood. Mt. Horeb, WI: Perishable, 1977

AUSTER, Paul
207. Wall writing. Berkeley: The Figures, 1976
208. Facing the music. Barrytown, NY: Station Hill, 1980
209. White spaces. Barrytown, NY: Station Hill, 1980

11   Axelrod

AXELROD, Alan
210. Conclusions from memory. Chicago: Ommation, 1976
211. Records of a chance meeting. Chicago: Ad Hoc, 1977

AXELROD, David B.
212. Myths, dreams and dances. Northampton, MA: Despa,
      1974
213. A dream of feet. Merrick, NY: Cross-Cultural Com-
      munications, 1976

AXINN, Donald Everett
214. Sliding down the wind. Chicago: Swallow, 1977
215. The hawk's dream and other poems. New York: Grove,
      1982

AXLEY, Jim
216. Oranges and sweet red wines. Santa Fe, NM: Lightning
      Tree, 1979

BAATZ, Ronald
217. All the days are. Tannersville, NY: Tideline, 1974

BACA, Jimmy Santiago
218. Immigrants in our land. Baton Rouge: Louisiana State
      University Press, 1979
219. [No entry]

BAGG, Robert
220. Scrawny sonnets. Urbana: University of Illinois Press,
      1973
221. Trompe l'ame. Urbana: University of Illinois Press,
      1973

BAILEY, Jane
222. Pomegranate. Missoula, MT: Black Stone, 1976
223. Still life. Pittsburgh: Slow Loris, 1976
224. Tuning. Pittsburgh: Slow Loris, 1978

BAILIE, Anne
225. In the soul's riptide. Midland Park, NJ: Chantry,
      1982

BAILIN, George
226. Collapsing spaces. Menemsha, MA: Stone Country,
      1981

BAKER, David
227. Laws of the land. Boise, ID: Ahsahta, 1981

BAKER, Donald W.
   228. Formal application: selected poems, 1960-1980. Dale-
         ville, IN: Barnwood, 1982

BAKER, Houston A.
   229. No matter where you travel, you still be black. Detroit:
         Lotus, 1979
   230. Spirit run. Detroit: Lotus, 1981

BAKKEN, Dick
   231. Here I am. Laurinburg, NC: St. Andrews, 1979

BALABAN, John
   232. After our war. Pittsburgh: University of Pittsburgh
         Press, 1974
   233. Blue Mountain. Greensboro, NC: Unicorn, 1982

BALAKIAN, Peter
   234. Father Fisheye. New York: Sheep Meadow, 1979
   235. Sad days of light. New York: Sheep Meadow, 1983

BALAZ, Joseph P.
   236. After the drought. Honolulu: Topgallant, 1983

BALDWIN, Deirdra
   237. Gathering time. Washington: Washington Writers', 1975
   238. The emerging detail. Washington: Word Works, 1977
   239. Totemic. Providence: Burning Deck, 1983

BALDWIN, Neil
   240. The bared and bended arm. Dennis, MA: Salt-Works,
         1976
   241. Seasons. Dennis, MA: Salt-Works, 1976
   242. On the trail of messages. Grenada, MS: Salt-Works,
         1978

BALDWIN, Petie W.
   243. Winds of imagination. Visalia, CA: Creative Ventures,
         1976

BALL, David
   244. Praise of Crazy. Providence: Diana's Bimonthly, 1974
   245. The garbage poems. Providence: Burning Deck, 1976

BALLARD, Nancer
   246. Dead reckoning. Boston: Good Gay Poets, 1980

BALLOWE, James
   247. The coal miners. Peoria, IL: Spoon River, 1979

BALOIAN, James C.
   248. The Ararat papers. New York: Ararat, 1979

BANGS, Carol Jane
    249. Irreconcilable differences. Lewiston, ID: Confluence,
          1979
    250. The bones of the Earth. New York: New Directions,
          1983

BANKS, C. Tillery
    251. Hello to me with love. New York: Morrow, 1980

BARAKA, Imamu Amiri
    252. Afrikan revolution. Newark, NJ: Jihad, 1973
    253. Hard facts. Newark, NJ: People's War, 1976
    254. AM/TRAK. New York: Phoenix Bookshop, 1979
    255. Selected poetry of Amiri Baraka. New York: Morrow,
          1979
    256. Reggae or not! New York: Contact II, 1981

BARANSKI, Johnny
    257. Pencil flowers: jail haiku. Whitehorn, CA: Holmgang-
          ers, 1983

BARBER, William
    258. Abyss. San Francisco: Manroot, 1975
    259. Getting over it. San Francisco: Hoddypoll, 1975

BARKER, David
    260. Inside the Big O. Long Beach, CA: Russ Haas, 1975
    261. Scenes from a marriage. Stockton, CA: Wormwood Re-
          view, 1979

BARKS, Coleman
    262. New Words. Austell, GA: Sweetwater, 1976

BARLOW, George
    263. Gabriel. Detroit: Broadside, 1974
    264. Gumbo. Garden City, NY: Doubleday, 1981

BARNARD, Mary
    265. Later. Portland: Prescott Street, 1975
    266. Collected poems. Portland: Breitenbush, 1979

BARNES, Dick
    267. A lake on the Earth. Santa Monica, CA: Momentum,
          1982

BARNES, Jane
    268. Extremes. Cambridge, MA: Blue Giant, 1981

BARNES, Jim
    269. The American book of the dead. Urbana: University
          of Illinois Press, 1982

BARNETT, Anthony
270. Poem about music. Providence: Burning Deck, 1974
271. A forest utilization family. Providence: Burning Deck, 1982

BARNSTONE, Willis
272. China poems. Columbia: University of Missouri Press, 1976
273. Stickball on 88th Street. Boulder: Colorado Quarterly, 1978
274. A snow salmon reached the Andes lake. Austin, TX: Curbstone, 1980

BARON, Mary
275. Letters for the New England dead. Boston: Godine, 1974
276. Wheat among bones. New York: Persea, 1979

BARR, James M.
277. The hanging at Silver Junction. New York: William-Frederick, 1978

BARTELS, Susan L.
278. Step carefully in night grass. Winston-Salem, NC: J. F. Blair, 1974

BARTH, R. L.
279. Forced-marching to the Styx: Vietnam War poems. Van Nuys, CA: Perivale, 1982

BARTLETT, Elizabeth
280. Memory is no stranger. Athens: Ohio University Press, 1981

BARTLETT, Tom
281. Dreams of a native son. Austin, TX: Pike, 1980

BARTMAN, Joeffrey
282. Habit blue. Cambridge, MA: Apple-wood, 1980

BARTON, David
283. Notes from the exile. New York: Elysian, 1983

BASILONE, Joe
283a. White noise, Elkins, WV: Cheat Mountain, 1982

BASS, Ellen
284. I'm not your laughing daughter. Amherst: University of Massachusetts Press, 1973
285. Haiti, August 13-28. Ventor, NJ: Bass, 1977
286. Of separateness and merging. Brookline, MA: Autumn, 1977
287. For earthly survival. Santa Cruz, CA: Moving Parts, 1980

BASS, Madeline Tiger
288. Keeping house in this forest. Madison, NJ: Journal of
     New Jersey Poets, 1977
289. Toward spring bank. Wescosville, PA: Damascus Road,
     1981

BASS, Tom
290. Fly free my love. Chicago: Makepeace, 1976

BASSEIN, Beth Ann
291. Why did I laugh tonight? Pueblo, CO: Pueblo Poetry
     Project, 1979

BASSETT, Lee
292. Gaughin and food. Story, WY: Dooryard, 1982

BATKI, John
293. Falling upwards. Cambridge, MA: Dolphin, 1976

BAXTER, Carolyn
294. Prison solitary, and other free government services.
     Greenfield Center, NY: Greenfield Review, 1979

BAXTER, Charles
295. The South Dakota guidebook. New York: New Rivers,
     1974

BAYES, Ronald H.
296. King of August. Laurinburg, NC: Curveship, 1975
297. Tokyo annex. Laurinburg, NC: St. Andrews, 1977
298. Fram. Atlanta: Pynyon, 1979

BEACH, Mary
299. The electric banana. Cherry Valley, NY: Cherry Valley,
     1975

BEALL, Jim
300. Hickey, the days. Washington: Word Works, 1980

BEASLEY, William Conger
301. Over Desoto's bones. Boise, ID: Ahsahta, 1979

BEAUSOLEIL, Beau
302. Witness. San Francisco: Panjandrum, 1975
303. Red light with blue sky. Palo Alto, CA: Matrix, 1980

BEAUSOLEIL, Laura
304. Autograph. San Francisco: Gallimaufry, 1975

BEAUVAIS, John H.
305. A flight of arrows. Cambridge, MA: Pitcairn, 1975

BECK, Art
306. The discovery of music. Ellensburg, WA: Vagabond,
      1977
307. Enlightenment. Fairfax, CA: Red Hill, 1977

BECK, Regina
308. Looking at the sun. New York: Telephone, 1974

BECKER, Robin
309. Backtalk. Cambridge, MA: Alice James, 1982

BEECHER, John
310. Collected poems, 1924-1974. New York: Macmillan,
      1974

BEELER, Janet N.
311. Dowry. Columbia: University of Missouri Press, 1978

BELDEN
312. Snake blossoms. Berkeley: Berkeley Poets', 1976

BELITT, Ben
313. The double witness: poems 1970-1976. Princeton, NJ:
      Princeton University Press, 1978

BELL, Carolyn
314. Delivery. Hermosa, SD: Lame Johnny, 1980

BELL, Marvin
315. Residue of song. New York: Atheneum, 1974
316. Stars which see, stars which do not see. New York:
      Atheneum, 1977
317. These green-going-to-yellow. New York: Atheneum,
      1981

BELLAMY, Joe David
318. Olympic gold medalist. Cedar Falls, IA: North Ameri-
      can Review, 1978

BENEDETTI, David
319. Nictitating membrane. Berkeley: The Figures, 1976

BENEDIKT, Michael
320. Night cries. Middletown, CT: Wesleyan University
      Press, 1976
321. The badminton at Great Barrington. Pittsburgh: Univer-
      sity of Pittsburgh Press, 1980

BENET, George
322. A place in Colusa. San Pedro, CA: Singlejack, 1977

BENNANI, B. M.
323. Splinters of bone. Greenfield Center, NY: Greenfield

Review, 1974
324. A bowl of sorrow.   Greenfield Center, NY: Greenfield
     Review, 1977

BENNETT, Bruce
325. The strange animal.   Pittsford, NY: State Street, 1981

BENNETT, John
326. Al la poems: Lansing, MI: Ghost Dance, 1974
327. Anarchistic murmurs from a high mountain valley.
     Ellensburg, WA: Vagabond, 1975
328. White screen. New York: New Rivers, 1976
329. Whiplash on the couch. Fallon, NV: Duck Down, 1977
330. Crazy girl on the bus. Ellensburg, WA: Vagabond,
     1979
331. Fire in the dust. Houghton, NY: Houghton College,
     1980

BENNETT, John M.
332. Works. New York: New Rivers, 1973
333. [No entry]

BENNETT, Mary V.
334. Imprints of a heart: poems. Detroit: Harlo, 1974

BENNETT, Paul
335. A strange affinity. Granville, OH: Orchard House,
     1975
336. The eye of reason. Granville, OH: Orchard House,
     1976

BENNETT, Susan Sanders
337. Still life. Cleveland: Cleveland State University Poetry
     Center, 1973

BENSEN, Robert
338. Near misses. Oneonta, NY: Nocturnal Canary, 1979

BENSON, Steve
339. As is. Berkeley: The Figures, 1978
340. The busses. Berkeley: Tuumba, 1981

BENSKO, John
341. Green soldiers. New Haven, CT: Yale University
     Press, 1981

BENTIVEGNA, Philip A.
342. September inventory. New Berlin, NY: Grandma's
     Attic, 1977

BENTLEY, Beth
343. Country of resemblances. Athens: Ohio University
     Press, 1976

BENTLEY, Lemuel Elihu
344. African in America. Chicago: DuSable Museum, 1976

BENTLEY, Nelson
345. Iron man of the Hoh. Port Townsend: WA: Copper
     Canyon, 1978

BENTLEY, Sean
346. Instances. Lewiston, ID: Confluence, 1979

BENTON, William
347. Eye la view. Santa Barbara: Capra, 1975

BERG, Stephen
348. Grief; poems and versions of poems. New York: Gross-
     man, 1975
349. With Akhmatova at the black gates. Urbana: University
     of Illinois Press, 1981

BERGAN, Brooke
350. Windowpane. Chicago: Wine, 1974
351. Distant topologies, poems, 1974-1976. Chicago: Wine,
     1976

BERGÉ, Carol
352. Rituals and gargoyles. Bowling Green, OH: Newedi,
     1976
353. The unexpected. Milwaukee: Membrane, 1976
354. A song, a chant. Albuquerque, NM: Amalgamated Sen-
     sitivity, 1978
355. Alba genesis. Woodstock, NY: Aesopus, 1979
356. Alba nemesis: the China poems. Albuquerque, NM:
     Amalgamated Sensitivity, 1979

BERGER, Suzanne E.
357. These rooms. Lincoln, MA: Penmaen, 1979

BERKSON, Bill
358. Recent visitors. New York: Angel Hair, 1973
359. Ants. Berkeley: Arif, 1974
360. Hymns of St. Bridget. New York: Adventures in Poetry,
     1974
361. 100 women. Chicago: Simon and Schuchat, 1974
362. Quiet world. San Francisco: Grape, 1974
363. Enigma Variations. Bolinas, CA: Big Sky, 1975
364. Blue is the hero: poems 1960-1975. Kensington, CA:
     L Publications, 1976
365. Parts of the body. Bolinas, CA: Tombouctou, 1979

BERKSON, Lee
366. Away from home. Peoria, IL: Spoon River, 1980

19   Berman

BERMAN, Mark
367. In winter, they. Bowling Green, OH: Armchair, 1974
368. Eyes. Bowling Green, OH: Brain Dream, 1975

BERNAYS, Doris Fleischman
369. Progression. Cambridge, MA: Beach Tree, 1977

BERNHEIMER, Alan
370. Cafe isotope. Berkeley: The Figures, 1980
371. State lounge. Berkeley: Tuumba, 1981

BERNSTEIN, Charles
371a. Asylums. New York: Asylum's, 1976
372. Parsing. New York: Asylum's, 1978
373. Shade. College Park, MD: Sun & Moon, 1978
374. Controlling interests. New York: Segue Foundation, 1980
375. Disfrutes. Elmwood, CT: Potes & Poets, 1981
376. Stigma. Barrytown, NY: Station Hill, 1981

BERNSTEIN, Joel
377. For the going. Chatham, NY: Omphalos, 1973

BERRIGAN, Daniel
378. Selected and new poems. Garden City, NY: Doubleday, 1973
379. Prison poems. Greensboro, NC: Unicorn, 1974

BERRIGAN, Sandy
380. Daily rites. New York: Telephone, 1974
381. Summer sleeper. New York: Telephone, 1981

BERRIGAN, Ted
382. A feeling for leaving. New York: Frontward, 1975
383. Red wagon. Chicago: Yellow, 1976
384. Tell it like it is. Chicago: Ommation, 1977
385. Nothing for you. New York: United Artists, 1978
386. Train ride. New York: Vehicle, 1978
387. So going around in circles; new and selected poems, 1958-1979. Berkeley: Blue Wind, 1980
388. The sonnets. New York: United Artists, 1982
389. The sonnets. New York: United Artists, 1983

BERRY, John Stevens
390. Darkness of snow. San Luis Obispo, CA: Solo, 1973

BERRY, Wendell
391. The country of marriage. New York: Harcourt, Brace, 1973
392. An Eastward look. Berkeley: Sand Dollar, 1974
393. Horses. Monterey, KY: Larkspur, 1975
394. Sayings & doings. Lexington, KY: Gnomon, 1975
395. To what listens. Crete, NE: Best Cellar, 1975

396. The Kentucky River. Owenton, KY: Larkspur, 1976
397. There is singing around me. Austin, TX: Cold Mountain, 1976
398. Clearing. New York: Harcourt Brace Jovanovich, 1977
399. Three memorial poems. Berkeley: Sand Dollar, 1977
400. A part. San Francisco: North Point, 1980
401. The wheel. San Francisco: North Point, 1982

BERRYMAN, John
402. Henry's fate & other poems. New York: Farrar, Straus and Giroux, 1977

BERSSENBRUGGE, Mei-mei
403. Summits move with the tide. Greenfield Center, NY: Greenfield Review, 1974
404. Random possession. Berkley: I. Reed, 1979
405. The heat bird. Providence: Burning Deck, 1983
406. Pack rat sieve. New York: Contact II, 1983

BERTAGNOLI, Leslie
407. Family photographs. Urbana, IL: Red Herring, 1979

BERTOLINO, James
408. Soft rock. Tacoma, WA: Charas, 1973
409. The gestures. Providence: Bonewhistle, 1975
410. Making space for our living. Port Townsend, WA: Copper Canyon, 1975
411. Terminal placebos. New York: New Rivers, 1975
412. New and selected poems. Pittsburgh: Carnegie-Mellon University Press, 1978
413. Are you tough enough for the eighties? St. Paul: New Rivers, 1980

BIALY, Harvey
414. The broken pot. Berkeley: Sand Dollar, 1975
415. Susanna Martin. Berkeley: Sand Dollar, 1975

BIDART, Frank
416. Golden state. New York: Braziller, 1973
417. The book of the body. New York: Farrar, Straus and Giroux, 1977
418. The sacrifice. New York: Random House, 1983

BIG EAGLE, Duane
419. Bidato: Ten Mile River poems. Berkeley: Workingman's, 1976

BIGGS, Margaret Key
420. Swampfire. Richford, VT: Samisdat, 1980
421. Sister to the sun. Miami: Earthwise, 1981
422. Magnolias and such. Port St. Joe, FL: Red Key, 1982
423. Petals from the woman flower. East Hampton, MA: Adastra, 1983

BISHOP, Elizabeth
424. Geography III. New York: Farrar, Straus and Giroux, 1976
425. The complete poems, 1927-1979. New York: Farrar, Straus, Giroux, 1983

BISSELL, Norman R.
426. Struggle for the dawn. Easthampton, MA: Adastra, 1982

BISSERT, Ellen Marie
427. The immaculate conception of the blessed virgin dyke. New York: Violet, 1976

BITA, Lili
428. Sacrifice, exile, and night. Birmingham, AL: Ragnarok, 1976

BIZZARO, Patrick
429. Violence. Syracuse, NY: Tamarack, 1979
430. The taste of rope. Olean, NY: Allegany Mountain, 1980

BLACK, Charles Lund
431. Owls bay in Babylon. Paradise, CA: Dustbooks, 1980

BLACK, Patsie
432. Tapestry, a finespun grace & mercy. Portland: Multnomah, 1982

BLACKBURN, Paul
433. The journals. Santa Barbara: Black Sparrow, 1975
434. Halfway down the coast. Northampton, MA: Mulch, 1975
435. Against the silences. New York: Permanent, 1980
436. The selection of heaven. Mt. Horeb, WI: Perishable, 1980

BLACKMUR, R. P.
437. From Jordan's delight. Norwood, PA: Norwood, 1975

BLAISDELL, Gus
438. Fractionally awake monad. Berkeley: Sand Dollar, 1974
439. Dented fenders. Bowling Green, OH: Tribal, 1976

BLAKE, Howard
440. The island self. Boston: Godine, 1973

BLAKELY, Henry
441. Windy place. Detroit: Broadside, 1974

BLASING, Randy
442. The particles. Providence: Copper Beech, 1983

BLAZEK, Douglas
443.   Inner marathons.   London, Ont.:   Killaly, 1973
444.   Lethal paper.   Okemos, MI: Stone, 1974
445.   I am a weapon.   Marshall, MN: Ox Head, 1975
446.   If you are going to be famous.   London: Second Aeon,
       1975
447.   Exercises in memorizing myself.   Berkeley: Two Win-
       dows, 1976
448.   Edible fire.   Milwaukee: Morgan, 1978

BLESSING, Randy
449.   For the birds.   Isla Vista, CA: Turkey, 1975
450.   Winter constellations.   Boise, ID: Ahsahta, 1977
451.   A closed book.   Seattle: University of Washington Press,
       1981

BLOOM, Clare
452.   Dreams and memories.   Santa Fe, NM: Sunstone,
       1976

BLOSSOM, Laurel
453.   Any minute.   Santa Cruz, CA: Greenhouse Review, 1979

BLUE CLOUD, Peter
454.   White corn sister.   New York: Strawberry, 1979

BLUM, Etta
455.   The space my body fills.   Santa Fe, NM: Sunstone,
       1981

BLUMENTHAL, Michael
456.   Sympathetic magic.   Huntington, NY: Water Mark, 1980

BLUMENTHAL, P. J.
457.   Slow train to Cincinnati.   San Francisco: Other Voices,
       1975

BLY, Robert
458.   Point Reyes poems.   San Francisco: Mudra, 1973
459.   Old man rubbing his eyes.   Greensboro, NC: Unicorn,
       1974
460.   The morning glory.   New York: Harper & Row, 1975
461.   Kabir, try to live to see this!   London: Sceptre, 1976
462.   The loon.   Marshall, MN: Ox Head, 1977
463.   This body is made of camphor and gopherwood.   New
       York: Harper & Row, 1977
464.   This tree will be here for a thousand years.   New York:
       Harper & Row, 1979
465.   What the fox agreed to do.   Athens, OH: Croissant,
       1979
466.   Finding an old ant mansion.   Knotting, Eng.:   Martin
       Booth, 1981

467. The man in the black coat turns. New York: Dial,
        1981
468. The traveler who repeats his cry. New York: Red
        Ozier, 1982
469. Four ramages. Daleville, IN: Barnwood, 1983

BOCKRIS, Victor
470. In America. Norwood, PA: Telegraph, 1973

BODE, Carl
471. Practical magic. Chicago: Swallow, 1981

BODE, Elroy
472. Home and other moments. El Paso, TX: Texas Western,
        1975

BOER, Charles
473. Varmit Q. Chicago: Swallow, 1976

BOGAR, Rosa
474. Black woman sorrow. Robbinsdale, MN: Guild, 1983

BOGIN, George
475. In a surf of strangers: poems. Orlando: University
        Presses of Florida, 1981

BOHANON, Mary
476. Strictly personal. Reseda, CA: Mojave, 1976

BOHM, Robert
477. Kali uyga. Amherst, MA: Lynx House, 1976

BONA, Mercy
478. Sleeping obsessions. Brooklyn: Release, 1976

BONAZZI, Robert
479. Living the borrowed life. New York: New Rivers, 1974

BOND, Alec
480. Poems for an only daughter. Peoria, IL: Spoon River,
        1982

BOND, Harold
481. The way it happens to you. New York: Ararat, 1979

BONESTEEL, Michael
482. Poems. Milwaukee: Morgan, 1974
483. Beyond mars. Madison, WI: Quest, 1975

BOOKER, Stephen Todd
484. Waves & license. Greenfield Center, NY: Greenfield
        Review, 1983

BOOTH, Martin
485.   Brevities.   New Rochelle, NY: Elizabeth,   1974

BOOTH, Philip
486.   Available light.   New York: Viking,   1976
487.   Before sleep.   New York: Viking,   1980

BORENSTEIN, Emily
488.   Finding my face.   Birmingham, AL: Thunder City, 1978
489.   Women chopping.   Mason, TX: Timberline, 1978
490.   Night of the broken glass: poems of the Holocaust.
       Mason, TX: Timberline, 1981

BORICH, Michael
491.   The Black Hawk songs.   Urbana: University of Illinois
       Press, 1975

BOSQUE, Gloria
492.   Strange meat; poems, 1968-1974.   Winters, CA: Konocti,
       1974

BOSS, Martha
493.   Christmas tree.   Dennis, MA: Salt-Works, 1975
494.   Winter contracts.   Dennis, MA: Salt-Works, 1975
495.   Building poems.   Dennis, MA: Salt-Works, 1976

BOTTOMS, David
496.   Jamming with the band at the VFW.   Austell, GA: Burnt
       Hickory, 1978
497.   Shooting rats at the Bibb County dump.   New York: Mor-
       row, 1980
498.   In a U-Haul north of Damascus.   New York: Morrow,
       1983

BOTTORFF, Leslie
499.   A thin volume of hate.   Santa Fe, NM: Sunstone, 1973

BOULDING, Kenneth E.
500.   Sonnets from the interior life and other autobiographical
       verse.   Boulder: Colorado Associated University
       Press, 1975

BOUND, Charles R.
501.   Incantations.   New York: Harcourt Brace Jovanovich,
       1978

BOURNS, Juanita
502.   Inward a jungle.   Houston: Bellerophon, 1981

BOWERS, Edgar
503.   Living together; new and selected poems.   Boston:
       Godine, 1973

504. Living together; new and selected poems. New York:
        Godine, 1973; Manchester, Eng.: Carcanet, 1977

BOWERS, Neal
505. The golf ball diver. St. Paul: New Rivers, 1983

BOWLES, Paul Frederic
506. Next to nothing. Santa Barbara: Black Sparrow, 1981

BOYD, Melba Joyce
507. Cat eyes and dead wood. Highland Park, MI: Fallen
        Angel, 1978

BOYER, Jill Witherspoon
508. Dream farmer. Detroit: Broadside, 1975

BOYLES, Denis
509. Maxine's flattery. Washington: Dryad, 1977

BOYLES, Richard
510. Severing the cause. Reseda, CA: Mojave Books, 1975

BRACKER, Jonathan
511. Duplicate keys. Berkeley: Thorp Springs, 1977

BRADBURY, Ray
512. When elephants last in the dooryard bloomed. New York:
        Random House, 1973
513. This attic where the meadow greens. Northridge, CA:
        Lord John, 1979
514. The haunted computer and the android pope. New York:
        Knopf, 1981

BRADLEY, Ardyth
515. Inside the bones is flesh. Ithaca, NY: Ithaca House,
        1978

BRADLEY, Carol W.
516. Empty your body in mine. San Francisco: Mother Hen,
        1974

BRAGG, Linda Brown
517. A love song to Black men. Detroit: Broadside, 1975

BRAHAM, Jeanne
518. One means of telling time. Tunnel, NY: Geryon, 1981
519. Primary sources: poems. Meadville, PA: Heatherstone,
        1981

BRAINARD, Joe
520. I remember Christmas. New York: Museum of Modern
        Art, 1973

521. More, I remember more. New York: Angel Hair, 1973
522. New work. Los Angeles: Black Sparrow, 1973
523. I remember. New York: Full Court, 1975

BRANDI, John
524. The Phoenix gas slam. Bolinas, CA: Nail, 1974
525. In a December Storm. Bowling Green, OH: Tribal, 1975
526. Looking for minerals. Cherry Valley, NY: Cherry Valley, 1975
527. Narrowgauge to Riobamba. Santa Barbara: Christopher's Books, 1975
528. Andean town circa 1980. Santa Fe, NM: Tooth of Time, 1978
529. Diary from Baja. Oakland, CA: Christopher's, 1978
530. Poems from four corners. Fort Kent, ME: Great Raven, 1978
531. Sky hourse. Santa Fe, NM: Tooth of Time, 1980
532. That crow that visited was flying backwards. Santa Fe, NM: Tooth of Time, 1982
533. Poems on the edge of day. Buffalo, NY: White Pine, 1983
534. Rite for the beautification of all beings. West Branch, IA: Toothpaste, 1983
535. That back road in. Berkeley: Wingbow, 1983
536. Zuleika's book. Santa Barbara: Doggerel, 1983

BRAUTIGAN, Richard
537. Loading mercury with a pitchfork. New York: Simon and Schuster, 1975
538. June 30th, June 30th. New York: Delacorte Press/Seymour Lawrence, 1978
539. The Tokyo-Montana express. New York: Targ, 1979

BRAVERMAN, Kate
540. Milk run. Santa Monica, CA: Momentum, 1977
541. Poems. New York: Harper, 1979
542. Lullaby for sinners. New York: Harper & Row, 1980

BRAXTON, Jodi
543. Sometimes I think of Maryland. Bronx, NY: Sunbury, 1976

BRECHT, Stefan
544. Poems. San Francisco: City Lights, 1978

BREEN, Nancy
545. Dancing the slack wire. Cincinnati: La Reina, 1983

BREMSER, Ray
546. Blowing mouth: the jazz poems, 1958-1970. Cherry Valley, NY: Cherry Valley, 1978

BRENNAN, Joseph Payne
547.   Edges of night.   Grand Rapids, MI: Pilot, 1973

BRICUTH, John
548.   The Heisenberg variations.   Athens: University of Geor-
       gia Press, 1976

BRIDWELL, Tom
549.   & collected conjunctions.   Dennis, MA: Salt-Works,
       1973
550.   Axis: parataxis.   Dennis, MA: Salt-Works, 1973
551.   Ciderman.   Dennis, MA: Salt-Works, 1973
552.   The interstate poem; south on 75.   Dennis, MA: Salt-
       Works, 1973
553.   Rafting Quivet Creek.   Dennis, MA: Salt-Works, 1976
554.   Humours run deep.   Grenada, MS: Salt-Works, 1979

BRIGHT, Susan
555.   Julia.   Houston, TX: Wing, 1977

BRISTOL, David
556.   Paradise & cash.   Washington: Washington Writers',
       1980

BRITT, Alan
557.   I suppose the darkness is ours.   Tampa: University of
       Tampa Press, 1978

BRIZENDENE, Nancy
558.   The braless express.   San Diego: Realities, 1977

BROCK, Van K.
559.   Weighing the penalties.   Austell, GA: Sweetwater, 1977.
560.   Spelunking & other poems.   Sarasota, FL: New Collage,
       1978
561.   The hard essential landscape.   Orlando: University
       Presses of Florida, 1979
562.   The window.   Winter Park, FL: Chase Avenue, 1981

BRODEY, Jim
563.   Blues of the Egyptian kings.   Bolinas, CA: Big Sky,
       1975
564.   Judyism.   New York: United Artists, 1980

BRODINE, Karen
565.   Slow juggling.   Berkeley: Berkeley Poets, 1975
566.   Workweek.   Berkeley: Kelsey Street, 1977
567.   Illegal assembly.   Brooklyn: Hanging Loose, 1980

BROMIGE, David
568.   Birds of the West.   Toronto: Coach House, 1973
569.   Spells & blessing.   Vancouver, BC: Talon, 1974
570.   Tight corners and what's around them.   Los Angeles:
       Black Sparrow, 1974

BRONK, William
571. Looking at it. Rushden, Eng.: Sceptre, 1973
572. Silence and metaphor. New Rochelle, NY: Elizabeth, 1975
573. The stance. Port Townsend, WA: Graywolf, 1975
574. Finding losses. New Rochelle, NY: Elizabeth, 1976
575. The meantime. New Rochelle, NY: Elizabeth, 1976
576. My father photographed with friends. New Rochelle, NY: Elizabeth, 1976
577. Twelve losses found. Lumb Bank, Eng.: Grosseteste, 1976
578. That beauty still. Providence: Burning Deck, 1978
579. The force of desire. New Rochelle, NY: Elizabeth, 1979
580. Life supports; new and collected poems. San Francisco: North Point, 1981

BROOK, Donna
581. Notes on space/time. Brooklyn: Hanging Loose, 1977

BROOKS, Gwendolyn
582. Beckonings. Detroit: Broadside, 1975
583. Primer for Blacks. Chicago: Black Position, 1980

BROUGHTON, Irv
584. The blessing of the fleet. Fayetteville, AR: Lost Roads, 1977

BROUGHTON, James
585. Going through customs. San Francisco: Arion, 1976
586. The water circle. San Francisco: Manroot, 1976
587. Erogeny. San Francisco: Manroot, 1977
588. Odes for odd occasions. San Francisco: Manroot, 1977
589. Song of the godbody. San Francisco: Manroot, 1978
590. Hymns to Hermes. San Francisco: Manroot, 1979

BROUGHTON, T. Alan
591. Adam's dream. La Crosse, WI: Juniper, 1975
592. In the face of descent. Pittsburgh: Carnegie-Mellon University Press, 1975
593. The others we are. La Crosse, WI: Juniper, 1979

BROUMAS, Olga
594. Beginning with O. New Haven, CT: Yale University Press, 1977
595. Soie sauvage. Port Townsend, WA: Copper Canyon, 1980
596. Pastoral jazz. Port Townsend, WA: Copper Canyon, 1983

BROWN, Rita Mae
597. Songs to a handsome woman. Oakland, CA: Diana, 1973

BROWN, Robert Edward
598. Gathering the light. Fairfax, CA: Red Hill, 1976

BROWN, Rosellen
599. Cora Fry. New York: Norton, 1977

BROWN, Spencer
600. Child's game, on a journey and other poems. New
     Rochelle, NY: Elizabeth, 1979

BROWN, Sterling A.
601. The last ride of Wild Bill. Detroit: Broadside, 1975
602. The collected poems. New York: Harper & Row, 1983

BROWNE, Michael Dennis
603. Fox. Duluth, MN: Knife River, 1974
604. Sun exercises. Loretto, MN: Red Studio, 1976
605. The sun fetcher. Pittsburgh: Carnegie-Mellon University
     Press, 1978

BROWNSTEIN, Michael
606. American tantrums. New York: Angel Hair, 1973
607. Strange days ahead. Calais, VT: Z, 1975

BRUCE, Debra
608. Dissolves. Providence: Burning Deck, 1977
609. Pure daughter. Fayetteville: University of Arkansas
     Press, 1983

BRUCE, Lennart
610. Subpoemas. San Francisco: Panjandrum, 1974
611. Exposure. Berkeley: Cloud Marauder, 1975
612. Subpoemas. San Francisco: Panjandrum, 1975

BRUCHAC, Joseph
613. The buffalo in the Syracuse zoo. Greenfield Center, NY:
     Greenfield Review, 1973
614. The last stop. Greenfield Center, NY: Greenfield Re-
     view, 1974
615. The Manabozho poems. Marvin, SD: Blue Cloud Quar-
     terly, 1974
616. Flow. Austin, TX: Cold Mountain, 1975
617. This earth is a drum. Austin, TX: Cold Mountain,
     1976
618. The good message of Handsome Lake. Greensboro, NC:
     Unicorn, 1977
619. Entering Onondaga. Austin, TX: Provision House, 1978

BRUNDAGE, Burr
620. No chance encounter. St. Petersburg, FL: Valkyrie,
     1974
621. The juniper palace. St. Petersburg, FL: Valkyrie, 1976

BRYAN, Sharon
   622. Salt air. Middleton, CT: Wesleyan University Press,
       1983

BRYAND, F. J. Jr.
   623. Songs from ragged streets. Greenfield Center, NY:
       Greenfield Review, 1974

BUCK, Peggy
   624. I'm divorced, are you listening, Lord? Valley Forge,
       PA: Judson, 1976

BUCKLEY, Christopher
   625. Looking up. Santa Cruz, CA: Greenhouse Review, 1977
   626. Last rites. Ithaca, NY: Ithaca House, 1980
   627. Blue hooks in weather. Santa Cruz, CA: Moving Parts,
       1983

BUDBILL, David
   628. The chain saw dance. Wolcott, VT: Crow's Mark,
       1977
   629. From down to the village. New York: Ark, 1981

BUELL, Frederick
   630. Full summer. Middletown, CT: Wesleyan University
       Press, 1979

BUGGS, George
   631. Music from the middle passage. St. Louis: Corner-
       stone, 1974

BUKOWSKI, Charles
   632. Burning in water, drowning in flame: selected poems
       1955-1973. Los Angeles: Black Sparrow, 1974
   633. Africa, Paris, Greece. Los Angeles: Black Sparrow,
       1975
   634. Scarlet. Santa Barbara: Black Sparrow, 1976
   635. Love is a dog from hell; poems, 1974-1977. Santa
       Barbara: Black Sparrow, 1977
   636. Maybe tomorrow. Santa Barbara: Black Sparrow, 1977
   637. Play the piano drunk like a percussion instrument until
       the fingers begin to bleed a bit. Santa Barbara:
       Black Sparrow, 1979
   638. Dangling in the tournefortia. Santa Barbara: Black Spar-
       row, 1981

BULLEN, David
   639. TV poems. Berkeley: Cloud Marauder, 1975

BULLIS, Jerald
   640. Taking up the serpent. Ithaca, NY: Ithaca House, 1973

641. Adorning the buckhorn helmet. Ithaca, NY: Ithaca
      House, 1976
642. Orion. Winston-Salem, NC: Jackpine, 1976

BULLOCK, Mark
643. Sensually yours. North Babylon, NY: J. Mark, 1974

BUNIN, Patricia Ann
644. Do you think we could have made it? and other love
      poems for the separated and divorced. Pasadena,
      CA: Newaves, 1977

BURKARD, Michael
645. In a white light. Fort Collins, CO: L'Epervier, 1977
646. None, river. Tucson, AZ: Ironwood, 1979
647. Ruby for grief. Pittsburgh: University of Pittsburgh
      Press, 1981

BURKE, Carol
648. Close quarters. Ithaca, NY: Ithaca House, 1975

BURLINGAME, Robert
649. Eighteen poems. Texas City, TX: College of the Main-
      land Press, 1976

BURNETT, Mary
650. The solera poems. Seattle: L'Epervier, 1980

BURNS, Ralph
651. US. Cleveland: Cleveland State Poetry Center, 1983

BURNS, William
652. Dark leverage. Hancock, MD: Trunk, 1977

BURNSHAW, Stanley
653. Mirages. Garden City, NY: Doubleday, 1977

BURROWAY, Janet
654. Material goods. Tallahassee: University Presses of
      Florida, 1980

BURROWS, E. G.
655. The crossings. Kalamazoo, MI: New Moon/Humble
      Hills, 1976
656. Kiva. Ithaca, NY: Ithaca House, 1976
657. On the road to Bailey's. Highland Park, MI: Fallen
      Angel, 1979

BURSK, Christopher
658. Standing watch. Boston: Houghton Mifflin, 1978
659. Making wings. Pittsford, NY: State Street, 1983
660. Place of residence. West Lafayette, IN: Sparrow, 1983

BURSTYN, Joan N.
    661. Song cycle. Woods Hole, MA: Woods Hole, 1976

BURWELL, Cora
    662. Of this and that. Reseda, CA: Mojave Books, 1975

BURWELL, Rex
    663. Anti-history. Missoula, MT: SmokeRoot, 1977

BUSH, Barney
    664. Petroglyphs. Greenfield Center, NY: Greenfield Review,
        1982

BUSH, Darrin S.
    665. Through the eyes of man. Reseda, CA: Mojave, 1976
    666. Thoughtful roads. Reseda, CA: Mojave, 1979

BUTCHER, Grace
    667. Before I go out on the road. Cleveland: Cleveland
        State University Poetry Center, 1979
    668. Rumors of ecstasy, rumors of death. Daleville, IN:
        Barnwood, 1981

BUTLER, Robert Olen
    669. The alleys of Eden. New York: Horizon, 1981

BUTSCHER, Edward
    670. Poems about silence. New York: Seabury, 1976

BUTTORFF, Leslie see BOTTORFF, Leslie
    671. [No entry]

BYRD, Bobby
    672. Here. Plainfield, VT: North Atlantic, 1975
    673. Pomegranates. Philadelphia: Tamarisk, 1982

BYRNE, Vincent
    674. Miracles & other poems. Old Greenwich, CT: Devin-
        Adair, 1979

CABRAL, Olga
    675. The darkness in my pockets. San Francisco: Gallimau-
        fry, 1976
    676. Occupied country. New York: New Rivers, 1976
    677. In the empire of ice and other poems. Cambridge, MA:
        West End, 1980

CAGE, John
    678. Themes & variations. Barrytown, NY: Station Hill,
        1982

CALDWELL, E. T.
    679. Evidence of light. Milwaukee: Peacock, 1975

CALDWELL, Justin
    680. The sleeping porch. Fayetteville, AR: Lost Roads,
        1979

CALLAWAY, Kathy
    681. Heart of the garfish. Pittsburgh: University of Pitts-
        burgh Press, 1982

CALLOW, Philip
    682. The bare wires. Middletown, CT: Wesleyan University
        Press, 1973

CAMP, James
    683. Carnal refreshment. Providence: Burning Deck, 1975

CAMPBELL, Libby Marsh
    684. Make me a falcon. Worcester, MA: Commonwealth,
        1974

CANN, John Allen
    685. Lemurian rhapsodies. Santa Barbara: Mudborn, 1976

CANNON, Marion
    686. Another light. Charlotte, NC: Red Clay, 1976
    687. Second wind. Charlotte, NC: Red Clay, 1977
    688. Collected poems. Charlotte, NC: Red Clay, 1980

CAPUTO, Thomas Head
    689. 50 selected poems 1970-1976. Berkeley: Thorp Springs,
        1977

CARDIFF, Gladys
    690. To frighten a storm. Port Townsend, WA: Copper
        Canyon, 1976

CARDONA-HINE, Alvaro
    691. Words on paper. Fairfax, CA: Red Hill, 1974

CAREY, John
    692. Hand to hand. Willimantic, CT: Curbstone, 1983

CAREY, Macdonald
    693. A day in the life. New York: Coward, McCann &
        Geoghegan, 1982

CAREY, Steve
    694. Gentle subsidy. Bolinas, CA: Big Sky, 1975

CARLILE, Henry
    695. Running lights. Port Townsend, WA: Dragon Gate, 1981

CARLSON, Douglas
    696. Climbing and diving, flying and swimming. Bigfork, MN:
          Northwoods, 1975
    697. Waiting to disappear. Olean, NY: Allegany Mountain,
          1978

CARNEY, Margaret
    698. Margaret of Cortona. Derry, PA: Rook, 1976
    699. Ours for the love. Derry, PA: Rook, 1976

CARPENTER, William
    700. The hours of morning. Charlottesville: University
          Press of Virginia, 1981

CARR, Dan
    701. Li Po's sandlewood boat. Ashulot, NH: Four Zoas
          Night House, 1975
    702. Living in fear. Ashulot, NH: Four Zoas Night House,
          1975
    703. Notice the star. Ashulot, NH: Four Zoas Night House,
          1976
    704. Antedeluvian dream songs. Charleston, MA: Four Zoas,
          1978
    705. The ennead of Set-Heru. Ashulot, NH: Four Zoas Night
          House, 1983

CARR, Harriett
    706. Cape Canaveral cape of storms and wild cane fields. St.
          Petersburg, FL: Valkyrie, 1974

CARR, Pat
    707. The women in the mirror. Iowa City: University of
          Iowa Press, 1977

CARRIER, Constance
    708. The angled road. Chicago: Swallow, 1973

CARRIER, Warren
    709. Leave your sugar for the cold morning. Laurinburg, NC:
          St. Andrews, 1977

CARRIGAN, Andrew G.
    710. To read to read: new & selected poems. Ann Arbor,
          MI: Crowfoot, 1981

CARROLL, Jim
    711. Living at the movies. New York: Goliard/Grossman,
          1973

CARROLL, Paul
    712. New and selected poems. Chicago: Yellow, 1978

CARRUTH, Hayden
713. From snow and rock, from chaos. New York: New
        Directions, 1973
714. Dark world. Santa Cruz, CA: Kayak, 1974
715. The Bloomingdale papers. Athens: University of Georgia
        Press, 1975
716. Loneliness: an outburst of hexasyllables. West Burke,
        VT: Janus, 1976
717. Aura. West Burke, VT: Janus, 1977
718. Brothers, I loved you all. New York: Sheep Meadow,
        1978
719. The mythology of dark and light. Syracuse, NY: Tama-
        rack, 1982
720. The sleeping beauty. New York: Harper & Row, 1982
721. If you call this cry a song. Woodstock, VT: Country-
        man, 1983

CARTER, Jared
722. Early warning. Daleville, IN: Barnwood, 1979
723. Work, for the night is coming. New York: Macmillan,
        1981

CARTER, Jefferson
724. Taking chances, taking chances, taking chances. Tucson,
        AZ: Desert First Works, 1976

CARVER, Raymond
725. At night the salmon move. Santa Barbara: Capra, 1976

CASSELLS, Cyrus
726. The mud actor. New York: Holt, Rinehart and Winston,
        1982

CASSITY, Turner
727. Steeplejacks in Babel. Brookline, MA: Godine, 1973
728. Yellow for peril, black for beautiful. New York: Bra-
        ziller, 1975
729. The defense of the Sugar Islands. Los Angeles: Sympo-
        sium, 1979

CASTRO, Michael
730. Ghost hiways & other homes. St. Louis: Cornerstone,
        1976

CAVALIERI, Grace
731. Why I cannot take a lover. Washington: Washington
        Writers', 1975
732. Swan research. Washington: Word Works, 1980
733. Creature comforts. Washington: Word Works, 1983

CAVANAUGH, Gregory S.
734. Poesie. San Francisco: Twowindows, 1980

CECIL, Otis Van
    735. OV's bicentennial book of poetry. Platte City, MO: C
          & K Enterprises, 1976

CERAVOLO, Joseph
    736. Transmigration solo. West Branch, IA: Toothpaste,
          1979
    737. Millennium dust. New York: Kulchur Foundation, 1982

CERVANTES, Lorna Dee
    738. Emplumada. Pittsburgh: University of Pittsburgh Press,
          1981

CHADWICK, Mark
    739. Into the icehouse. Bowling Green, OH: Newedi, 1976

CHAFFIN, Lillie D.
    740. 8th day, 13th moon. Pikeville, KY: Pikeville College
          Press, 1974
    741. Poems of Appalachia. Clinton, CT: Ashford, 1981

CHALONER, David
    742. Projections. Providence: Burning Deck, 1977

CHAMBERLAIN, Marsha
    743. Powers. St. Paul: New Rivers, 1983

CHANDRA, Sharat
    744. The ghost of meaning. Lewiston, ID: Confluence, 1978

CHAPIN, Harry
    745. Looking ... seeing. New York: Crowell, 1975

CHAPMAN, Frank Monroe
    746. The spell of Hungry Wolf. Santa Fe, NM: Sunstone, 1975

CHAPPELL, Fred
    747. River. Baton Rouge: Louisiana State University Press,
          1975
    748. The man twice married to fire. Greensboro; NC: Uni-
          corn, 1977
    749. Bloodfire. Baton Rouge: Louisiana State University
          Press, 1978
    750. Earthsleep. Baton Rouge: Louisiana State University
          Press, 1980
    751. Midquest: a poem. Baton Rouge: Louisiana State Uni-
          versity Press, 1981

CHARTERS, Samuel
    752. From a Swedish notebook. Berkeley: Oyez, 1973
    753. In Lagos. Berkeley, CA: Oyez, 1976
    754. Of those who died. Berkeley: Oyez, 1980

CHASIN, Helen
    755. Casting stones. Boston: Little, Brown, 1975

CHATFIELD, Hale
    756. What color are your eyes? La Crosse, WI: Juniper,
         1977
    757. Water colors. Gulfport, FL: Konglomerati, 1979
    758. Little fictions. Gulfport, FL: Konglomerati, 1981

CHEATWOOD, Kiarri T-H
    759. Valley of the anointers. Detroit: Lotus, 1979
    760. Psalms of redemption. Detroit: Lotus, 1983

CHEEVER, Mary
    761. The need for chocolate and other poems. New York:
         Stein and Day, 1980

CHERKOVSKI, Neeli
    762. The waters reborn. Fairfax, CA: Red Hill, 1975

CHERNOFF, Maxine
    763. Utopia TV store. Chicago: Yellow, 1980

CHERRY, Kelly
    764. Lovers & agnostics. Charlotte, NC: Red Clay, 1975
    765. Relativity. Baton Rouge: Louisiana State University
         Press, 1977

CHESTER, Laura
    766. Nightlatch. Bowling Green, OH: Tribal, 1974
    767. Chunk off and float. Austin, TX: Provision House,
         1978
    768. Proud and ashamed. Oakland, CA: Christopher's, 1978
    769. Watermark. Berkeley: The Figures, 1978
    770. My pleasure. Berkeley: The Figures, 1980

CHILDERS, David C.
    771. American dusk. San Francisco: Buffalo, 1977

CHISHOLM, Scott
    772. Desperate affections. Pittsford, NY: State Street, 1982

CHMIELARZ, Sharon
    773. Different arrangements. St. Paul: New Rivers, 1983

CHRISTENSEN, Marty
    774. My flashlight was attacked by bats. Portland: Out of
         the Ashes, 1975

CHRISTIAN, Diane
    775. Wide-ons. San Francisco: Synergistic, 1981

CHRISTOPHER, Nicholas
   776. On tour with Rita. New York: Knopf, 1982

CHURCH, Peggy Pond
   777. New & selected poems. Boise, ID: Ahsahta, 1976

CHURCHILL, Matilda
   778. And the master said. St. Petersburg, FL: Valkyrie,
         1975

CIARDI, John
   779. The little that is all. New Brunswick, NJ: Rutgers
         University Press, 1974
   780. For instance. New York: Norton, 1979

CITINO, David
   781. Last Rites and other poems. Columbus: Ohio State
         University Press, 1980
   782. The appassionata poems. Cleveland: Cleveland State
         Poetry Center, 1983

CLAIRE, William F.
   783. From a southern France notebook. Holly Springs, MS:
         Ragnarok, 1975

CLAMPITT, Amy
   784. The kingfisher. New York: Knopf, 1983

CLAREMON, Neil
   785. West of the American dream; poems to be read aloud.
         New York: Morrow, 1973

CLARK, Duane
   786. To catch the sun. Stevens Point, WI: Scopcraeft, 1979

CLARK, Gordon
   787. Sarah's gorilla. Berkeley: Samisdat, 1975

CLARK, Marden J.
   788. Moods of late. Provo, UT: Brigham Young University
         Press, 1975

CLARK, Naomi
   789. Burglaries and celebrations. Berkeley: Oyez, 1977

CLARK, Thomas A.
   790. Some particulars. Millerton, NY: Jargon, 1973

CLARK, Tom
   791. Blue. Los Angeles: Black Sparrow, 1974
   792. Chicago. Los Angeles: Black Sparrow, 1974
   793. Suite. Los Angeles: Black Sparrow, 1974
   794. At Malibu. New York: Kulchur Foundation, 1975

795. Baseball. Berkeley: The Figures, 1976
796. 35. Berkeley: Poltroon, 1976
797. How I broke in/Six modern masters. Bolinas, CA: Tom-
     bouctou, 1978
798. When things get tough on easy street; selected poems
     1963-1978. Santa Barbara: Black Sparrow, 1978
799. The master. Markesan, WI: Pentagon, 1980
800. Heartbreak Hotel. West Branch, IA: Toothpaste, 1981
801. A short guide to the high plains. Santa Barbara: Cad-
     mus, 1981
802. Nine songs. Isla Vista, CA: Turkey, 1982
803. Under the fortune palms. Isla Vista, CA: Turkey,
     1982

CLARK, Walter H.
804. View from Mount Paugus, and other poems. Omaha:
     Abattoir, 1976

CLARKE, Terence
805. The Englewood readings. Paradise, CA: Dustbooks,
     1976

CLAUSEN, Andy
806. Extreme unction. Salt Lake City: Litmus, 1974

CLAUSEN, Jan
807. After touch. Brooklyn: Out & Out, 1975
808. Waking at the bottom of the dark. Brooklyn: Long Haul,
     1979
809. Duration. Brooklyn: Hanging Loose, 1983

CLAYTON, Candyce
810. At the barre. Minneapolis: Holy Cow, 1978

CLEWELL, David
811. Room to breathe. Milwaukee: Pentagram, 1976

CLIFF, Michele
812. Claiming an identity they taught me to despise. Water-
     town, MA: Persephone, 1981

CLIFFORD, Robert E.
813. Pardon me your honor. Ann Arbor, MI: Crowfoot, 1979

CLIFTON, Lucille
814. An ordinary woman. New York: Random House, 1974
815. Two-headed woman. Amherst: University of Massachu-
     setts Press, 1980

CLIFTON, Merritt
816. From the Golan Heights. Richford, VT: Samisdat,
     1974

817.   From an age of cars. Easthampton, MA: Adastra, 1980
818.   Live free or die! Richford, VT: Samisdat, 1982

CLINTON, D.
819.   The conquistador dog texts. New York: New Rivers,
       1976
820.   The coyot: Inca texts. Bowling Green, OH: Newedi,
       1977
821.   Das illustrite Mississippithal revisped. Browns Mills,
       NJ: Ptolemy/Browns Mills Review, 1983

CLIPMAN, William
822.   Dog light. Irvington, NY: Columbia University Press,
       1981

CLOUTIER, David
823.   Ghost call. Providence: Copper Beech, 1976
824.   My grandfather's house. Whitehorn, CA: Holmgangers,
       1980
825.   Tongue and thunder. Providence: Copper Beech, 1980
826.   Soft lightenings. Providence: Copper Beech, 1982

CLUETT, Robert
827.   Turner. Emory, VA: Iron Mountain, 1976

COBB, Pamela
828.   Inside the devil's mouth. Detroit: Lotus, 1975

COBB, Thomas
829.   We shall curse the dead. Tucson, AZ: Desert First
       Works, 1975

COCHRANE, Shirley
830.   Burnsite. Washington: Washington Writers', 1979

CODRESCU, Andrei
831.   The history of the growth of heaven. New York: Bra-
       ziller, 1973
832.   A serious morning. Santa Barbara: Capra, 1973
833.   For Max Jacob. Berkeley: Tree, 1974
834.   Diapers on the snow. Ann Arbor, MI: Crowfoot, 1981
835.   Necrocorrida (bullfight with the dead). Los Angeles:
       Panjandrum, 1981
836.   In America's shoes. San Francisco: City Lights, 1983
837.   Selected poems, 1970-1980, New York: Sun, 1983

COFFIN, Lyn
838.   Human trappings. Omaha: Abattoir, 1980
839.   The poetry of wickedness and other poems. Ithaca, NY:
       Ithaca House, 1981

COGGESHALL, Rosanne
840.   Hymn for drum. Baton Rouge: Louisiana State Univer-
       sity Press, 1978

COHEN, Marty
  841. A traveller's alphabet. Portland: Prescott Street, 1979

COHEN, Robert
  842. There is a country. Cambridge, MA: West End, 1978

COHEN, Rosetta Marantz
  843. Domestic scenes. Chicago: Riverstone, 1982

COLBERT, Alison
  844. Let the circle be unbroken. New York: Women Writing,
        1976

COLBY, Joan
  845. Beheading the children. Chicago: Ommation, 1977
  846. Blue woman dancing in the nerve. Ithaca, NY: Alembic,
        1979
  847. Dream tree. Medina, OH: Jump River, 1980
  848. How the sky begins to fall. Peoria, IL: Ellis, 1982

COLEMAN, Elliott
  849. The tangerine birds. Baltimore: Harbor House, 1973
  850. In the canyon. Baltimore: Bay, 1974
  851. Oxford flow. Oxford: Duns Scotus, 1976

COLEMAN, Lucile
  852. The lyric return. St. Petersburg, FL: Valkyrie, 1977

COLEMAN, Mary Ann
  853. Disappearances. Tallahassee, FL: Anhinga, 1978

COLEMAN, Mary Joan
  854. Take one blood red rose. Cambridge, MA: West End,
        1978

COLEMAN, Wanda
  855. Mad dog black lady. Santa Barbara: Black Sparrow,
        1979
  856. Imagoes. Santa Barbara: Black Sparrow, 1983

COLES, Robert
  857. A festering sweetness. Pittsburgh: University of Pitts-
        burgh Press, 1978

COLIE, Rosalie L.
  858. Atlantic wall. Princeton, NJ: Princeton University
        Press, 1975

COLLEN, Robert
  859. A few pianos. Amherst, MA: Lynx House, 1978

COLLEY, Peter see COOLEY, Peter
  860. [No entry]

861. [No entry]

COMPTON, Thelma J.
    862. The glass tree. Radford, VA: Commonwealth, 1975

CONCHA, Joseph L.
    863. Chokecherry hunters and other poems. Santa Fe, NM: Sunstone, 1976

CONDEE, Nancy
    864. The rape of St. Emad. Providence: Burning Deck, 1974
    865. Explosion in the puzzle factory. Providence: Burning Deck, 1983

CONGDON, Kirby
    866. Black sun. Grand Rapids, MI: Pilot, 1973
    867. Fantoccini: a little book of memories. New York: Little Caesar, 1980
    868. [No entry]

CONNELLAN, Leo
    869. Penobscot poems. New Haven, CT: New Quarto, 1974
    870. Another poet in New York: Brooklyn: Living Poets, 1975
    871. Crossing America. Lincoln, MA: Penmaen, 1976
    872. First selected poems. Pittsburgh: University of Pittsburgh Press, 1976
    873. Massachusetts poems. Chester, MA: Hollow Spring, 1981
    874. Shatterhouse. Chester, MA: Hollow Spring, 1983

CONNOLLY, James
    875. Sax's songs. Gulfport, FL: Konglomerati, 1975

CONTOSKI, Victor
    876. Broken treaties. New York: New Rivers, 1973
    877. Names. St. Paul: New Rivers, 1979
    878. A Kansas sequence. Lawrence, KS: Cottonwood, 1983

COOK, Albert Spaulding
    879. Adapt the living. Athens: Ohio University Press, 1981

COOK, Geoffrey
    880. Tolle lege. San Francisco: Peace & Pieces, 1974

COOLEY, Peter
    881. The company of strangers. Columbia: University of Missouri Press, 1975
    882. Miracle, miracles. LaCrosse, WI: Juniper, 1976

883. The room where summer ends. Pittsburgh: Carnegie-
        Mellon University Press, 1979
884. Nightseasons. Pittsburgh: Carnegie-Mellon University
        Press, 1983

COOLIDGE, Clark
885. The Maintains. San Francisco: This, 1974
886. Polaroid. New York: Adventures in Poetry, 1975
887. Own face. New York: United Artists, 1978
888. Quartz hearts. Berkeley: This, 1978
889. A geology. Elmwood, CT: Potes & Poets, 1981
890. Research. Berkeley: Tuumba, 1982

COON, Betty
891. Seaward. Berkeley: Berkeley Poets, 1978

COONEY, Rian
892. Icarus. Whitehorn, CA: Holmgangers, 1982

COOPER, Dennis
893. The tenderness of the wolves. Trumansburg, NY:
        Crossing, 1982

COOPER, Jane
894. Calling me from sleep; new and selected poems 1961-
        1973. Bronxville, NY: Sarah Lawrence College,
        1974
895. Maps & windows. New York: Macmillan, 1974

COOPERMAN, Stanley
896. Canadian gothic and other poems. Burnaby, BC: West
        Coast Review, 1977
897. Greco's last book. Vancouver BC: Intermedia, 1980

COPE, David
898. Gas. Grand Rapids, MI: Nada, 1974
899. The clouds. Grand Rapids, MI: Free, 1975
900. Quiet lives. Clifton, NJ: Humana, 1983

COPPOCK, John
901. Regardless of title. Berkeley: Samisdat, 1974

CORBETT, William
902. Columbus Square journal. New York: United Artists,
        1976
903. Spoken in sleep. New York: United Artists, 1980
904. Runaway Pond. Cambridge, MA: Apple-wood, 1981

CORDRESCU, Andrei see CODRESCU, Andrei
905. [No entry]

COREY, Stephen
906. The last magician. Huntington, NY: Water Mark, 1981
907. Fighting death. Pittsford, NY: State Street, 1983

CORINO, Michael
  908. Unfree associations. Berkeley: Berkeley Poets, 1982

CORMAN, Cid
  909. So far. New Rochelle, NY: Elizabeth, 1973
  910. O/I, . New Rochelle, NY: Elizabeth, 1974
  911. RSVP. Knotting, Eng.: Sceptre, 1974
  912. Yet. New Rochelle, NY: Elizabeth, 1974
  913. For dear life. Los Angeles: Black Sparrow, 1975
  914. Once and for all; poems for William Bronk. New Ro-
            chelle, NY: Elizabeth, 1975
  915. Unless. Kyoto: Origin, 1975
  916. 'S. New Rochelle, NY: Elizabeth, 1976
  917. Auspices. Markesan, WI: Pentagram, 1978
  918. Of course. Boston: Origin, 1978
  919. So. Boston: Origin, 1978
  920. Aegis; selected poems 1970-1980. Barrytown, NY:
            Station Hill, 1983
  921. Tu. West Branch, IA: Toothpaste, 1983

CORN, Alfred
  922. All roads at once. New York: Viking, 1976
  923. A call in the midst of the crowd. New York: Viking,
            1978
  924. The various light. New York: Viking, 1980

CORNISH, Sam
  925. Sometimes. Cambridge, MA: Pym-Randall, 1973
  926. Streets. Chicago: Third World, 1973
  927. Sam's world. Washington: Decatur House, 1978

CORR, Michael
  928. Brooming to paradise. Berkeley: Workingman's, 1976
  929. To leave the standing grain. Port Townsend, WA: Cop-
            per Canyon, 1977

CORSO, Gregory
  930. Earth egg. New York: Unmuzzled Ox, 1974
  931. The Japanese notebook. New York: Unmuzzled Ox, 1974
  932. Gasoline; the vestal lady on Brattle. San Francisco:
            City Lights, 1976

CORSSON, Robert
  933. Geographies: William James, Gertrude Stein, General
            Booth & Ives. Los Angeles: Red Hill, 1980

COSTANZO, Gerald/
  934. Badlands. Denver: Copper Canyon, 1973
  935. South moccasin. Orangeburg, SC: Peaceweed, 1973
  936. In the aviary. Columbia: University of Missouri Press,
            1974

COSTLEY, Bill
    937.   Mundo Ragas. Lansing, MI: Ghost Dance, 1974
    938.   Knosh 1 Cir. Lansing, MI: Ghost Dance, 1975
    939.   RAG(a)S. East Lansing, MI: Ghost Dance, 1977

COTT, Jonathan
    940.   Charms. West Branch, IA: Toothpaste, 1981

COURCIER, Helen M.
    941.   November burning. Reseda, CA: Mojave, 1974

COURSEN, H. R.
    942.   Lookout point. Berkeley: Samisdat, 1974
    943.   Inside the piano bench. Richford, VT: Samisdat, 1975
    944.   Fears of the night. Richford, VT: Samisdat, 1976
    945.   Walking away. Richford, VT: Samisdat, 1977
    946.   Hope Farm: new and selected poems. Stratford, CT:
          Cider Mill, 1979
    947.   Winter dreams. Stratford, CT: Cider Mill, 1982

COVIN, Michael <u>see</u> CORINO, Michael
    948.   [No entry]

COX, Carol
    949.   Woodworking and places near by. Brooklyn: Hanging
          Loose, 1979
    950.   The water in the pearl. Brooklyn: Hanging Loose,
          1982

COX, Connie
    951.   Unhooked. San Diego: Boondocks, 1976

COX, Ed
    952.   Waking. San Francisco: Gay Sunshine, 1977

COXE, Louis
    953.   Passage; selected poems, 1943-1978. Columbia: Univer-
          sity of Missouri Press, 1979

CRANNY, Robert
    954.   On us thy poor children. New York: Dial, 1982

CRASE, Douglas
    955.   The revisionist. Boston: Little Brown, 1981

CREELEY, Bobbie
    956.   Own your body. Los Angeles: Black Sparrow, 1977

CREELEY, Robert
    957.   For my mother. Rushden, Eng.: Sceptre, 1973
    958.   His idea. Toronto: Coach House, 1973

959. Kitchen. Chicago: Wine, 1973
960. Sitting here. Storrs: University of Connecticut Library, 1974
961. Thirty things. Los Angeles: Black Sparrow, 1974
962. Backwards. Knotting, Eng.: Sceptre, 1975
963. Away. Santa Barbara: Black Sparrow, 1976
964. Hello. Christchurch, NZ: Hawk, 1976
965. Presences. New York: Scribner, 1976
966. Selected poems. New York: Scribner, 1976
967. Myself. Knotting, Eng.: Sceptre, 1977
968. Desultory days. Knotting, Eng.: Sceptre, 1978
969. Hello: a journal, February 23--May 3, 1976. New York: New Directions, 1978
970. Later. West Branch, IA: Toothpaste, 1978; New York: New Directions, 1979
971. The collected poems, 1945-1975. Berkeley: University of California Press, 1982
972. Echoes. West Branch, Iowa: Toothpaste, 1982
973. Calendar. West Branch, IA: Toothpaste, 1983
974. Mirrors. New York: New Directions, 1983
975. Sad advice. New York: Hard, 1983

CRENNER, James
976. The airplane burial ground. Syracuse, NY: Hoffstadt, 1976
977. My hat flies on again. Seattle: L'Epervier, 1981

CREW, Louie
978. Sunspots. Detroit: Lotus, 1976

CREWS, Judson
979. Nations and peoples. Cherry Valley, NY: Cherry Valley, 1976
980. Nolo contendere. Houston: Wing, 1978
981. Selected poems. Berkeley: Thorp Springs, 1979
982. The noose; retrospective of 3 decades. Placitas, NM: Duende, 1980
983. A tree grown straight. Chicago: Ommation, 1980
984. If I: 79 poems. Stockton, CA: Wormwood Review, 1981
985. The clock of moss. Boise, ID: Ahsata, 1983

CRIDISQUE, L.
986. Aba. East Lansing, MI: Ghost Dance, 1977

CRIST, Lyle
987. Runaways. New Philadelphia, OH: Pale Horse, 1976

CROCKETT, Eleanor Earle
988. '53 Ford. Houston: Wings, 1979

CROWELL, Robert Merle
    989. Brief but warm the rain.   Fairhope, AL: Windhover,
          1974

CROZIER, Andrew
    990. The veil poem.   Providence: Burning Deck, 1974

CRUZ, Victor Hernandex
    991. Mainland.   New York: Random House, 1973
    992. Tropicalization.   New York: Reed, Canon & Johnson,
          1976
    993. El clutch y los klinkies.   New York: # Magazine, 1980
    994. By lingual wholes.   San Francisco: Momo's, 1982

CUDAHY, Sheila
    995. The bristle cone pine & other poems.   New York: Har-
          court Brace Jovanovich, 1976

CUDDIHY, Michael
    996. Celebrations.   Port Townsend, WA: Copper Canyon,
          1980

CUELHO, Art
    997. The last foot of shade.   Diablo, CA: Holmgangers, 1975
    998. Death's legacy.   Big Timber, MT: Seven Buffaloes,
          1977
    999. A caged bird in spring.   Big Timber, MT: Seven Buf-
          faloes, 1978
  1000. Evening comes slow to a fieldhand.   Big Timber, MT:
          Seven Buffaloes, 1982

CULROSS, Michael
  1001. The lost heroes.   Pittsburgh: University of Pittsburgh
          Press, 1974

CUMMING, Patricia
  1002. Afterwards.   Cambridge, MA: Alice James, 1974
  1003. Letter from an outlying province.   Cambridge, MA:
          Alice James, 1976

CUMMINGS, D.
  1004. Ain't no melody like the tune.   Berkeley: Vital, 1975

CUMMINGS, Peter
  1005. Bicycle consciousness.   Greenfield Center, NY: Green-
          field Review, 1979

CUNEO, Louis
  1006. Haiku revisited.   San Francisco: Mother's Hen, 1973
  1007. Day to day.   San Francisco: Mother's Hen, 1975

CUNNINGHAM, Robert S.
  1008. Rationale.   Reseda, CA: Mojave, 1974

1009. Love Poems. Reseda, CA: Mojave, 1975
1010. Rippling rhymes and fairy tales. Reseda, CA: Mojave
         Books, 1975

CURRY, David
   1011. Theatre. Crete, NE: Best Cellar, 1973
   1012. Contending to be the dream. St. Paul: New Rivers,
            1979

CURTIS, Walt
   1013. The roses of Portland. Portland: Out of the Ashes,
            1974
   1014. The sunflower. Portland: Out of the Ashes, 1975

CUSHMAN, Don
   1015. Jim and the evil. San Francisco: Gallimaufry, 1975

CUTLER, Bruce
   1016. The doctrine of selective depravity. La Crosse, WI:
            Juniper, 1980
   1017. The maker's name. La Crosse, WI: Juniper, 1980

CUTTS, Simon
   1018. Quelques pianos. Millerton, NY: Jargon, 1976

CZAPLA, Cathy Young
   1019. Heirloom. Richford, VT: Samisdat, 1981
   1020. Genetic memories. Richford, VT: Samisdat, 1983

D'ABATE, Richard
   1021. To keep the house from falling in. Ithaca, NY: Ithaca
            House, 1973

DACEY, Philip
   1022. How I escaped from the labyrinth, and other poems.
            Pittsburgh: Carnegie-Mellon University Press, 1977
   1023. The condom poems. Marshall, MN: Ox Head, 1979
   1024. Men at table. Milton, MA: Chowder, 1979
   1025. The boy under the bed. Baltimore: Johns Hopkins
            University Press, 1981
   1026. Gerard Manley Hopkins meets Walt Whitman in heaven.
            Lincoln, MA: Penmaen, 1982

DAHLEN, Beverly
   1027. Out of the third. San Francisco: Momo's, 1974

DAIGON, Ruth
   1028. Learning not to kill you. Chaplin, CT: Daigon, 1975
   1029. On my side of the bed. Chicago: Ommation, 1978

DAILEY, Joel
   1030. Exploring another leg. Milwaukee: Pentagram, 1975

DALE, Peter
1031. Mortal fire. Athens: Ohio University Press, 1976

DAMALI
1032. I am that we may be. Chicago: Third World, 1974

DAME, Enid
1033. Between revolutions. Brooklyn: Downtown Poets, 1977
1034. Interesting times. Brooklyn: Downtown Poets, 1978
1035. On the road to Damascus, Maryland. Brooklyn: Down-
       town Poets, 1980

DANA, Robert
1036. The Watergate elegy. Chicago: Wine, 1973
1037. Tryptych. Chicago: Wine, 1974
1038. In a fugitive season. Chicago: Swallow, 1980

DANFORD, Richard
1039. Unfinished poems. San Francisco: Cranium, 1973

DANIELL, Rosemary
1040. A sexual tour of the Deep South. New York: Holt,
       Rinehart and Winston, 1975
1041. The feathered trees. Austell, GA: Sweetwater, 1976

DANIELS, Lou
1042. Reflections. Chicago: Adams, 1976

DANKLEFF, Richard
1043. Popcorn girl. Corvallis: Oregon State University
       Press, 1979

DANN, Jack
1044. Christs and other poems. Binghamton, NY: Bellevue,
       1974

DARLING, Dorothea
1045. Arachnids and other friends. Dennis, MA: Salt-Works,
       1974

DARR, Ann
1046. The myth of a woman's fist. New York: Morrow, 1973
1047. Cleared for landing. Washington: Dryad, 1978
1048. Riding with the fireworks! Cambridge, MA: Alice
       James, 1981

DAVIDE
1049. Astralphonic voices. San Francisco: Isthmus, 1976

DAVIDSON, Michael
1050. Two views of pears. Albany, CA: Sand Dollar, 1973
1051. The mutabilities. Albany, CA: Sand Dollar, 1976
1052. The prose of fact. Berkeley: The Figures, 1981

DAVIDSON, Richard
1053. Glass roads. New York: Home Planet, 1976

DAVIS, Glover
1054. August fires and other poems. Omaha: Abattoir, 1978

DAVIS, Helene
1055. Nightblind. Woods Hole, MA: Pourboire, 1976

DAVIS, Jon
1056. West of New England. Missoula: University of Montana
       Press, 1982

DAVIS, Lloyd
1057. Fishing the lower Jackson. Crete, NE: Best Cellar,
       1974
1058. The way all rivers run. Omaha: University of Nebras-
       ka at Omaha Press, 1982

DAVIS, Ron
1059. Women & horses. Pomeroy, OH: Carpenter, 1981

DAVIS, William Virgil
1060. One way to reconstruct the scene. New Haven, CT:
       Yale University Press, 1981

DAVISON, Peter
1061. Walking the boundaries: poems, 1957-1974. New York:
       Atheneum, 1974
1062. A voice in the mountain. New York: Atheneum, 1977

DAWSON, Fielding
1063. The miracle. Los Angeles: Black Sparrow, 1973
1064. Tiger lilies. Los Angeles: Black Sparrow, 1974
1065. Delayed, not postponed. New York: Telephone, 1978

DAY, Jean
1066. Linear C. Berkeley: Tuumba, 1983

DAY, Lucille
1067. Self-portrait with hand microscope. Berkeley: Poets
       Workshop, 1983

DAYTON, David
1068. The lost body of childhood. Providence: Copper Beech,
       1979

DEAGON, Ann
1069. Carbon 14. Amherst: University of Massachusetts
       Press, 1974
1070. Indian Summer. Greensboro, NC: Unicorn, 1976
1071. Women and children first. Emory, VA: Iron Mountain,
       1976

1072. There is no balm in Birmingham. Boston: Godine,
       1978
1073. Habitats. University Center, MI: Green River, 1982

DEAL, Susan Strayer
1074. No moving parts. Boise, ID: Ahsahta, 1980

DEATON, Clyde F.
1075. Foot-prints in the sands of time. Chicago: Adams,
       1976

DEEMER, Bill
1076. All wet. Brunswick, ME: Blackberry, 1975

DeFOE, Mark
1077. Bringing home breakfast. Norristown, PA: Black
       Willow, 1982

De FREES, Madeline
1078. Imaginary ancestors. Missoula, MT: SmokeRoot, 1978
1079. When sky lets go. New York: Braziller, 1978
1080. Magpie on the gallows. Port Townsend, WA: Copper
       Canyon, 1982

de la TORRIENTE, Donna
1081. In the shadow of a bell. Reseda, CA: Mojave, 1981
1082. Bay is the land. Reseda, CA: Mojave, 1982

DeLONGCHAMPS, Joanne
1083. The hungry lions. Westport, CT: Greenwood, 1974
1084. Warm-bloods, cold-bloods. Reno, NV: West Coast
       Poetry Review, 1981

DEMING, Barbara
1085. On Anger. Palo Alto, CA: Frog in the Wall, 1974

DEMISE, Phil
1086. What I don't know for sure. Providence: Burning
       Deck, 1978

Den BOER, James
1087. Lost in the blue canyon. Oakland, CA: Christopher's,
       1980

DENBY, Edwin
1088. Snoring in New York. New York: Angel Hair, 1974
1089. Collected poems. New York: Full Court, 1975

DENNIS, Carl
1090. A house of my own. New York: Braziller, 1974
1091. Climbing down. New York: Braziller, 1976
1092. Signs and wonders. Princeton, NJ: Princeton Univer-
       sity Press, 1979

DENNIS, Pauli
    1093. Chrysalis. Indianola, WA: Watermark, 1974

DEPEW, Wally
    1094. 100 Poems. Livermore, CA: PN Books, 1973
    1095. BPQD. Livermore, CA: Ironwhorse/Ironhores, 1974
    1096. EMPO. Livermore, CA: Ironwhorse/Ironhores, 1974
    1097. Grey G. Livermore, CA: Ironwhorse/Ironhores, 1974
    1098. This Bag. Livermore, CA: PN Books, 1974

DEPTA, Victor
    1099. The creek. Athens: Ohio University Press, 1973
    1100. The house. St. Paul: New Rivers, 1978

DER HOVANESSIAN
    1101. How to choose your past. New York: Ararat, 1978

DERLETH, August William
    1102. Last light. Mt. Horeb, WI: Perishable, 1978

DERRICOTTE, Toi
    1103. The empress of the death house. Detroit: Lotus, 1978
    1104. Natural birth. Trumansburg, NY: Crossing, 1983

DETRO, Gene
    1105. Mary Militant. Whitehorn, CA: Holmgangers, 1979
    1106. Moon horns/razor door. Whitehorn, CA: Holmgangers, 1981
    1107. The Mary caper. Portland: Sunburst, 1982
    1108. When all the wild summer. Whitehorn, CA: Holmgang-ers, 1983

DEZA, E. C.
    1109. New laugh poems. Bigfork, MN: Northwoods, 1975

DICKERSON, George-Therese
    1110. Striations. Boston: Good Gay Poets, 1976

DICKEY, James
    1111. The zodiac. Bloomfield Hills, MI: Bruccoli Clark, 1976; Garden City, NY: Doubleday, 1976
    1112. The owl king. New York: Red Angel, 1977
    1113. Tucky the hunter. New York: Crown, 1978
    1114. The strength of fields. Garden City, NY: Doubleday, 1979
    1115. The early motion. Middletown, CT: Wesleyan University Press, 1981
    1116. Falling, May Day sermon, and other poems. Middletown, CT: Wesleyan University Press, 1981
    1117. Puella. Garden City, NY: Doubleday, 1982
    1118. The central motion; poems 1968-1979. Middletown, CT: Wesleyan University Press, 1983

DICKEY, R. P.
1119. Concise dictionary of Lead River, MO. Taos, NM:
      Black Bear, 1973
1120. Drunk on a Greyhound. Shawnee Mission, KS: BkMk,
      1973
1121. McCabe wants chimes. Taos, NM: Talmaneh, 1973

DICKEY, William
1122. The rainbow grocery. Amherst: University of Massa-
      chusetts Press, 1978
1123. The sacrifice consenting. San Francisco: Pterodactyl,
      1981

DICKSON, Ronald
1124. Much. Carmel Valley, CA: Oakcrest, 1975

DILLARD, Annie
1125. Tickets for a prayer wheel. Columbia: University of
      Missouri Press, 1974

DILLARD, R. H. W.
1126. The greeting: new & selected poems. Salt Lake City:
      University of Utah Press, 1981

DILSAVER, Paul
1127. Malignant blues. Omaha: Abattoir, 1976

DINGLEY, Fred R.
1128. Six hundred acres. Thorndike, ME: Thorndike, 1980

DIORIA, Margaret Toarello
1129. Bring in the plants. Riderwood, MD: Icarus, 1981

DiPALMA, Ray
1130. Max, a sequel. Providence: Burning Deck, 1974
1131. Soli. Ithaca, NY: Ithaca, 1974
1132. Marquise. New York: Asylum, 1976
1133. Cuiva sails. College Park, MD: Sun & Moon, 1978
1134. Observatory gardens. Berkeley: Tuumba, 1979

DiPIERO, W. S.
1135. Country of survivors. Berkeley: Rasmussen, 1974
1136. Solstice. Tempe, AZ: Porch Publications, 1981

DiPRIMA, Diane
1137. Loba. Santa Barbara: Capra, 1973
1138. Dinners and nightmares. New York: Corinth, 1974
1139. Freddie poems. Point Reyes, CA: Eidolon, 1974
1140. Brass furnace going out. Syracuse, NY: Pulpartforms,
      1975
1141. Loba as Eve. New York: Phoenix Book Shop, 1975
1142. Selected poems. Plainfield, VT: North Atlantic, 1975

1143. Brass furnace going out. Buffalo, NY: Intrepid, 1976
1144. Loba, parts 1-8. Berkeley: Wingbow, 1978

DiPRISCO, Joseph
1145. Wit's end. Columbia: University of Missouri Press,
       1975

DISCH, Thomas M.
1146. Orders of the retina. West Branch, Iowa: Toothpaste,
       1982

DIXON, Melvin
1147. Change of territory. Lexington: University of Kentucky
       Press, 1983

DiZAZZO, Raymond
1148. Clovin's head. Fairfax, CA: Red Hill, 1976

DLUGOS, Tim
1149. High there. Washington: Some of Us, 1973
1150. A fast life. Chatsworth, CA: Sherwood, 1982

DOBYNS, Stephen
1151. Griffon. New York: Atheneum, 1976
1152. Heat death. New York: Atheneum, 1980
1153. The Balthus poems. New York: Atheneum, 1982

DODD, Wayne
1154. We will wear white roses. Crete, NE: Best Cellar,
       1974
1155. Made in America. Athens, OH: Croissant & Company,
       1975
1156. The names you gave it. Baton Rouge: Louisiana State
       University Press, 1980
1157. The general mule poems. La Crosse, WI: Juniper,
       1981

DOLGIN, Steven Alfred
1158. Between Lunatic Ears. Springfield, IL: Sangamon,
       1974

DONNELLY, Dorothy
1159. Kudzu. Providence: Burning Deck, 1979

DORESKI, William
1160. The testament of Israel Potter. New York: Seven
       Woods, 1976
1161. Half of the map. Providence: Burning Deck, 1980

DORMAN, Sonya
1162. Stretching fence. Athens: Ohio University Press, 1975
1163. A paper raincoat. Orono, ME: Puckerbrush, 1976
1164. [No entry]

1165. Pomegranate. Binghamton, NY: Bellevue, 1977
1166. The far traveller. La Crosse, WI: Juniper, 1980

DORN, Ed
1167. Recollections of Gran Apacheria. San Francisco: Tur-
       tle Island, 1974
1168. The collected poems, 1956-1974. Bolinas, CA: Four
       Seasons, 1975
1169. Gunslinger. Berkeley: Wingbow, 1975
1170. Manchester Square. New York: Permanent, 1975
1171. The poet, the people, the spirit. Vancouver, BC: Tal-
       on, 1976
1172. Selected poems. Bolinas, CA: Grey Fox, 1978
1173. Hello La Jolla. Berkeley: Wingbow, 1978
1174. Selected poems. Bolinas, CA: Grey Fox, 1978
1175. Yellow Lola. Santa Barbara: Cadmus, 1980
1176. [No entry]

DORRANCE, Don
1177. Morituri. Richford, VT: Samisdat, 1975

DOSTAL, Cyril A.
1178. Emergency exit. Cleveland: Cleveland State University,
       1975

DOUBIAGO, Sharon
1179. Hard country. Minneapolis: West End, 1983

DOUGLAS, Max
1180. Collected poems. Washington: White Dot, 1978

DOUSKEY, Franz
1181. Rowing across the dark. Athens: University of Georgia
       Press, 1981

DOVE, Rita
1182. The Manila series: No. 4, ten poems. Lisbon, IA:
       Penumbra, 1977
1183. Ten poems. Lisbon, IA: Penumbra, 1977
1184. Museum. Pittsburgh: Carnegie-Mellon University
       Press, 1983

DOVICHI, A.
1185. The morning after midnight. Franklin, MI: Iron, 1983

DRACHLER, Rose
1186. Digging in, burrowing out. Berkeley: Tree, 1974
1187. The choice. Berkeley: Tree, 1977

DRAFTS, C. Gene
1188. Bloodwhispers/blacksongs. Detroit: Broadside, 1974

DRAGONWAGON, Crescent
    1189. Message from the avocadoes. Little Rock, AR: August House, 1982

DRAKE, Albert
    1190. Assuming the position. Grand Rapids, MI: Pilot, 1973
    1191. Riding bike in the 'fifties. Okemos, MI: Stone, 1973
    1192. By breathing in and out. Pittsburgh: Three Rivers, 1974
    1193. Thirteen ways of looking at a Model A. Okemos, MI: Stone, 1974
    1194. Cheap thrills. Rock Hill, SC: Peaceweed, 1975
    1195. Poems pro/found. Okemos, MI: Stone, 1975
    1196. Returning to Oregon. Columbus, OH: Cider, 1975
    1197. Roadsalt. Poynette, WI: Bieler, 1976
    1198. Tilamook Burn. Union City, CA: Fault, 1977
    1199. Reaching for the sun. San Jose, CA: Laughing Bear, 1979
    1200. Garage. Santa Barbara: Mudborn, 1980

DRAKE, Barbara
    1201. Narcissa Notebook. Okemos, MI: Stone, 1973
    1202. Case history. Okemos, MI: Stone, 1974
    1203. Field poems. Okemos, MI: Stone, 1975
    1204. Love at the Egyptian Theatre. East Lansing, MI: Red Cedar, 1978
    1205. Life in a gothic novel. Adelphi, MD: White Ewe, 1981

DRESSLER, Muriel Miller
    1206. Appalachia. Charleston, WV: MHC, 1977

DRISCOLL, Jack
    1207. Home grown. Orangeburg, SC: Peaceweed, 1973

DROZD, John
    1208. Between two rivers. Montclair, NJ: Montclair State College, 1976

DRYER, Lynne
    1209. Lamplights used to feed the deer. Washington: Some of Us, 1974

DUBERSTEIN, Helen
    1210. Changes. East Lansing, MI: Ghost Dance, 1977

DUBIE, Norman
    1211. In the dead of the night. Pittsburgh: University of Pittsburgh Press, 1975
    1212. Popham of the new song. Port Townsend, WA: Graywolf, 1975
    1213. The prayers of the North American martyrs. Lisbon, IA: Penumbra, 1975

1214. The illustrations. New York: Braziller, 1977
1215. Odalisque in white. Bisbee, AZ: Porch, 1978
1216. A thousand little things, and other poems. Omaha:
       Abattoir, 1978
1217. The city of the Olesha fruit. Garden City, NY: Double-
       day, 1979
1218. The everlastings. Garden City, NY: Doubleday, 1980
1219. Selected and new poems. New York: Norton, 1983

DUBIE, William
1220. Closing the moviehouse. Belfast, ME: Wings, 1981

DUCKETT, Alfred
1221. Raps. Chicago: Nelson-Hall, 1973

DuFAULT, Peter Kane
1222. On balance. Sand Lake, NY: Sagarin, 1978

DUFF, Gerald
1223. Calling collect. Orlando: University Presses of
       Florida, 1982

DUFFANY, Brett
1224. An illustrated voice. Canton, NY: Dreambooks, 1975

DUGAN, Alan
1225. Poems 4. Boston: Little, Brown, 1974
1226. Sequence. Cambridge, MA: Dolphin, 1976
1227. New and collected poems, 1961-1983. New York: Ecco,
       1983

DUGAN, Thomas
1228. A modern bestiary. Barrytown, NY: Cordella, 1982

DUKES, Norman
1229. The reckless sleeper. Woods Hole, MA: Pourboire,
       1975

DUNAWAY, Judith
1230. Genealogy. Bowling Green, OH: Newedi, 1976

DUNCAN, Robert
1231. Opening of the field. New York: New Directions, 1973
1232. Dante. Canton, NY: Institute of Further Studies, 1974
1233. An ode and Arcadia. Berkeley: Ark, 1974
1234. The Venice poem. Sydney, NSW, Aus.: Prism, 1976

DUNN, Si
1235. Waiting for water. Dallas: Calliope, 1977

DUNN, Stephen
1236. Looking for holes in the ceiling. Amherst: University
       of Massachusetts Press, 1974

1237.   Full of lust and good usage. Pittsburgh: Carnegie-
        Mellon University Press, 1976
1238.   A circus of needs. Pittsburgh: Carnegie-Mellon Uni-
        versity Press, 1978
1239.   Work & love. Pittsburgh: Carnegie-Mellon University
        Press, 1981

DUNNING, Stephen
1240.   Handfuls of us. Athens, OH: Croissant, 1979
1241.   Walking home dead. Menemsha, MA: Stone Country,
        1981
1242.   Do you fear no one. San Francisco: Pancake, 1982

DWYER, David
1243.   Ariana Olisvos: her last works and days. Amherst:
        University of Massachusetts Press, 1976

DWYER, Frank
1244.   Looking wayward. Washington: Dryad, 1974
1245.   [No entry]

DYAK, Miriam
1246.   Fire under water. Lebanon, NH: New Victoria, 1977
1247.   Dying. Lebanon, NH: New Victoria, 1978

DYBEK, Stuart
1248.   Brass knuckles. Pittsburgh: University of Pittsburgh
        Press, 1979

EADDY, Felton
1249.   If i hold my tongue. Davenport, WA: Peaceweed, 1973
1250.   Living by the sword. St. Paul: Truck, 1977

EAGELFELD, Glen
1251.   Glen with one n. Mamaroneck, NY: Artmore Graphics,
        1974

EAKINS, Patricia
1252.   Oono. Chapel Hill, NC: I-74, 1982

EATON, Charles Edward
1253.   The man in the green chair. South Brunswick, NJ:
        A. S. Barnes, 1977
1254.   Colophon of the rover. South Brunswick, NJ: A. S.
        Barnes, 1980
1255.   The thing king. New York: Cornwall, 1983

EBELT, Alfred
1256.   Shoulder the sky. St. Petersburg, FL: Valkyrie,
        1975

EBERHART, Richard
  1257. Collected poems, 1930-1976. New York: Oxford Uni-
          versity Press, 1976
  1258. Poems to poets. Lincoln, MA: Penmaen, 1976
  1259. Hour, Gnats. Davis, CA: Putah Creek, 1977
  1260. Ways of light. New York: Oxford University Press,
          1980
  1261. Florida poems. Gulfport, FL: Konglomerati, 1981
  1262. The long reach: new and uncollected poems, 1948-
          1984. New York: New Directions, 1983

ECKELS, Jon
  1263. Firesign. San Jose, CA: Firesign, 1973
  1264. Back to black basics. Oakland, CA: Firesign, 1981

ECKLES, Georgiana
  1265. Gold diggers, sex junkies, needful lovers. Cleveland:
          Cleveland State University Poetry Center, 1981

ECKMAN, Fred
  1266. Nightmare township. Bowling Green, OH: Newedi,
          1976

ECONOMOU, George
  1267. Ameriki. New York: Sun, 1977

EDGCOMB, Gabrielle Simon
  1268. Moving violation. Washington: Some of Us: 1973

EDMUNDS, John
  1269. Hesperides. Georgetown, CA: Dragon's Teeth, 1975

EDSON, Russell
  1270. The clam theater. Middletown, CT: Wesleyan Univer-
          sity Press, 1973
  1271. A roof with some clouds behind it. Hartford, CT:
          Bartholomew's Cobble, 1975
  1272. The intuitive journey. New York: Harper & Row, 1976
  1273. The reason why the closet-man is never sad. Middle-
          town, CT: Wesleyan University Press, 1977
  1274. With sincerest regrets. Providence: Burning Deck,
          1981

EDWARDS, Eric
  1275. Ancestors to come. Woods Hole, MA: Pourboire, 1975

EHRHART, W. D.
  1276. A generation of peace. New York: New Voices, 1975
  1277. An awkward silence. South Thomaston, ME: North-
          woods, 1980
  1278. The Samisdat poems of W. D. Ehrhart. Richford, VT:
          Samisdat, 1980
  1279. Matters of the heart: poems. Easthampton, MA: Ad-
          astra, 1981

EHRLICH, Gretel
    1280. To touch the water. Boise: ID: Ahsahta, 1981

EIGNER, Larry
    1281. Shape, shadow, elements move. Los Angeles: Black
          Sparrow, 1973
    1282. Words touching ground under. Belmont, MA: Hellric,
          1973
    1283. Anything on its side. New Rochelle, NY: Elizabeth,
          1974
    1284. No radio. Boulder, CO: Lodestar, 1974
    1285. Things stirring together or far away. Los Angeles:
          Black Sparrow, 1974
    1286. My God the proverbial. Kensington, CA: L Press,
          1975
    1287. Suddenly it gets light and dark in the street: poems
          1961-74. Winchester, Eng.: Green Horse, 1975
    1288. The music variety. Newton, MA: Roxbury, 1976
    1289. Watching how or why. New Rochelle, NY: Elizabeth,
          1977
    1290. The world & its streets, places. Santa Barbara: Black
          Sparrow, 1977
    1291. Cloud, invisible air. Barrytown, NY: Station Hill,
          1978
    1292. Flagpole riding. Alverstoke, Eng.: Stingy Artist, 1978
    1293. Heat simmers cold. Paris: Orange Export, 1978
    1294. Running around. Providence: Burning Deck, 1978
    1295. Lined up bulk senses. Providence: Burning Deck, 1979
    1296. Time, details of a tree. New Rochelle, NY: Elizabeth,
          1979
    1297. Earth birds: forty six poems written between May 1964
          and June 1972. Guildford, Eng.: Circle, 1981
    1298. Now there's a morning, hulk of the sky. Berkeley:
          Small Press Distribution, 1981
    1299. Waters, places, a time. Santa Barbara: Black Sparrow,
          1983

EINZIG, Barbara
    1300. Color. Milwaukee: Membrane, 1976
    1301. Disappearing work. Berkeley: The Figures, 1979

EISELEY, Loren C.
    1302. The innocent assassins. New York: Scribner, 1973
    1303. Another kind of autumn. New York: Scribner, 1977
    1304. All the night wings. New York: Times Books, 1979

ELANNER, Hildegrade
    1305. The hearkening eye. Boise, ID: Ahsahta, 1979

ELDER, Gary
    1306. A vulgar elegance. Berkeley: Thorp Springs, 1974
    1307. Arnulfsaga. Paradise, CA: Dustbooks, 1979
    1308. Eyes on the land. Los Cerrillos, NM: San Marcos
          Press, 1980

ELDRED, Bonnie
    1309. Mother nature is a bitch. St. Petersburg, FL: Val-
           kyrie, 1974

ELETHEA, Abba
    1310. The Anitoch suite-jazz. Detroit: Lotus, 1980

ELLIOTT, George P.
    1311. Reaching. Northridge, CA: Santa Susana, 1979

ELLIOTT, Harley
    1312. All beautyfull & foolish souls. Trumansburg, NY:
           Crossing, 1974
    1313. Sky heart. Milwaukee: Pentagram, 1975
    1314. Animals that stand in dreams. Brooklyn: Hanging
           Loose, 1976
    1315. The secret lover. Tempe, AZ: Emerald City, 1977
    1316. Darkness at each elbow. Brooklyn: Hanging Loose,
           1981

ELLIOTT, William
    1317. Eco-catastrophe. Bemidji, MN: Bemidji State College,
           1973
    1318. Pine and jack pine. Bemidji, MN: Bemidji State Col-
           lege, 1973
    1319. Winter in the rex. Bemidji, MN: Bemidji State College,
           1973

ELLISON, Jessie
    1320. In the running. Chicago: Ommation, 1976

ELMAN, Richard M.
    1321. Homage to Fats Navarro. New York: New Rivers,
           1978
    1322. In chontales. Port Jefferson, NY: Street, 1980

ELMSLIE, Kenward
    1323. ZZ. Calais, VT: Z Press, 1974
    1324. Tropicalism. Calais, VT: Z Press, 1975
    1325. The alphabet work. Washington: Titanic, 1977
    1326. Communications equipment. Providence: Burning Deck,
           1979
    1327. Moving right along. Calais, VT: Z Press, 1980

ELY, Carolanne
    1328. Love wounds & multiple fractures. New York: Sun,
           1975

EMANUEL, James A.
    1329. Black man abroad. Detroit: Lotus, 1978
    1330. A chisel in the dark. Detroit: Lotus, 1980
    1331. The broken bowl. Detroit: Lotus, 1983

EMANUEL, Lynn
    1332. Oblique light. Pittsburgh: Slow Loris, 1979

ENGELS, John
    1333. Signals from the safety coffin. Pittsburgh: University
          of Pittsburgh Press, 1975
    1334. Blood mountain. Pittsburgh: University of Pittsburgh
          Press, 1977
    1335. Vivaldi in early fall. Athens: University of Georgia
          Press, 1981
    1336. The seasons of Vermont. Syracuse, NY: Tamarack,
          1982
    1337. Weather-fear: new and selected poems, 1958-1982.
          Athens: University of Georgia Press, 1983

ENGLISH, Maurice
    1338. A savaging of roots. Waterloo, ON: Pasdeloup, 1974

ENSLIN, Theodore
    1339. In the keeper's house. Dennis, MA: Salt-Works, 1973
    1340. Sitio. Hanover, NH: Granite, 1973
    1341. The swamp fox. Dennis, MA: Salt-Works, 1973
    1342. With light reflected. Fremont, MI: Sumac, 1973
    1343. Fever poems. Brunswick, ME: Blackberry, 1974
    1344. Forms, coda. New Rochelle, NY: Elizabeth, 1974
    1345. The last days of October. Dennis, MA: Salt-Works,
          1974
    1346. The median flow; selected poems, 1943-1973. Los
          Angeles: Black Sparrow, 1974
    1347. The mornings. Berkeley: Shaman/Drum, 1974
    1348. Some pastorals. Dennis, MA: Salt-Works, 1974
    1349. Landler. New Rochelle, NY: Elizabeth, 1975
    1350. Synthesis 1-24. Plainfield, VT: North Atlantic, 1975
    1351. Carmina. Dennis, MA: Salt-Works, 1976
    1352. The July book. Berkeley: Sand Dollar, 1976
    1353. Papers. New Rochelle, NY: Elizabeth, 1976
    1354. The further regions. Milwaukee: Pentagram, 1977
    1355. Concentrations. Dennis, MA: Salt-Works, 1978
    1356. Ranger, Vol. 1. Berkeley: North Atlantic, 1978
    1357. Tailings. Markesan, WI: Pentagram, 1978
    1358. Opus 31. Markesan, WI: Pentagram, 1979
    1359. Opus O. Milwaukee: Membrane, 1979
    1360. The fifth direction. Markesan, WI: Pentagon, 1980
    1361. Ranger, Vol. 2. Berkeley: North Atlantic, 1980
    1362. Axes 52. Willimantic, CT: Ziesing, 1981
    1363. Markings. Milwaukee: Membrane, 1981
    1364. F. P. Willimantic, CT: Ziesing, 1982
    1365. Meditations on various grounds. Elmwood, CT: Potes
          & Poets, 1982

ENTREKIN, Charles
    1366. All pieces of a legacy. Berkeley: Berkeley Poets
          Workshop, 1975

1367.   Casting for the cutthroat & other poems.   Berkeley,
        CA: Berkeley Poets' Workshop, 1980

EPES, W. Perry
   1368.   Tidewater salt & other poems.   Boston: Godine, 1974

EPSTEIN, Daniel
   1369.   No vacancies in hell.   New York: Liveright, 1973
   1370.   The follies.   Woodstock, NY: Overlook, 1977

EPSTEIN, Judy
   1371.   Keeping score.   Ithaca, NY: Ithaca House, 1975

ESHLEMAN, Clayton
   1372.   Coils.   Los Angeles: Black Sparrow, 1973
   1373.   Human wedding.   Santa Barbara: Black Sparrow, 1973
   1374.   The last judgment.   Los Angeles: Plantin, 1973
   1375.   Aux morts.   Los Angeles: Black Sparrow, 1974
   1376.   Realignment.   Philadelphia: Treacle, 1974
   1377.   The gull wall.   Los Angeles: Black Sparrow, 1975
   1378.   Cogollo.   Newton, MA: Roxbury, 1976
   1379.   The woman who saw through paradise.   Lawrence, KS:
           Tansy, 1976
   1380.   Core meander.   Santa Barbara: Black Sparrow, 1977
   1381.   Grotesca.   London: New London Pride, 1977
   1382.   On Mules sent from Chavin.   Swansea: Galloping Dog,
           1977
   1383.   The gospel of Celine Arnaud.   Berkeley: Tuumba, 1978
   1384.   The name encanyoned river.   Providence: Treacle, 1978
   1385.   What she means.   Santa Barbara: Black Sparrow, 1978
   1386.   A note on apprenticeship.   Chicago: Two Hands, 1979
   1387.   The lich gate.   Barrytown, NY: Station Hill, 1980
   1388.   Nights we put the rock together.   Santa Barbara: Cad-
           mus, 1980
   1389.   Hades in manganese.   Santa Barbara: Black Sparrow,
           1981
   1390.   Fracture.   Santa Barbara: Black Sparrow, 1983
   1391.   Visions of the fathers of Lascaux.   San Francisco:
           Panjandrum, 1983

ESTES, Kathleen
   1392.   Omphalos.   Port Townsend, WA: Copper Canyon, 1979

ESTEVES, Sandra Maria
   1393.   Yerba buena.   Greenfield Center, NY: Greenfield Re-
           view, 1981

ETTER, Dave
   1394.   Bright Mississippi.   La Crosse, WI: Juniper, 1975
   1395.   Strangers.   La Crosse, WI: Juniper, 1975
   1396.   Well, you needn't.   Independence, MO: Raindust, 1975
   1397.   Open to the wind.   Mount Carroll, IL: Uzzano, 1979
   1398.   Cornfields.   Peoria, IL: Spoon River, 1980

1399.   West of Chicago. Peoria, IL: Spoon River, 1981
1400.   Alliance, Illinois. Ann Arbor, MI: Kylix, 1978; Peoria,
        IL: Spoon River, 1983

EVANS, David Allan
1401.   Train windows. Athens: Ohio University Press, 1976

EVANS, Mari
1402.   JD. Garden City, NY: Doubleday, 1973
1403.   Whisper. Berkeley: University of California Center for
        African American Studies, 1979

EVERETT, Graham
1404.   Strange coast. Syracuse, NY: Tamarack, 1979

EVERHARD, Jim
1405.   Cute, and other poems. San Francisco: Gay Sunshine,
        1982

EVERSON, William
1406.   Black hills. San Francisco: Didymus, 1973
1407.   Tendril in the mesh. Aromas, CA: Cayucos, 1973
1408.   Man-fate; the swan song of Brother Antoninus. New
        York: New Directions, 1974
1409.   Missa defunctorum. Santa Cruz, CA: Lime Kiln, 1976
1410.   River-root. Berkeley: Oyez, 1976
1411.   The mate-flight of eagles. Newcastle, CA: Blue Oak,
        1977
1412.   Blackbird sundown. Northridge, CA: Lord John, 1978
1413.   Blame it on the jet stream! Santa Cruz, CA: Lime
        Kiln, 1978
1414.   Cutting the firebreak. Swanton, CA: Kingfisher, 1978
1415.   Rattlesnake August. Northridge, CA: Santa Susana,
        1978
1416.   The veritable years: poems 1949-1966. Santa Barbara:
        Black Sparrow, 1978
1417.   A man who writes. Northridge, CA: Shadows, 1980
1418.   The masks of drought. Santa Barbara: Black Sparrow,
        1980

EVERWINE, Peter
1419.   Collecting the animals. New York: Atheneum, 1973
1420.   Keeping the night. New York: Atheneum, 1977

FABILLI, Mary
1421.   The animal kingdom. Berkeley: Oyez, 1975

FAGIN, Larry
1422.   Rhymes of a jerk. New York: Kulchur Foundation,
        1974
1423.   Seven poems. Bolinas, CA: Big Sky, 1976
1424.   I'll be seeing you; poems, 1962-1976. New York: Full
        Court, 1978

FAHY, Christopher
 1425. The end beginning.   Albuquerque, NM: Red Earth,
        1978

FAIR, Ronald
 1426. Rufus.   Detroit: Lotus, 1980

FARBER, Norma
 1427. A desperate thing: marriage is a desperate thing.
        Boston: Plowshare, 1973
 1428. House hold poems. Jamaica Plain, MA: Hellric, 1975
 1429. Something further. Ann Arbor, MI: Kylix, 1979

FARINELLA, Salvatore
 1430. The orange telephone, the San Francisco experience.
        Boston: Good Gay Poets, 1975
 1431. Night blooming. Boston: Fag Rag, 1976

FARROW, Peter
 1432. What use are moose? Thorndike, ME: Thorndike, 1983

FAUST, Naomi F.
 1433. All beautiful things. Detroit: Lotus, 1983

FAWBUSH, James
 1434. Great-grandpa Nettestad was blind. Moorhead, MN:
        Territorial, 1973

FEDERMAN, Raymond
 1435. Me too. Reno, NV: West Coast Poetry Review, 1975

FEIBLEMAN, James Kern
 1436. Collected poems. New York: Horizon, 1974

FELDMAN, Alan
 1437. The happy genius. New York: Sun, 1978

FELDMAN, Irving
 1438. Leaping clear and other poems. New York: Viking,
        1976
 1439. New and selected poems. New York: Viking, 1979
 1440. Teach me, dear sister. New York: Viking, 1983

FELDMAN, Ruth
 1441. The ambition of ghosts. University Center, MI: Green
        River, 1979

FELL, Mary
 1442. The triangle fire. Minneapolis: Shadow, 1983

FENTON, Elizabeth
 1443. Public testimony. Cambridge, MA: Alice James, 1975

FERGUSON, William
    1444.   Light of paradise.   Lincoln, MA: Penmaen, 1973

FERICANO, Paul F.
    1445.   Beneath the smoke rings.   Millbrae, CA: Poor Souls/
            Scaramouche, 1976
    1446.   Cancer quiz.   Millbrae, CA: Poor Souls/Scaramouche,
            1977
    1447.   Loading the revolver with real bullets.   San Francisco:
            Second Coming, 1977
    1448.   Commercial break.   Millbrae, CA: Poor Souls/Scara-
            mouche, 1982

FERLINGHETTI, Lawrence
    1449.   Open eye, open heart.   New York: New Directions,
            1973
    1450.   Director of alienation.   Clinton, NJ: Main Street, 1976
    1451.   Who are we now?   New York: New Directions, 1976
    1452.   Northwest ecolog.   San Francisco: City Lights, 1978
    1453.   Landscapes of living & dying.   New York: New Direc-
            tions, 1979
    1454.   Mule Mountain dreams.   Bisbee, AZ: Bisbee, 1980
    1455.   Endless life.   New York: New Directions, 1981
    1456.   The populist manifestos.   San Francisco: Grey Fox,
            1981

FERRARI, Mary
    1457.   The isle of the little god.   New York: Kulchur Foun-
            dation, 1981

FERRINI, Vincent
    1458.   Selected poems.   Storrs: University of Connecticut
            Library, 1976
    1459.   Know fish.   Storrs: University of Connecticut Library,
            1979

FERRY, David
    1460.   Strangers.   Chicago: University of Chicago Press,
            1983

FETHERSTON, Patrick
    1461.   His many & himself.   Providence: Burning Deck, 1974
    1462.   The world was a bubble.   Providence: Burning Deck,
            1979

FIALKOWSKI, Barbara
    1463.   Framing.   Athens, OH: Croissant, 1977

FIELD, Edward
    1464.   A full heart.   New York: Sheep Meadow, 1977
    1465.   Stars in my eyes.   New York: Sheep Meadow, 1977
    1466.   Sweet Gwendolyn and the countess.   Gulfport, FL: Kong-
            lomerati, 1977

FIELD, Greg
1467. The end of this set. Kansas City, MO: BkMk, 1980

FIELDS, Kenneth
1468. Sunbelly. Boston: Godine, 1973

FIFER, Ken
1469. Falling man. Ithaca, NY: Ithaca House, 1979

FINCH, Donald G.
1470. Georgia. Reseda, CA: Mojave, 1976

FINKEL, Donald
1471. A mote in heaven's eye. New York: Atheneum, 1975
1472. Going under and Endurance: an Arctic idyll: two poems.
       New York: Atheneum, 1978
1473. What manner of beast: poems. New York: Atheneum,
       1981

FINLEY, Mike
1474. Lucky you. Salt Lake City: Litmus, 1976
1475. The movie under the blindfold. Minneapolis: Vanilla,
       1978

FIRER, Susan
1476. My life with the Tsar & other poems. St. Paul: New
       Rivers, 1979

FISHER, Allen
1477. Place I-xxxVII. St. Paul: Truck, 1976

FISHER, David
1478. The book of madness. San Francisco: Gallimaufry,
       1975
1479. Teachings. Cotati, CA: Back Roads, 1977

FISHER, Elizabeth
1480. The world does not belong to old ladies. Emory, VA:
       Iron Mountain, 1977

FISHER, Harrison
1481. The gravity. Washington: Washington Writers', 1977
1482. Blank like me. Washington: Paycock, 1980
1483. The text's boyfriend. Providence: Burning Deck, 1980
1484. Curtains for you. Washington: Word Works, 1981
1485. UHFO. Providence: Diana's, 1982

FISHER, T. M.
1486. ImAges. East Lansing, MI: Ghost Dance, 1978

FISHER, Will
1487. Jabbergod. Minneapolis: Vanilla, 1975

FISHMAN, Charles
  1488. Aurora; 10 poems. Berkeley: Tree, 1974
  1489. Mortal companions. Wantagh, NY: Pleasure Dome,
        1977
  1490. Warm-blooded animals. La Crosse, WI: Juniper, 1977

FITZSIMMONS, Thomas
  1491. Playseeds. Grand Rapids, MI: Pilot, 1973

FIXEL, Lawrence
  1492. Time to destroy/to discover. San Francisco: Panjan-
        drum, 1974

FLAHERTY, Doug
  1493. Near the bone. Milwaukee: Pentagram, 1975
  1494. To keep the blood from drowning. San Francisco:
        Second Coming, 1976
  1495. Love-tangle of roots. Ithaca, NY: Ithaca House, 1977

FLANDERS, Jane
  1496. The students of snow. Amherst: University of Mas-
        sachusetts Press, 1982

FLAVIN, Jack
  1497. Circle of fire. Springfield, MA: Pines, 1977

FLEMING, Gerann
  1498. Starting with coquille. Portland: Prescott Street, 1978

FLETCHER, Marjorie
  1499. Us: women. Cambridge, MA: Alice James, 1973
  1500. 33. Cambridge, MA: Alice James, 1976

FLINT, Roland
  1501. And morning. Washington: Dryad, 1975
  1502. Say it. Washington: Dryad, 1979
  1503. Resuming green: selected poems, 1965-1982. New
        York: Dial, 1983

FLOOK, Maria
  1504. Reckless wedding. Boston: Houghton Mifflin, 1982

FLOYD, Bryan Alec
  1505. The long war dead. New York: Avon, 1976

FLUCK, Sandra
  1506. Forgiving the beasts. Lancaster, PA: Risser-Fluck,
        1982

FOGEL, Daniel
  1507. A trick of resilience. Ithaca, NY: Ithaca House, 1975

FORBES, Calvin
    1508. Blue Monday. Middleton, CT: Wesleyan University
          Press, 1974
    1509. From the book of shine. Providence: Burning Deck,
          1979

FORCHÉ, Carolyn
    1510. Gathering the tribes. New Haven, CT: Yale Univer-
          sity Press, 1976
    1511. The country between us. Port Townsend, WA: Copper
          Canyon, 1981

FORD, Charles Henri
    1512. Om Krishna. Cherry Valley, NY: Cherry Valley, 1979

FOREMAN, Paul
    1513. Texas liveoak. Berkeley: Thorp Springs, 1977

FORTUNATO, Peter
    1514. A bell or a hook. Ithaca, NY: Ithaca House, 1977

FOSTER, Charles
    1515. Victoria Mundi. New York: The Smith, 1973
    1516. Dial artemis. Berkeley: Aldebaran, 1975
    1517. Peyote Toad. Salt Lake City: Litmus, 1975

FOURNET, Paul
    1518. The tortured stem. Roslyn Heights, NY: Libra, 1976

FOWLER, Gene
    1519. Vivisection. Berkeley: Thorp Springs, 1974
    1520. Felon's Journal. San Francisco: Second Coming, 1975
    1521. Fires; selected poems 1963-1976. Berkeley: Thorp
          Springs, 1975
    1522. Truckstop dance. San Francisco: Second Coming, 1976
    1523. Return of the shaman. San Francisco: Second Coming,
          1981
    1524. The quiet poems. Chapel Hill, NC: Wren, 1982

FOX, Hugh
    1525. Huaca. East Lansing, MI: Ghost Dance, 1975
    1526. Yo Yo poems. East Lansing, MI: Allegra, 1975
    1527. The face of Guy Lombardo. Union City, CA: The
          Fault, 1976
    1528. Happy deathday. Ellensburg, WA: Vagabond, 1977
    1529. Almazora 42. San Jose, CA: Laughing Bear, 1982

FOX, Siv Cedering
    1530. Cup of cold water. New York: New Rivers, 1973
    1531. Letters from the island. Fredericton, NB: Fiddlehead,
          1973
    1532. Letters from Helge. New York: New Rivers, 1974

1533. Mother is. New York: Stein and Day, 1975
1534. How to eat a fortune cookie. New York: New Rivers,
      1977
1535. The juggler. Chatham, NY: Sagarin, 1977
1536. Color poems. Missoula, MT: Calliopea, 1978
1537. The blue horse, and other night poems. New York:
      Seabury, 1979

FOX, William
1538. Election. Pittsburgh: Three Rivers, 1974
1539. Monody. Woodinville, WA: Laughing Bear, 1977

FRAIRE, Isabel
1540. Poems. Athens: Ohio University Press, 1975

FRANCIS, Robert
1541. Like ghosts of eagles. Amherst: University of Mas-
      sachusetts Press, 1974
1542. A certain distance. Woods Hole, MA: Pourboire, 1976
1543. Collected poems, 1936-1976. Amherst: University of
      Massachusetts Press, 1976

FRANK, Jacqueline
1544. No one took a country from me. Cambridge, MA:
      Alice James, 1982

FRANK, Thaisa
1545. Desire. Berkeley: Kelsey Street, 1982

FRANKE, Christopher
1546. Title. Cleveland: Cleveland Poets Series, 1975

FRANKENBERG, Lloyd
1547. The stain of circumstances; selected poems. Athens:
      Ohio University Press, 1974

FRASER, Kathleen
1548. What I want. New York: Harper & Row, 1974
1549. Magritte series. Willits, CA: Tuumba, 1977
1550. New shoes. New York: Harper & Row, 1978
1551. Each next. Berkeley: The Figures, 1980

FREED, Ray
1552. Necessary lies. Mastic, NY: Street, 1975

FRENCH, David
1553. Salt. Chico: California State University Poetry Center,
      1975

FRIEBERT, Stuart
1554. Up in bed. Cleveland: Cleveland State University
      Poetry Center, 1974

1555.   Uncertain health.   Andes, NY: Woolmer/ Brotherson,
        1979

FRIED, Emanuel
1556.   The dodo bird.   Buffalo, NY: Labor Arts, 1975

FRIEDMAN, Richard
1557.   Straight poems.   Chicago: Yellow, 1975
1558.   Physical culture.   Chicago: Yellow, 1980

FRIEDRICK, Paul
1559.   Bastard moons.   Chicago: Benjamin and Martha Waite,
        1979

FROSCH, Thomas R.
1560.   Plum Gut.   St. Paul: New Rivers, 1979

FROST, Carol
1561.   The salt lesson.   Port Townsend, WA: Graywolf, 1976
1562.   Liar's dice.   Ithaca, NY: Ithaca House, 1978
1563.   The fearful child.   Ithaca, NY: Ithaca House, 1982

FROST, Celestine
1564.   An inhuman rival.   New York: New Rivers, 1977

FRUMKIN, Gene
1565.   The mystic writing pad.   San Francisco: Red Hill, 1977
1566.   Clouds and red earth.   Chicago: Swallow, 1981

FUKFUKA, Karoma
1567.   My daddy is a cool dude, and other poems.   New York:
        Dial, 1975

FULLER, Chester
1568.   Spend sad Sundays singing songs to sassy sisters.
        Chicago: Third World, 1974

FULTON, Alice
1569.   Anchors of light.   Oneonta, NY: Swamp, 1979
1570.   Dance script with electric ballerina.   Philadelphia:
        University of Pennsylvania Press, 1983

FUNGE, Robert
1571.   The lie the lamb knows.   Peoria, IL: Spoon River,
        1979

FUNKHOUSER, Erica
1572.   Natural affinities.   Cambridge, MA: Alice James,
        1983

FUSCO, Tony
1573.   Short-lived phenomena.   Boston: Madeira, 1978

FUSSELL, Edwin S.
 1574. Your name is you. San Diego, CA: Aeolian, 1975

GABEL, John
 1575. Beach glass. Cleveland: Cleveland State University
    Poetry Center, 1979

GABRIEL, Daniel
 1576. Sacco & Vanzetti: a narrative longpoem. Brooklyn:
    Gull, 1983

GALARZA, Ernesto
 1577. Kodachromes in rhyme. Notre Dame, IN: University
    of Notre Dame Press, 1982

GALE, Vi
 1578. Clearwater. Chicago: Swallow, 1974
 1579. Eight poems. Portland: Prescott Street, 1974

GALEY, Pat
 1580. Echoes from an ivory tower. N. Babylon, NY: J.
    Mark, 1974

GALL, Gretchen
 1581. Touch earth. Vermillion, SD: Dakota, 1973

GALLAGHER, Tess
 1582. Stepping outside. Lisbon, IA: Penumbra, 1975
 1583. Instructions to the double. Port Townsend, WA: Gray-
    wolf, 1976
 1584. On your own. Port Townsend, WA: Graywolf, 1978
 1585. Portable kisses. Seattle: Sea Pen, 1978
 1586. Under stars. Port Townsend, WA: Graywolf, 1978

GALLAHER, Cynthia
 1587. Pretend it's all a movie. Chicago: Ommation, 1976

GALLOWAY, Terry Lynn
 1588. Buncha crocs in surch of snac. Austin, TX: Curb-
    stone, 1980

GALLUP, Dick
 1589. The wacking of the fruit trees. West Branch, IA:
    Toothpaste, 1975
 1590. Above the treeline. Bolinas, CA: Big Sky, 1976

GALT, Tom
 1591. The world has a familiar face. Wellfleet, MA: Shear-
    water, 1981

GALVIN, Brendan
 1592. No time for good reasons. Pittsburgh: University of
    Pittsburgh Press, 1974

1593. The minutes no one owns. Pittsburgh: University of
       Pittsburgh Press, 1977
1594. Atlantic flyway. Athens: University of Georgia Press,
       1980
1595. Winter Oysters. Athens: University of Georgia Press,
       1983

GALVIN, James
1596. Imaginary timber. Garden City, NY: Doubleday, 1980

GANCY, Doreen
1597. Poems for twelve moods. Georgetown, CA: Dragon's
       Teeth, 1979

GARCIA, Luis
1598. A blue book. Oakland, CA: Cloud Marauder, 1976

GARITANO, Rita
1599. We do what we can. Tucson, AZ: Desert First Works,
       1975

GARRETT, George
1600. Welcome to the medicine show. Winston-Salem, NC:
       Palaemon, 1978

GARRETT, Joshua H.
1601. Come in and get lost. San Diego: Grossmont, 1975

GARRIGUE, Jean
1602. Studies for an actress. New York: Macmillan, 1973

GEISSBUHLER, Elizabeth
1603. Variations on a theme. Dennis, MA: Salt-Works, 1974

GEKKER, Katherine
1604. Childhood poems. Annandale, VA: Huffman, 1975

GELFOND, Rhoda
1605. Laughing past history. Providence: Copper Beech, 1976

GENSER, Cynthia
1606. Taking on the local color. Middletown, CT: Wesleyan
       University Press, 1977

GENSLER, Kinereth D.
1607. Without roof. Cambridge, MA: Alice James, 1981

GEORGE, Charley
1608. A more. Salt Lake City: Litmus, 1975

GEORGE, Diana
1609. The evolution of love. Dennis, MA: Salt-Works, 1977

GERBER, Dan
    1610. Departure. Fremont, MI: Sumac, 1973
    1611. The Chinese poems. Fremont, MI: Sumac Press,
          1978

GERNER, Ken
    1612. The red dreams. Port Townsend, WA: Copper Canyon,
          1978

GERNES, Sonia
    1613. Brief lives. South Bend, IN: University of Notre
          Dame Press, 1981

GERSHGOREN, Sid
    1614. Negative space. Fairfax, CA: Red Hill, 1975

GHIRADELLA, Robert
    1615. Fragments. Cambridge, MA: Applewood, 1980

GHISELIN, Brewster
    1616. Light. Omaha: Abattoir, 1978
    1617. Windrose: poems, 1929-1979. Salt Lake City: Univer-
          sity of Utah Press, 1980

GIAMMARINO, Jaye
    1618. A certain hunger. Milwaukee: Peacock, 1974

GIBBONS, Reginald
    1619. The ruined motel. Boston: Houghton Mifflin, 1981

GIBBS, Barbara
    1620. The meeting place of colors. West Branch, IA: Cum-
          mington, 1973

GIBSON, Grace Evelyn
    1621. Home in time. Laurinburg, NC: Curveship, 1977

GIBSON, Margaret
    1622. Lunes. Washington: Some of Us, 1973
    1623. On the cutting edge. Willimantic, CT: Curbstone, 1976
    1624. Sings. Baton Rouge: Louisiana State University Press,
          1979
    1625. Long walks in the afternoon. Baton Rouge: Louisiana
          State University Press, 1982

GIERACH, John
    1626. Motel thought in the 70's. Boulder, CO: Lodestar,
          1976
    1627. Signs of life. Cherry Valley, NY: Cherry Valley, 1977

GIFFORD, Barry
    1628. Letters to Proust. Buffalo, NY: White Pine, 1976
    1629. A quinzaine in return for the portrait of Mary Sun.
          Berkeley: Workingman, 1977

GILBERT, Celia
  1630. Queen of darkness. New York: Viking, 1977
  1631. Bonfire. Cambridge, MA: Alice James, 1983

GILBERT, Jack
  1632. Monolithos. New York: Knopf, 1982

GILBERT, Sandra M.
  1633. In the fourth world. University: University of Alabama
         Press, 1979

GILCHRIST, Ellen
  1634. The land surveyor's daughter. Fayetteville, AR: Lost
         Roads, 1979

GILDNER, Gary
  1635. Nails. Pittsburgh: University of Pittsburgh Press,
         1975
  1636. Letters from Vicksburg. Greensboro, NC: Unicorn,
         1977
  1637. The runner. Pittsburgh: University of Pittsburgh
         Press, 1978
  1638. Jabon. Portland: Breitenbush, 1981

GILES, Laurence
  1639. Goat cottage dream poems. Mt. Horeb, WI: Perish-
         able, 1978

GILFILLAN, Merrill
  1640. To creature. Berkeley: Blue Wind, 1975
  1641. Truck/9:15. Berkeley: Blue Wind, 1976
  1642. Light years. Berkeley: Blue Wind, 1977
  1643. River through Rivertown. Berkeley: The Figures, 1982

GILL, John
  1644. Country pleasures. Trumansburg, NY: Crossing, 1975
  1645. From the diary of Peter Doyle. Plainfield, IN: Alem-
         bic, 1982

GILLILAND, Mary
  1646. Gathering fire. Ithaca, NY: Ithaca House, 1982

GILLON, Adam
  1647. Summer morn ... winter weather. New York: Astra,
         1976

GILMOUR, Bruce
  1648. Alone. New York: Stonehouse, 1973
  1649. Lovers. New York: Morrow, 1975

GILPIN, Laura
  1650. The hocus-pocus of the universe. Garden City, NY:
         Doubleday, 1977

GINSBERG, Allen
  1651. Iron horse. San Francisco: City Lights, 1974
  1652. First blues. New York: Full Court, 1975
  1653. Sad dust glories. Berkeley: Workingman's, 1975
  1654. Mind breaths; poems 1972-1977. San Francisco: City
        Lights, 1978
  1655. Poems all over the place, mostly 'seventies. Cherry
        Valley, NY: Cherry Valley, 1978
  1656. Mostly sitting Haiku. Fanwood, NJ: From Here, 1982
  1657. Plutonian ode: poems, 1977-1980. San Francisco:
        City Lights, 1982

GIORNO, John
  1658. Cancer in my left ball. Barton, VT: Something Else,
        1973

GIOVANNI, Nikki
  1659. The women and the men. New York: Morrow, 1975
  1660. Cotton candy on a rainy day. New York: Morrow, 1978
  1661. Those who ride the night winds. New York: Morrow,
        1983

GISCOMBE, C. S.
  1662. Postcards. Ithaca, NY: Ithaca House, 1977

GITIN, David
  1663. City air. Ithaca, NY: Ithaca House, 1974
  1664. This once; new and selected poems, 1965-1978. Ber-
        keley: Blue Wind, 1979

GITIN, Maria
  1665. Little movies. Ithaca, NY: Ithaca House, 1975
  1666. Night shift. Berkeley: Blue Wind, 1977

GITLIN, Todd
  1667. Busy being born. San Francisco: Straight Arrow, 1974

GIZZI, Ippy
  1668. Letters to Pauline. Providence: Burning Deck, 1975

GIZZI, Michael
  1669. Carmela Bianca. Providence: Copper Beech, 1974
  1670. Bird as. Providence: Burning Deck, 1976
  1671. Avis. Providence: Burning Deck, 1979
  1672. Species of intoxication. Providence: Burning Deck,
        1983

GLASS, Malcolm
  1673. Bone love. Orlando: University Presses of Florida,
        1978

GLAZE, Andrew
  1674. A masque of surgery. London: Menard, 1974

1675. The trash dragon of Shensi. Providence: Copper Beech,
       1978
1676. I am the Jefferson County Courthouse. Birmingham,
       AL: Thunder, 1981
1677. A city. Amherst, MA: Swamp, 1983

GLAZIER, Lyle
1678. Two continents. Montpelier, VT: Council on the Arts,
       1976

GLEASON, Madeline
1679. Here comes everybody. San Francisco: Panjandrum,
       1975

GLIDZEN, Alex
1680. Funny ducks. East Lansing, MI: Ghost Dance, 1973

GLOSSER, Pete
1681. The light. Charlottesville, VA: Alderman, 1976

GLOVER, Al
1682. Paradise valley. Binghamton, NY: Bellevue, 1975

GLÜCK, Louise
1683. The house on marshland. New York: Ecco, 1974
1684. The garden. New York: Antaeus, 1976
1685. Descending figure. New York: Ecco, 1980
1686. Firstborn. New York: Ecco, 1982

GLUCK, Robert
1687. Andy. San Francisco: Panjandrum, 1973
1688. Elements of a coffee service. San Francisco: Four
       Seasons Foundation, 1983

GODFREY, John
1689. Dabble: poems, 1966-1980. New York: Full Court,
       1981

GOEDICKE, Patricia
1690. For the four corners. Ithaca, NY: Ithaca House, 1976
1691. The trail that turns on itself. Ithaca, NY: Ithaca
       House, 1978
1692. Crossing the same river. Amherst: University of
       Massachusetts Press, 1980
1693. The dog that was barking yesterday. Amherst, MA:
       Lynx House, 1980

GOHLKE, Madelon Sprengnether
1694. The normal heart. St. Paul: New Rivers, 1981

GOICHBERG, Rena
1695. Spiked flower. San Francisco: Cassandra, 1975

GOLDBARTH, Albert
  1696. Coprolites. New York: New Rivers, 1973
  1697. Under cover. Crete, NE: Best Cellar, 1973
  1698. Jan. 31. Garden City, NY: Doubleday, 1974
  1699. Optiks. New York: Seven Woods, 1974
  1700. Keeping. Ithaca, NY: Ithaca House, 1975
  1701. Comings back. Garden City, NY: Doubleday, 1976
  1702. Curve. New York: New Rivers, 1977
  1703. Different fleshes. Geneva, NY: Hobart and William
        Smith Colleges Press, 1979
  1704. Ink, blood, semen. Cleveland: Bits, 1980
  1705. Eurekas. Memphis, TN: St. Luke's, 1981
  1706. The smuggler's handbook. Milton, MA: Chowder, 1981
  1707. Who gathered and whispered behind me. Seattle:
        L' Epervier, 1981
  1708. Faith. St. Paul: New Rivers, 1982
  1709. Goldbarth's book of occult phenomena. Des Moines, IA:
        Blue Buildings, 1982
  1710. Original light: new and selected poems, 1973-1983.
        Princeton, NJ: Ontario Review, 1983

GOLDBERG, Natalie
  1711. Chicken & in love. Minneapolis: Holy Cow!, 1980

GOLDENSOHN, Barry
  1712. Saint Venus Eve. Iowa City: Cummington, 1973

GOLDFARB, Sidney
  1713. Curve in the road. Cambridge, MA: H. Ferguson,
        1980

GOLDMAN, Beate
  1714. Letters to a stranger. Washington: Washington
        Writers', 1981

GOLDSTEIN, Laurence
  1715. Altamira. Omaha: Abattoir, 1978

GOLFFING, Francis
  1716. Collected poems. Omaha: Abattoir, 1980

GOOCH, Brad
  1717. The daily news. Calais, VT: Z Press, 1977

GOODMAN, Miriam
  1718. Permanent wave. Cambridge, MA: Alice James, 1977
  1719. Signal-noise. Cambridge, MA: Alice James, 1982

GOODMAN, Paul
  1720. Collected poems. New York: Random House, 1973
  1721. Collected poems. New York: Vintage, 1977

GORDON, Bonnie
    1722. Release the breathless. Port Jefferson, NY: Street
           Magazine, 1976
    1723. A childhood in Reno. Port Jefferson, NY: Street, 1982

GORDON, Don
    1724. On the ward. Reno, NV: West Coast Poetry Review,
           1977
    1725. Excavations. Reno, NV: West Coast Poetry Review,
           1979

GORDON, Jaimy
    1726. The bend, the lip, the kid. New York: Sun, 1978

GOREN, Judith
    1727. Coming alive. Okemos, MI: Stone, 1975

GOTTLIEB, Darcy
    1728. No witness but ourselves. Columbia: University of
           Missouri Press, 1973

GRABILL, James
    1729. One river. Santa Monica, CA: Momentum, 1975
    1730. To other beings. Amherst, MA: Lynx House, 1981

GRAFF, John
    1731. Variety is. Reseda, CA: Mojave, 1974

GRAHAM, Jorie
    1732. Hybrids of plants and of ghosts. Princeton, NJ: Prince-
           ton University Press, 1980
    1733. Erosion. Princeton, NJ: Princeton University Press,
           1983

GRAHAM, Neile
    1734. Seven robins. Lisbon, IA: Penumbra, 1983

GRAHAM, Philip
    1735. The vanishings. Brooklyn: Release, 1978

GRAHN, Judy
    1736. The work of a common woman. New York: St. Mar-
           tin's, 1978
    1737. The queen of wands. Trumansburg, NY: Crossing,
           1983

GRAUERHOLZ, James
    1738. Rusty Jack. Cherry Valley, NY: Cherry Valley, 1975

GRAY, Darrell
    1739. Scattered brains. West Branch, IA: Toothpaste, 1975

GRAZIANO, Frank
    1740. Desemboque. Point Reyes, CA: Floating Island, 1979
    1741. From Sheepshead, from Paumanok. Bisbee, AZ:
          Porch, 1979

GREASYBEAR, Charles John
    1742. Songs. Boise, ID: Ahsahta, 1979

GREBANIER, Bernard
    1743. Last harvest. Larchmont, NY: Estate of Bernard
          Grebanier, 1980

GREEN, J. Charles
    1744. First words. Greenfield Center, NY: Greenfield Re-
          view, 1975

GREEN, Jaki Shelton
    1745. Dead on arrival. Chapel Hill, NC: Carolina Wren,
          1983

GREEN, Rose Basile
    1746. Songs of ourselves. New York: Cornwall, 1982

GREENBERG, Alvin
    1747. Dark lands. Ithaca, NY: Ithaca House, 1973
    1748. Metaform. Amherst: University of Massachusetts
          Press, 1975
    1749. In. Boston: Godine, 1978

GREENBERG, Barbara L.
    1750. The spoils of August. Middletown, CT: Wesleyan
          University Press, 1974

GREENBERG, Judith Anne
    1751. Antelope are running. Lewiston, ID: Confluence, 1978

GREENE, Jonathan
    1752. Glossary of the everyday. Toronto: Coach House, 1974
    1753. Scaling the walls. Lexington, KY: Gnomon, 1974
    1754. Once a kingdom again. Albany, CA: Sand Dollar, 1978
    1755. Peripatetics. St. Paul: Truck, 1978
    1756. Quiet goods. Monterey, KY: Larkspur, 1979
    1757. Trickster tabs. West Branch, IA: Toothpaste, 1983

GREENHORN, Billy
    1758. We'll see who's a peasant. Beckley, WV: Mountain
          Union, 1977

GREENSPAN, Judy
    1759. To lesbians everywhere. New York: Violet, 1976

GREENWALD, Ted
    1760. The life. Bolinas, CA: Big Sky, 1974

1761. Makes sense. Lenox, MA: Angel Hair, 1974
1762. Native land. Washington: Titanic, 1977
1763. You bet! Berkeley: This, 1978
1764. Licorice chronicles. New York: Kulchur Foundation, 1979
1765. Use no hooks. New York: Asylum's, 1980
1766. Smile. Berkeley: Tuumba, 1981

GREENWAY, William
1767. Pressure under grace: poems. Portland: Breitenbush, 1982

GREENWOOD, William
1768. Into the center of America. Santa Cruz, CA: Green Horse, 1976

GREGER, Debora
1769. Cartography. Lisbon, IA: Penumbra, 1980
1770. Movable islands. Princeton, NJ: Princeton University Press, 1980

GREGERSON, Linda
1771. Fire in the conservatory. Port Townsend, WA: Dragon's Gate, 1983

GREGG, Linda
1772. Too bright to see. Port Townsend, WA: Graywolf, 1981

GREGOR, Arthur
1773. The past now. Garden City, NY: Doubleday, 1975
1774. Embodiment. New York: Sheep Meadow, 1982
1775. A longing in the land. New York: Schocken, 1983

GREGORY, Eric
1776. The musics. Laurinburg, NC: St. Andrews, 1974

GREINKE, L. Eric
1777. Iron rose. Grand Rapids, MI: Pilot, 1973
1778. The broken lock. Grand Rapids, MI: Pilot, 1975
1779. Masterpiece theater. Grand Rapids, MI: Pilot, 1975

GRENFELL, Cynthia
1780. Stone run: tidings. Santa Fe, NM: Sunstone, 1983

GRIFFIN, Howard
1781. Four poems. New York: Eudora, 1976

GRIFFIN, Susan
1782. Dear sky. San Lorenzo, CA: Shameless Hussy, 1973
1783. Like the iris of an eye. New York: Harper & Row, 1976
1784. Woman and nature. New York: Harper & Row, 1978

GRIFFIN, Walter
    1785. Night Music. New Philadelphia, OH: Pale Horse, 1974
    1786. Port Authority. Nashville, TN: Brevity, 1976
    1787. Machineworks. Austell, GA: Sweetwater, 1977

GRIGSBY, Gordon
    1788. Tornado watch. Columbus: Ohio State University Press,
           1977

GRILLO, Paul
    1789. Video ranger. Milwaukee: Morgan, 1974
    1790. Vibes of the saints. Cherry Valley, NY: Cherry Valley,
           1977
    1791. Skin of doubt. Olean, NY: Allegany Mountain, 1979

GROSHOLZ, Emily
    1792. The river painter. Urbana: University of Illinois
           Press, 1983

GROSS, Mary E.
    1793. Penny on the floor. St. Petersburg, FL: Valkyrie,
           1974

GROSSINGER, Richard
    1794. The provinces. Plainfield, VT: North Atlantic, 1975

GROSSMAN, Allen R.
    1795. And the dew lay all night upon my branch. Lexington,
           MA: Aleph, 1976
    1796. The woman on the bridge over the Chicago River. New
           York: New Directions, 1979
    1797. Of the great house: a book of poems. New York: New
           Directions, 1982

GROSSMAN, Martin
    1798. The arable mind. Kalamazoo, MI: Blue Mountain, 1977

GROSSMAN, Richard
    1799. Tycoon boy. Santa Cruz, CA: Kayak, 1977
    1800. The animals. Minneapolis: Zygote, 1983

GROSSMAN, Ronald
    1801. Kiss the sky. North Babylon, NY: J. Mark, 1974

GUERNSEY, Bruce
    1802. Lost wealth. Fredonia, NY: Basilisk, 1974
    1803. January thaw. Pittsburgh: University of Pittsburgh
           Press, 1982

GUEST, Barbara
    1804. Moscow mansions. New York: Viking, 1973
    1805. The countess from Minneapolis. Providence: Burning
           Deck, 1976

1806. The Turler losses. Montreal: Mansfield, 1979
1807. Biography. Providence: Burning Deck, 1980

GULLANS, Charles
    1808. Imperfect correspondences. Los Angeles: Symposium,
        1978
    1809. A diatribe to Dr. Steele. Los Angeles: Symposium,
        1982
    1810. Under red skies. Florence, KY: Barth, 1983

GURLEY, George
    1811. Home movies. Independence, MO: Raindust, 1975
    1812. Fugues in the plumbing. Kansas City, MO: BkMk,
        1980

GUSTAFSON, Jim
    1813. Tales of virtue and transformation. Bolinas, CA: Big
        Sky, 1974
    1814. Bright eyes talks crazy to Rembrandt. Brooklyn:
        Hanging Loose, 1975

GUSTAFSON, Richard C.
    1815. The arc from now. Ames: Iowa State University Press,
        1978

GUSTAFSSON, Lars
    1816. Warm rooms and cold. Providence: Copper Beech,
        1975

GUTHRIE, James
    1817. Legerdemain. Rochester, NY: Grace Note, 1977

HAAGENSEN, Jan
    1818. Like a diamondback in the trunk of a witness's Buick.
        Cleveland: Cleveland State University Poetry Center,
        1977

HABERMAN, Daniel
    1819. Poems. New York: Art Direction, 1977
    1820. The furtive wall. New York: Art Direction, 1982

HACKER, Marilyn
    1821. Presentation piece. New York: Viking, 1974
    1822. Separations. New York: Knopf, 1976
    1823. Taking notice. New York: Knopf, 1980

HACKMAN, Neil
    1824. Ode to Jack Spicer and other poems. Chicago: Om-
        mation, 1976

HACKNEY, Jim
    1825. 19, in celebration. Spartanburg, SC: Wofford Library,
        1975

HADAS, Pamela White
    1826. Designing women. New York: Knopf, 1979
    1827. Beside herself; Pocahontas to Patty Hearst. New York:
        Knopf, 1983

HADAS, Rachel
    1828. Starting from Troy. Boston: Godine, 1975
    1829. Slow transparency. Middleton, CT: Wesleyan Universi-
        ty Press, 1983

HAGEDORN, Jessica-Tarahata
    1830. Dangerous music. San Francisco: Momo's, 1975
    1831. Pet food and tropical apparitions. San Francisco:
        Mom's, 1982

HAGUE, Richard
    1832. Ripening. Columbus: Ohio State University Press, 1983

HAHN, Robert
    1833. Collectibles. Hollywood, CA: Pygmalion, 1976
    1834. Crimes. Amherst, MA: Lynx House, 1976
    1835. Routine risks. Omaha: Abattoir, 1976

HAIMSOHN, Naomi
    1836. The happy tree. Milwaukee: Peacock, 1974

HAINES, John
    1837. Leaves and ashes. Santa Cruz, CA: Kayak, 1973
    1838. Leaves and ashes. Santa Cruz, CA: Kayak, 1974
    1839. In five years time. Missoula, MT: SmokeRoot, 1976
    1840. The sun on your shoulder. Port Townsend, WA: Gray-
        wolf, 1976
    1841. Cicada. Middletown, CT: Wesleyan University Press,
        1977
    1842. In a dusty light. Port Townsend, WA: Graywolf, 1977
    1843. News from the glacier; selected poems 1960-1980.
        Middletown, CT: Wesleyan University, 1982
    1844. Winter news (rev. ed.). Middletown, CT: Wesleyan
        University Press, 1983

HAKIM, Seymour
    1845. Substituting memories. New York: Poet Gallery, 1975

HALE, Janet Campbell
    1846. Owl's song. Garden City, NY: Doubleday, 1973
    1847. Custer lives in Humboldt County & other poems. Green-
        field Center, NY: Greenfield Review, 1978

HALL, D. J.
    1848. Journey into morning. Middletown, CT: Wesleyan
        University Press, 1973

HALL, Donald
    1849. A blue wing tilts at the edge of the sea; selected poems
            1964-1974. London: Secker and Warburg, 1975
    1850. Kicking the leaves. Mt. Horeb, WI: Perishable, 1975;
            New York: Harper & Row, 1978
    1851. The town of Hill. Boston: Godine, 1975

HALL, J. C.
    1852. A house of words. Middletown, CT: Wesleyan Univer-
            sity Press, 1973

HALL, James B.
    1853. The hunt within. Baton Rouge: Louisiana State Univer-
            sity Press, 1973

HALL, Jim
    1854. The lady from the green hills. Pittsburgh: Three
            Rivers, 1976
    1855. Ham operator. Bristol, RI: Ampersand, 1980
    1856. The mating reflex. Pittsburgh: Carnegie-Mellon Uni-
            versity Press, 1980

HALL, Joan Joffe
    1857. The rift zone. Willimantic, CT: Curbstone, 1977
    1858. The aerialist's fall. Willimantic, CT: Ziesing, 1981

HALL, John
    1859. The dreams of Mercurius. Santa Cruz, CA: Green-
            house Review, 1977
    1860. Jack the Ripper. Santa Cruz, CA: Greenhouse Review,
            1978
    1861. The hiding place. Santa Cruz, CA: Greenhouse Review,
            1982

HALL, Walter
    1862. Glowing in the dark. Providence: Burning Deck, 1973
    1863. Vestiges. Providence: Diana's Bimonthly 1974
    1864. Miners getting off the graveyard; selected poems, 1969-
            1977. Providence: Burning Deck, 1977

HALLEY, Anne
    1865. The beared mother. Amherst: University of Massa-
            chusetts Press, 1979

HALPERIN, Mark
    1866. Backroads. Pittsburgh: University of Pittsburgh Press,
            1976
    1867. The white coverlet. Waldron Island, WA: Jawbone,
            1979
    1868. A place made fast. Port Townsend, WA: Copper Can-
            yon, 1982

HALPERN, Daniel
    1869. [No entry]
    1870. The lady knife-thrower. Binghamton, NY: Bellevue,
          1975
    1871. Street fire. New York: Viking, 1975
    1872. Life among others. New York: Viking, 1978
    1873. Seasonal rights. New York: Penguin, 1982

HAMADY, Walter
    1874. Seeds & chairs. Mt. Horeb, WI: Perishable, 1979

HAMILL, Janet
    1875. The temple. New York: Telephone, 1980

HAMILL, Juan
    1876. Troublante. New York: Oliphant, 1975

HAMILL, Sam
    1877. Heroes of the Teton mythos. Denver: Copper Canyon,
          1973
    1878. Uintah blue. Port Townsend, WA: Copper Canyon,
          1975
    1879. The calling across forever. Port Townsend, WA:
          Copper Canyon, 1976
    1880. Dead letter. Waldron Island, WA: Jawbone, 1978
    1881. Sam Hamill's Triada. Port Townsend, WA: Copper
          Canyon, 1978
    1882. Animae. Port Townsend, WA: Copper Canyon, 1980
    1883. Requiem. Port Townsend, WA: Copper Canyon, 1983

HAMILTON, Alfred Starr
    1884. The big parade. Crete, NE: Best Cellar, 1982

HAMMER, Adam
    1885. Magnito star mine. Boston: Barn Dream, 1973

HAMMER, Louis
    1886. To burn California. Chatham, NY: Omphalos, 1974
    1887. [No entry]
    1888. Lying on the earth. Santa Cruz, CA: Kayak, 1975
    1889. Birth sores/bands. Old Chatham, NY: Sachem, 1981

HAMMOND, Karla
    1890. The unicorn's choice. Chicago: Ommation, 1976

HAMMOND, Mac
    1891. Six Dutch hearts. Binghamton, NY: Bellevue, 1978

HAMPL, Patricia
    1892. Woman before an aquarium. Pittsburgh: University of
          Pittsburgh Press, 1978
    1893. Resort and other poems. Boston: Houghton Mifflin,
          1983

HANDKE, Russell
1894. Rainbow melody. Flushing, NY: New Voices, 1973

HANKLA, Cathryn
1895. Phenomena. Columbia: University of Missouri Press,
1983

HANKLA, Susan
1896. Mistral for Daddy and Van Gogh. Seattle: Mill Moun-
tain, 1976
1897. I am running home. Providence: Burning Deck, 1979

HANNAN, Greg
1898. Instincts for the jugular. Washington: Washington
Writers', 1980

HANNIGAN, Paul
1899. Bringing back slavery. Cambridge, MA: Dolphin, 1976

HANRAHAN, Janne
1900. Light from new steel. Springfield, IL: Sangamon,
1974

HANSEN, Dorothy Lee
1901. Africa to me. Napa, CA: Adinkra, 1983

HANSON, Jim
1902. Reasons for the sky. West Branch, IA: Toothpaste,
1979

HANSON, Kenneth O.
1903. The uncorrected world. Middletown, CT: Wesleyan
University Press, 1973
1904. Portraits, friends, artists. Portland: Press-22, 1978
1805. Lighting the night sky. Portland: Breitenbush, 1983

HANZLICEK, C. G.
1906. Stars. Columbia: University of Missouri Press, 1977
1907. Calling the dead. Pittsburgh: Carnegie-Mellon Univer-
sity Press, 1982
1908. A dozen for Leah. Santa Barbara: Brandenburg, 1982

HARASYMOWICZ, Jerzy
1909. Planting beeches. New York: New Rivers, 1975

HARDISON, O. B.
1910. Pro musica antiqua. Baton Rouge: Louisiana State
University Press, 1977

HARER, Katherine
1911. In these bodies. Santa Cruz, CA: Moving Parts, 1983

HARJO, Joy
 1912. What moon drove me to this. Berkeley: I. Reed, 1980
 1913. She had some horses. New York: Thunder's Mouth,
    1982

HARKNESS, Edward
 1914. Long eye, lost wind, forgive me. Port Townsend, WA:
    Copperhead, 1975

HARMON, William
 1915. Legion: civic courses. Middletown, CT: Wesleyan
    University Press, 1973
 1916. The intussusception of Miss Mary America. Santa Cruz,
    CA: Kayak, 1976
 1917. One long poem. Baton Rouge: Louisiana State Univer-
    sity Press, 1982

HARPER, Michael S.
 1918. Department. Garden City, NY: Doubleday, 1973
 1919. Nightmare begins responsibility. Urbana: University
    of Illinois Press, 1974
 1920. Images of kin. Urbana: University of Illinois Press,
    1977

HARRIS, Blanche E.
 1921. Changing-ever changing. University: University of
    Alabama, 1978

HARRIS, Jana
 1922. Pin money. Fairfax, CA: Jungle Garden, 1977
 1923. Who's that pushy bitch? Fairfax, CA: Jungle Garden,
    1981
 1924. Manhattan as a second language and other poems. San
    Francisco: Harper & Row, 1982

HARRIS, John Stirling
 1925. Barbed wire. Provo, UT: Brigham Young University
    Press, 1974

HARRIS, Judith
 1926. Poppies. Washington: Washington Writers' Pub. House,
    1981

HARRIS, Marie
 1927. Herbal. Bowling Green, OH: Tribal, 1973
 1928. Raw honey. Cambridge, MA: Alice James, 1975
 1929. Interstate. Pittsburgh: Slow Loris, 1980

HARRIS, William J.
 1930. Hey fella, would you mind holding this piano a moment.
    Ithaca, NY: Ithaca House, 1974
 1931. In my own dark way. Ithaca, NY: Ithaca House, 1977

HARRISON, Jim
- 1932. Letters to Yesenin. Fremont, MI: Sumac, 1973
- 1933. Returning to Earth. Ithaca, NY: Ithaca House, 1977
- 1934. Letters to Yesenin. Returning to Earth. Los Angeles: Center, 1979
- 1935. Selected & new poems. New York: Delacorte Press/ Seymour Lawrence, 1982
- 1936. Natural world. Barrytown, NY: Station Hill, 1983

HARRYMAN, Carla
- 1937. Percentage. Berkeley: Tuumba, 1979

HARSHMAN, Marc
- 1938. Turning out the stones. Pittsford, NY: State Street, 1983

HART, Edward LeRoy
- 1939. To Utah. Provo, UT: Brigham Young University Press, 1979

HART, John
- 1940. The climbers. Pittsburgh: University of Pittsburgh Press, 1978

HARTER, Penny
- 1941. The orange balloon. Fanwood, NJ: From Here, 1980
- 1942. Lovepoems. Fanwood, NJ: From Here, 1981
- 1943. White flowers in the snow. St. Paul: New Rivers, 1981
- 1944. Hiking the crevass; poems on the way to divorce. West Orange, NJ: Warthog, 1983

HARTMAN, Charles O.
- 1945. The pigfoot rebellion. Boston: Godine, 1982

HARTMAN, Geoffrey H.
- 1946. Akiba's children. Emory, VA: Iron Mountain, 1978

HARTMAN, Susan
- 1947. Dumb show. Orlando: University Presses of Florida, 1979

HARTMAN, Yuki
- 1948. Hot footsteps. New York: Telephone, 1976

HARWOOD, Grace
- 1949. Half a loaf. San Francisco: Peace & Pieces, 1973

HASKINS, Anne
- 1950. The rain has no self. Chicago: Ommation, 1977

HASS, Robert
- 1951. Field guide. New Haven, CT: Yale University Press, 1973

1952. Winter morning in Charlottesville. Knotting, Eng.: Sceptre, 1977
1953. Praise. New York: Ecco, 1979

HASTE, Gwendolen
1954. The selected poems of Gwendolen Haste. Boise, ID: Ahsahta, 1976

HATHAWAY, Baxter
1955. The petulant children. Ithaca, NY: Ithaca House, 1978

HATHAWAY, James
1956. Foraging. Ithaca, NY: Ithaca House, 1978

HATHAWAY, William
1957. A wilderness of monkeys. Ithaca, NY: Ithaca House, 1975
1958. The gymnast of inertia. Baton Rouge: Louisiana State University Press, 1982

HAUSMAN, Gerald
1959. Night herding song. Port Townsend, WA: Copper Canyon, 1978
1960. The runner. Santa Fe, NM: Sunstone, 1983

HAVELIN, Jim
1961. What the diamond does is hold it all in. Buffalo, NY: White Pine, 1979

HAWKES, John
1962. The bestowal. West Lafayette, IN: Sparrow, 1983

HAWKINS, Bobbie Louise
1963. Own your body. Los Angeles: Black Sparrow, 1973

HAWKINS, Bruce
1964. Wordrows. Berkeley: Berkeley Poets' Workshop, 1975
1965. The ghost of the Buick. Berkeley: Berkeley Poets, 1982

HAWLEY, Beatrice
1966. Making the house fall down. Cambridge, MA: Alice James, 1977
1967. Nothing is lost. Cambridge, MA: Apple-wood, 1979

HAXO, Tom
1968. The lesser light. Amherst, MA: Swamp, 1982

HAYDEN, Robert
1969. Angle of ascent; new and selected poems. New York: Liveright, 1975

1970. The legend of John Brown. Detroit: Detroit Institute
       of Art, 1978
1971. American journal. New York: Liveright, 1982

HAYES, Ann
1972. A dancer's step. Pittsburgh: Three Rivers, 1973
1973. The living and the dead. Pittsburgh: Carnegie -Mellon
       University Press, 1975

HAYES, Dorsha
1974. New poems from the bell -branch. Georgetown, CA:
       Dragon's Teeth, 1980
1975. [No entry.]

HAYS, H. R.
1976. Inside my own skin. Santa Cruz, CA: Kayak, 1974
1977. Portraits in mixed media. Rockville Center, NY:
       Survivor's Manual, 1978

HAZARD, James
1978. A hive of souls. Trumansburg, NY: Crossing, 1977
1979. Fire in Whiting, Indiana. La Crosse, WI: Juniper,
       1983

HAZO, Samuel
1980. Quartered. Pittsburgh: University of Pittsburgh Press,
       1974
1981. Inscripts. Athens: Ohio University Press, 1975
1982. To Paris. New York: New Directions, 1981
1983. Thank a bored angel: selected poems. New York: New
       Directions, 1983

HEAD, Gwen
1984. Special effects. Pittsburgh: University of Pittsburgh
       Press, 1975
1985. The ten thousandth night. Pittsburgh: University of
       Pittsburgh Press, 1979

HEARNE, Vicki
1986. Nervous houses. Austin: University of Texas Press,
       1980
1987. In the absence of horses. Princeton, NJ: Princeton
       University Press, 1983

HEARST, James
1988. Dry leaves. Holly Springs, MS: Ragnarok, 1975
1989. Proved by trial. La Crosse, WI: Juniper, 1977
1990. Snake in the strawberries. Ames: Iowa State Univer-
       sity Press, 1979

HECHT, Anthony
1991. Millions of strange shadows. New York: Atheneum, 1977
1992. The Venetian vespers. New York: Atheneum, 1979

HECHT, Roger
    1993.   Parade of ghosts.   Santa Fe, NM: Lightning Tree,
            1976

HECKLER, Mary
    1994.   Love pommes.   Salt Lake City: Litmus,   1977

HEDIN, Robert
    1995.   Snow country.   Port Townsend, WA: Cooper Canyon,
            1975
    1996.   On the day of the bulls.   Waldron Island, WA: Jaw-
            bone, 1979

HEDLEY, Leslie Woolf
    1997.   On my way to the cemetery.   San Francisco: Amper-
            sand, 1981

HEFFERNAN, Michael
    1998.   Booking passage.   Shawnee Mission, KS: BkMk, 1973
    1999.   A figure of plain force.   Milton, MA: Chowder, 1978
    2000.   The cry of Oliver Hardy.   Athens: University of Geor-
            gia Press, 1979

HEFFERNAN, Thomas
    2001.   Mobiles, the sadness of Cerberus and the bitch.   Laurin-
            burg, NC: St. Andrews College, 1974
    2002.   The Liam poems.   Georgetown, CA: Dragon's Teeth,
            1981

HEJINIAN, Lyn
    2003.   A thought is the bride of what thinking.   Berkeley:
            Tuumba, 1976
    2004.   A mask of motion.   Providence: Burning Deck, 1977

HELLER, Michael D.
    2005.   Figures of speaking.   Mt. Horeb, WI: Perishable, 1977
    2006.   Knowledge.   New York: Sun, 1979

HEMSCHEMEYER, Judith
    2007.   I remember the room was filled with light.   Middletown,
            CT: Wesleyan University Press, 1973
    2008.   Very close and very slow.   Middletown, CT: Wesleyan
            University Press, 1975

HENDERSON, Arn
    2009.   Document for an anonymous Indian.   Norman, OK:
            Point Riders, 1974
    2010.   The surgeon general's collection.   Norman, OK: Point
            Riders, 1976

HENDERSON, David
    2011.   The low east.   Richmond, CA: North Atlantic, 1980

HENDRICKS, Geoff
    2012. Ring piece. West Glover, VT: Something Else, 1973.

HENLEY, Patricia
    2013. Learning to die. Pittsburgh: Three Rivers, 1978

HENRI, Raymond
    2014. Dispatches from the fields. Georgetown, Dragon's Teeth, 1981

HENRICHSEN, Dennis see HINRICHSEN, Dennis
    2015. [No entry]

HENSON, Lance
    2016. Poems for the Cheyenne. Norman, OK: Point Riders, 1976
    2017. Mistah. New York: Strawberry, 1977
    2018. Buffalo marrow on black. Edmond, OK: Full Count, 1980

HEPWORTH, James
    2019. Silence as a method of birth control. Lewiston, ID: Confluence, 1977

HERNTON, Calvin C.
    2020. Medicine man; collected poems. Berkeley: Reed, Cannon and Johnson, 1976

HERRON, Bill
    2021. Rituals of our time. Chapel Hill, NC: Carolina Wren, 1980

HERSHON, Robert
    2022. Little red wagon painted blue. Greensboro, NC: Unicorn, 1973
    2023. Rock and chairs. Washington: Some of us, 1975; Brooklyn: Hanging Loose, 1975
    2024. A blue shovel. Brooklyn: Hanging Loose, 1979
    2025. The public hug: new and selected poems. Baton Rouge: Louisiana State University Press, 1980

HERZ, Robert
    2026. White smoke. Seattle: L'Epervier, 1977
    2027. Stream. Berkeley: L'Epervier, 1983

HESSELGESSER, Debra
    2028. Guy's poem. San Francisco: Smoking Mirror, 1974
    2029. A small quirk in the fuselage. San Francisco: Smoking Mirror, 1974

HEWITT, Geof
    2030. Stone soup. Ithaca, NY: Ithaca House, 1974
    2031. I think they'll lay my egg tomorrow. Montpelier: Vermont Council on the Arts, 1976

HEYEN, William
    2032. The pigeons. Mt. Horeb, WI: Perishable, 1973
    2033. The trail beside the River Platte. Rushden, Eng.: Sceptre, 1973
    2034. Noise in the trees. New York: Vanguard, 1974
    2035. Mermaid. Derry, PA: Rook, 1975
    2036. Cardinals/The cardinal. Derry, PA: Rook, 1976
    2037. The Corrie White auction at Brockport, May, 1974. Derry, PA: Rook, 1976
    2038. Dusk. Derry, PA: Rook, 1976
    2039. Mare. Derry, PA: Rook, 1976
    2040. Of Palestine. Omaha: Abattoir, 1976
    2041. The pearl. Pittsburgh: Slow Loris, 1976
    2042. Pickerel. Derry, PA: Rook, 1976
    2043. XVII machines. Pittsburgh: Sisyphus, 1976
    2044. Sixteen poems and a story. Derry, PA: Rook, 1976
    2045. The trench. Derry, PA: Rook, 1976
    2046. Darkness. Derry, PA: Rook, 1977
    2047. The elm's home. Derry, PA: Scrimshaw, 1977
    2048. Fires. Athens, OH: Croissant, 1977
    2049. The swastika poems. New York: Vanguard, 1977
    2050. Brockport's poems. Brockport, NY: Challenger, 1978
    2051. Lord Dragonfly. Ruffsdale, PA: Rook, 1978
    2052. Son dream/daughter dream. Ruffsdale, PA: Rook, 1978
    2053. Witness. Madison, WI: Rara Avis, 1978
    2054. The ash. Syracuse, NY: Tamarack, 1979
    2055. The children. Knotting, Eng.: Sceptre, 1979
    2056. The city parables. Athens, OH: Croissant, 1979
    2057. The descent. Knotting, Eng.: Sceptre, 1979
    2058. Evening drowning. Concord, NH: Ewart, 1979
    2059. Long Island light. New York: Vanguard, 1979
    2060. The snow hen. Concord, NH: Ewart, 1979
    2061. The bees. Syracuse, NY: Tamarack, 1980
    2062. The city parables. Athens, OH: Croissant, 1980
    2063. December 31, 1979. Knotting, Eng.: Martin Booth, 1980
    2064. Lord Dragonfly. New York: Vanguard Press, 1981
    2065. The trains. Worcester, MA: Metacom, 1981
    2066. Along this water. Syracuse, NY: Tamarack, 1983
    2067. Erika: poems of the Holocaust. New York: Vanguard, 1983

HEYNEN, James
    2068. The funeral parlor. Port Townsend, WA: Graywolf, 1976
    2069. Notes from Custer. Hanover, NH: Bear Claw, 1976

2070. How the sow became a goddess. Lewiston, ID: Con-
      fluence, 1977
2071. A suitable church. Port Townsend, WA: Copper Can-
      yon, 1981

HEYNEN, Jim
2072. Maedra poems. Orangeburg, SC: Peaceweed, 1974

HIATT, Ben
2073. Poems. San Francisco: Second Coming, 1977

HIATT, David
2074. Vanish. Salt Lake City: Litmus, 1974

HICKY, Daniel Whitehead
2075. Poems of Daniel Whitehead Hicky. Atlanta: Cherokee,
      1975

HIFLER, Joyce
2076. Pathways. Garden City, NY: Doubleday, 1975

HIGGINS, Dick
2077. For Eugene in Germany. Barton, VT: Unpublished
      Editions, 1973
2078. The ladder to the moon. Barton, VT: Unpublished
      Editions, 1973
2079. Modular poems. Barton, VT: Unpublished Editions,
      1974
2080. Classic plays. Barton, VT: Unpublished Editions,
      1976
2081. Everyone has sher favorites (his or her). New York:
      Unpublished Editions, 1978
2082. Some recent snowflakes (and other things). New York:
      Printed Editions, 1979
2083. Of celebration of morning. New York: Printed Editions,
      1980

HILBERRY, Conrad
2084. Rust. Athens: Ohio University Press, 1974
2085. House marks. Mt. Horeb, WI: Perishable, 1980
2086. Man in the attic. Cleveland: Bits, 1980

HILDEBIDLE, John
2087. The old chore. Cambridge, MA: Alice James, 1981

HILDEBRAND, Tim
2088. Rotwang, or the delirious precision of dreams. Berke-
      ley: Blue Wind, 1976

HILL, Geoffrey
2089. Somewhere is such a kingdom. Boston: Houghton
      Mifflin, 1975

HILL, Pati
    2090. Impossible dreams. Cambridge, MA: Alice James, 1976

HILL, Russell
    2091. Letters from the mines. Fairfax, CA: Jungle Garden, 1978

HILL, Tom
    2092. Whales. San Francisco: Two Windows, 1973

HILLER, Tobey
    2093. Crossings. Berkeley: Oyez, 1980

HILTON, David
    2094. The candleflame. West Branch, IA: Toothpaste, 1976
    2095. Huladance. Trumansburg, NY: Crossing, 1976

HINE, Charles
    2096. No name stalks the land. Providence: Diana's Bi-monthly, 1974
    2097. Wild Indians. Providence: Burning Deck, 1975

HINE, Daryl
    2098. Resident alien. New York: Atheneum, 1975
    2099. Daylight saving. New York: Atheneum, 1978

HINRICHSEN, Dennis
    2100. The attraction of heavenly bodies. Middletown, CT: Wesleyan University Press, 1983

HIRSCH, Edward
    2101. For the sleepwalkers. New York: Knopf, 1981

HIRSCHMAN, Jack
    2102. Aur sea. Berkeley: Tree, 1974
    2013. Cantillations. Santa Barbara: Capra, 1974
    2014. Djackson. Salt Lake City: Rainbow Resin, 1974
    2105. Cockroach. San Francisco: Street, 1975
    2106. The cool boyetz cycle. San Francisco: Golden Mountain, 1975
    2107. Kashtaninyah Segodnyah. San Francisco: Beatitude, 1976
    2108. Lyripol. San Francisco: City Lights, 1976
    2109. The arcanes of Le Comte de St. Germain. San Francisco: Amerus, 1977
    2110. The Jonestown arcane. San Francisco: Poetry for the People, 1979
    2111. The proletarian arcane. San Pedro, CA: Angels Gate, 1980

HITCHCOCK, George
    2112. Notes of the siege year. Santa Cruz, CA: Kayak, 1975

2113. Lessons in alchemy. Reno, NV: West Coast Poetry
       Review, 1977
2114. The piano beneath the skin. Denver: Copper Canyon,
       1979

HOAG, David
2115. The robber's cook. San Francisco: Peace & Pieces,
       1973

HOBSON, Dale
2116. Second growth. Syracuse, NY: Tamarack, 1979

HOCHMAN, Sandra
2117. Futures. New York: Viking, 1974

HODGKINS, George
2118. Accidental postures. Providence: Burning Deck, 1973

HODGKINSON, Edith
2119. Season's edge. Brooklyn: Hanging Loose, 1980

HOEFER, Jacqueline
2120. Imagining the garden. San Francisco: Pterodactyl,
       1981

HOEY, Allen
2121. Evening in the Antipodes. Potsdam, NY: Banjo, 1977
2122. Naked as my bones in transit. Syracuse, NY: Tama-
       rack, 1979
2123. Relics. Syracuse, NY: Tamarack, 1979
2124. Cedar light. Port Jefferson, NY: Street, 1980
2125. Hymns to a tree. Syracuse, NY: Tamarack, 1983

HOFFMAN, Daniel
2126. The center of attention. New York: Random House,
       1974
2127. Able was I ere I saw Elba; selected poems 1954-1974.
       London: Hutchinson, 1977
2128. Brotherly love. New York: Vintage, 1981

HOFFMAN, Jill
2129. Mink coat. New York: Holt, Rinehart and Winston,
       1973

HOGAN, Judy
2130. Cassandra speaking. Berkeley: Thorp Springs, 1977

HOGAN, Linda
2131. Calling myself home. Greenfield Center, NY: Green-
       field Review, 1978

HOGAN, Michael
2132. If you ever get there, think of me. Tempe, AZ: Em-
       erald City, 1975.

2133. Letters for my son. Greensboro, NC: Unicorn, 1975
2134. If you ever get there, think of me. Tempe, AZ:
        Emerald City, 1976
2135. Soon it will be morning. Austin, TX: Cold Mountain,
        1976
2136. Risky business. Kent, ME: Great Raven, 1977
2137. Rust. Goleta, CA: Turkey, 1977
2138. A lion at a cocktail party. Arlington, VA: Gallimaufry,
        1978
2139. The broken face of summer: poems. Fallon, NV:
        Duck Down, 1981

HOLDEN, Jonathan
2140. Leverage. Charlottesville: University Press of Vir-
        ginia, 1983

HOLLAHAN, Eugene
2141. Stone Mountain escape. Atlanta: Work/shop, 1976

HOLLAND, Barbara
2142. Running backwards. West Orange, NJ: Warthog, 1983

HOLLAND, Patrick
2143. Horses in November. San Francisco: Cranium, 1976

HOLLAND, William
2144. How us white folks discovered rock & roll. Washington:
        Some of Us, 1974

HOLLANDER, John
2145. Town and country matters. Boston: Godine, 1973
2146. The head of the bed. Boston: Godine, 1974
2147. Tales told of the fathers. New York: Atheneum, 1975
2148. Reflections on espionage: the question of cupcake. New
        York: Atheneum, 1976
2149. In place. Omaha: Abattoir, 1978
2150. Spectral emanations. New York: Atheneum, 1978
2151. Blue wine and other poems. Baltimore: Johns Hopkins
        University Press, 1979
2152. Powers of thirteen. New York: Atheneum, 1983

HOLLANDER, Robert
2153. Walking on Dante. Princeton, NJ: At the Pilgrim,
        1974

HOLLOWAY, Roberta
2154. Poems. San Jose, CA: San Jose State University, 1979

HOLT, Rochelle
2155. Ballet of oscillations. Birmingham, AL: Ragnarok,
        1973
2156. Poems for Amaefula. Holly Springs, MS: Ragnarok
        Press, 1974

2157. The sun and the moon. Holly Springs, MS: Ragnarok, 1974
2158. Love in spring. Birmingham, AL: Ragnorok, 1975
2159. Raks Rochelle. Birmingham, AL: Ragnorok, 1975
2160. Yellow pears, smooth as silk. Holly Springs, MS: Ragnarok, 1975
2161. A summer of the heart. Westfield, NJ: Merging Media, 1977

HOLTHAUS, Gary
2162. Unexpected manna. Port Townsend, WA: Copper Canyon, 1978

HONGO, Garrett Kaoru
2163. Yellow light. Middletown, CT: Wesleyan University Press, 1982

HONIG, Edwin
2164. At sixes. Providence: Burning Deck, 1974
2165. Shake a spear with me, John Berryman. Providence: Copper Beech, 1975
2166. The affinities of Orpheus. Providence: Copper Beech, 1976
2167. The selected poems of Edwin Honig, 1955-1976. Dallas: Texas Center for Writers, 1979
2168. Gifts of light. Providence: Copper Beech, 1983
2169. Interrupted praise. Metuchen, NJ: Scarecrow, 1983

HOOVER, Paul
2170. The monocle thugs. Chicago: Oink!, 1978
2171. Somebody talks a lot. Chicago: Yellow, 1982

HOPES, David B.
2172. The glacier's daughters. Amherst: University of Massachusetts Press, 1981

HORAN, Leo
2173. In tranquil mood, and other poems. Detroit: Harlo, 1977

HORD, Fred
2174. After h(ours). Chicago: Third World, 1974

HOTCHKISS, Bill
2175. The graces of fire and other poems. Newcastle, CA: Blue Oak, 1974
2176. Climb to the high country. New York: Norton, 1978

HOUGH, Lindy
2177. The sun in cancer. Plainfield, VT: North Atlantic, 1975
2178. Outlands & inlands. St. Paul: Truck, 1978

HOUSTON, James D.
  2179. Three songs for my father. Santa Barbara: Capra, 1974

HOUSTON, Peyton
  2180. The changes. Columbia, MO: Open Places, 1977

HOWARD, Ben
  2181. Father of Waters. Omaha: Abattoir, 1979

HOWARD, Richard
  2182. Preferences. New York: Viking, 1973
  2183. Two-part inventions. New York: Atheneum, 1974
  2184. Fellow feelings. New York: Atheneum, 1976
  2185. Misgivings. New York: Atheneum, 1979

HOWE, Fanny
  2186. The Amerindian coastline poem. New York: Telephone, 1975
  2187. Poem from a single pallet. Berkeley: Kelsey St., 1980
  2188. Alsace-Lorraine. New York: Telephone, 1982

HOWE, Susan
  2189. Hinge picture. New York: Telephone, 1974
  2190. The western borders. Berkeley: Tuumba, 1976
  2191. Secret history of the dividing line. New York: Telephone, 1978
  2192. Pythagorean silence. New York: Montemora, 1982
  2193. The defenestration of Prague. New York: Kulchur Foundation, 1983

HOWELL, Christopher
  2194. The crime of luck. Sunderland, MA: Panache, 1977
  2195. Why shouldn't I. Fort Collins, CO: L'Epervier, 1977
  2196. Though silence: the Ling Wei texts. Seattle: L'Epervier, 1981

HOWES, Barbara
  2197. A private signal; poems new and selected. Middletown, CT: Wesleyan University Press, 1977

HOXMEIER, K. M.
  2198. Poems for now. Milwaukee: Peacock, 1974

HUBERT, Karen M.
  2199. In search of Fred & Ethel Mertz. Brooklyn: Release, 1979

HUDDLE, David
  2200. Paper boy. Pittsburgh: University of Pittsburgh Press, 1979

HUDSON, Marc
    2201. Afterlight. Amherst: University of Massachusetts
          Press, 1983

HUEY, Mark
    2202. The persistence of red dreams. Charlottesville, VA:
          Alderman, 1980

HUEY, Tom
    2203. Forcehymn. Chapel Hill, NC: Carolina Wren, 1979

HUFF, Robert
    2204. The ventriloquist. Chicago: Swallow, 1973
    2205. The ventriloquist. Charlottesville: University Press
          of Virginia, 1977

HUGHES, Daniel
    2206. Lost title, & other poems. Providence: Copper Beech,
          1975
    2207. Falling. Providence: Copper Beech, 1979

HUGO, Richard
    2208. The lady in Kicking Horse Reservoir. New York:
          Norton, 1973
    2209. Rain five days and I love it. Port Townsend, WA:
          Graywolf, 1975
    2210. What thou lovest well, remains American. New York:
          Norton, 1975
    2211. Duwamish head. Port Townsend, WA: Copper Canyon,
          1976
    2212. 31 letters and 13 dreams. New York: Norton, 1977
    2213. Road ends at Tahola. Pittsburgh: Slow Loris, 1978
    2214. Selected poems. New York: Norton, 1979
    2215. The right madness on Skye. New York: Norton, 1980
    2216. White Center. New York: Norton, 1980
    2217. Sea lanes out. Story, WY: Dooryard, 1982

HUMES, Harry
    2218. Winter weeds. Columbia: University of Missouri Press,
          1983

HUMMER, T. R.
    2219. Translation of light. Stillwater, OK: Cedar Creek,
          1976
    2220. The angelic orders. Baton Rouge: Louisiana State
          University Press, 1982

HUMPHREY, James
    2221. The re-learning. Providence: Hellcoal, 1976

HUNT, William
    2222. Of the map that changes. Chicago: Swallow, 1973

HUNTER, Paul
    2223. Pullman. Seattle: University of Washington Press,
           1976
    2224. Mockingbird. Waldron Island, WA: Jawbone, 1981

HUNTING, Constance
    2225. Beyond the summerhouse. Orono, ME: Puckerbrush,
           1976
    2226. Dream. Orono, ME: Puckerbrush, 1982

HYER, Helen von Kolnitz
    2227. What the wind forgets. Lexington, SC: Sandlapper,
           1975

IANNONE, Ron
    2228. An ethnic connection and goals beyond. Parsons, WV:
           McClain, 1975

IGNATOW, David
    2229. Facing the tree. Boston: Little, Brown, 1975
    2230. Selected poems. Middletown, CT: Wesleyan Univer-
           sity Press, 1975
    2231. The animal in the bush. Pittsburgh: Slow Loris, 1977
    2232. Tread the dark. Boston: Little, Brown, 1978
    2233. Open between us. Ann Arbor: University of Michigan
           Press, 1979
    2234. Conversations. Rockville Centre, NY: Survivors'
           Manual, 1980
    2235. Whisper to the earth. Boston: Little, Brown, 1981

IGNATOW, Yaedi
    2236. The flaw. New York: Sheep Meadow, 1982

INEZ, Colette
    2237. Alive and taking names, and other poems. Athens:
           Ohio University Press, 1977
    2238. Eight minutes from the sun. Upper Montclair, NJ:
           Saturday, 1983

INGALLS, Jeremy
    2239. This stubborn quantum. Tucson, AZ: Capstone, 1983

INGRAM, Marla
    2240. Maria. Charlotte, NC: Red Clay, 1976

INMAN, P.
    2241. What happens next. Washington: Some of Us, 1974
    2242. Platin. College Park, MD: Sun & Moon, 1979
    2243. Ocker. Berkeley: Tuumba, 1982

INMAN, Will
    2244. Voice of the beech oracle: a shaman song. San Fran-
           cisco: Manroot, 1977

2245. The wakers in the tongue. Marvin, SD: Blue Cloud,
       1977
2246. A way through for the damned. Canyon, TX: Pierides,
       1983

IRBY, Kenneth
2247. The snow queen. San Francisco: Turtle Island, 1973
2248. Archipelago. Willits, CA: Tuumba, 1976
2249. Catalpa; poems 1968-1973. Lawrence, KS: Tansy,
       1976
2250. Orexis. Barrytown, NY: Station Hill, 1981
2251. Riding the dog. Vandergrift, PA: Zelot, 1982

ISAACS, John Welborn
2252. Our embryonic world. Phoenix, AZ: Transition, 1975

JACKSON, Angela
2253. Voo doo/love magic. Chicago: Third World, 1974
2254. You don't love magic. Chicago: Third World, 1974

JACKSON, Richard
2255. Part of the story. New York: Grove, 1983

JACOB, John
2256. Knee: whip of occasions. Alamo, CA: Holmgangers,
       1977
2257. Scatter: selected poems. Chicago: Wine, 1979
2258. Summerbook. Peoria, IL: Spoon River, 1983

JACOBIK, Gray
2259. Sandpainting. Washington: Washington Writers', 1980

JACOBSEN, Josephine
2260. The shade-seller; new and selected poems. New York:
       Doubleday, 1974
2261. The Chinese insomniacs; new poems. Philadelphia:
       University of Pennsylvania Press, 1981

JACOBSON, Dale
2262. Dakota incantations. Moorhead, MN: Territorial, 1973

JAFFE, Sherril
2263. Young lust & others. Los Angeles: Black Sparrow,
       1973

JAFFIN, David
2264. As one. New Rochelle, NY: Elizabeth, 1975
2265. In the glass of winter. London: Abelard Schuman,
       1975
2266. The half of a circle. New Rochelle, NY: Elizabeth,
       1977
2267. Space of. New Rochelle, NY: Elizabeth, 1978

2268. Perceptions. New Rochelle, NY: Elizabeth, 1979

JAMA, Stephen
2269. Currently. Santa Cruz: University of California at
       Santa Cruz, 1974

JAMES, Thomas
2270. Letters to a stranger. Boston: Houghton Mifflin, 1973

JANDA, J.
2271. Hanbelachia. Marvin, SD: Blue Cloud Quarterly, 1978

JANET, Marie
2272. Heart's core. Madison, WI: Unicorn, 1974

JANOWITZ, Phyllis
2273. Rites of strangers. Charlottesville: University Press
       of Virginia, 1978
2274. Visiting rites. Princeton, NJ: Princeton University
       Press, 1982

JARMAN, Mark
2275. Tonight is the night of the poem. Pittsburgh: Three
       Rivers, 1974
2276. North Sea. Oberlin, OH: Cleveland State University
       Poetry Center, 1978
2277. The rote walker. Pittsburgh: Carnegie-Mellon Univer-
       sity Press, 1981

JARRELL, Randall
2278. Complete poems. New York: Farrar, Straus and
       Giroux, 1981

JARRETT, Emmett
2279. God's body. Brooklyn: Hanging Loose, 1975

JASON, Philip K.
2280. Shaping: new poems in traditional prosodies. Washing-
       ton: Dryad, 1978
2281. Thawing out. Washington: Dryad, 1979
2282. Near the fire. Washington: Dryad, 1983

JAY, T. E.
2283. River dogs. Port Townsend, WA: Copper Canyon,
       1976

JEFFERS, Lance
2284. When I know the power of my Black hand. Detroit:
       Broadside, 1975
2285. O Africa, where I baked my bread. Detroit: Lotus,
       1977
2286. Grandsire. Detroit: Lotus, 1979

JEFFREY, Susu
    2287.   Songs of the gypsy women. St. Paul: New Rivers,
           1979

JELLEMA, Roderick
    2288.   Something tugging on the line. Washington: Dryad,
           1974
    2289.   The lost faces. Washington: Dryad, 1979

JENKINS, Paul
    2290.   Forget the sky. Fort Collins, CO: L'Epervier, 1979

JENNINGS, Kate
    2291.   Second sight. Emory, VA: Iron Mountain, 1976

JENSEN, Laura
    2292.   Anxiety and ashes. Lisbon, IA: Penumbra, 1976
    2293.   Bad boats. New York: Ecco, 1977
    2294.   Memory. Port Townsend, WA: Dragon Gate, 1982

JEROME, Judson
    2295.   I never saw. Chicago: Whitman, 1974
    2296.   The village and other poems. Hancock, MD: Trunk,
           1976
    2297.   Public domain. Hancock, MD: Trunk, 1977
    2298.   Thirty years of poetry, 1949-1979. New Braunfels,
           TX: Cedar Rock, 1979
    2299.   Partita in nothing flat. Daleville, IN: Barnwood, 1983

JOANS, Ted
    2300.   Sure, really I is surrealist poems. Devon, Eng.:
           Transformaction, 1982

JOHANKNECHT, Susan
    2301.   Birthcords. Newark, VT: Janus, 1975
    2302.   Spring clay. Newark, VT: Janus, 1975

JOHN, Da Free
    2303.   Crazy Da must sing, inclined to his weaker side.
           Clearlake, CA: Dawn Horse, 1982

JOHNSON, Dan
    2304.   Suggestions from the border. Pittsford, NY: State
           Street, 1983

JOHNSON, Denis
    2305.   Inner weather. Port Townsend, WA: Graywolf, 1976
    2306.   The Incognito Lounge. New York: Random House,
           1982

JOHNSON, Halvard
    2307.   Eclipse. New York: New Rivers, 1974
    2308.   Winter journey. St. Paul: New Rivers, 1979

JOHNSON, Joe Donald
    2309. Not. New York: Telephone, 1977
    2310. The summit of sun & poems that dream peace. Peta-
           luma, CA: Johnson, 1977

JOHNSON, Lemuel
    2311. Highlife for Caliban. Ann Arbor, MI: Ardis, 1973

JOHNSON, Michael L.
    2312. Dry season. Lawrence, KS: Cottonwood Review, 1977
    2313. The unicorn captured. Lawrence, KS: Cottonwood
           Review, 1980

JOHNSON, Nan C.
    2314. Black of the wind-vane hen. Schenectady, NY: Washout
           Review, 1977

JOHNSON, Ronald
    2315. Maze/mane/wane. Cambridge, MA: Pomegranate, 1973
    2316. Eyes & objects. Millerton, NY: Jargon, 1976
    2317. Radio. Albany, CA: Sand Dollar, 1977

JOHNSON, Thomas
    2318. Footholds. Tucson, AZ: Ironwood, 1973
    2319. Homing signals. Ithaca, NY: Stone Marrow, 1974
    2320. Arriving at the nadir. Providence: Copper Beech,
           1975
    2321. The gardens of our going. Berkeley: Twowindows,
           1975
    2322. Ground zero. Reno, NV: West Coast Poetry Review,
           1975
    2323. The ice futures. Port Townsend, WA: Copper Canyon,
           1977
    2324. Swerving straight: poems, selected & new. Ithaca,
           NY: Alembic, 1981

JOHNSON, W. R.
    2325. Flowering time. West Burke, VT: Janus, 1976
    2326. Snow. Newark, VT: Janus, 1980
    2327. The town at dusk: poems. Newark, VT: Janus, 1980

JOHNSTON, Alastair
    2328. Cafe/Charivari, Charlatan/Chrom. Berkeley: Poltroon,
           1975

JOHNSTON, Elaine
    2329. Loves lost and found. Birmingham, AL: Thom Hen-
           ricks, 1975

JONES, Gayl
    2330. Song for Anninho. Detroit: Lotus, 1981
    2331. The hermit-woman. Detroit: Lotus, 1983

JONES, Robert L.
  2332. The space I occupy. Kalamazoo, MI: Blue Mountain,
         1977

JONES, Rodney
  2333. The story they told us of light. University: University
         of Alabama Press, 1980

JONES, Seaborn
  2334. Drowning from the inside out. Cherry Valley, NY:
         Cherry Valley, 1981

JONES, Sonya
  2335. The ultimate dare. Kalamazoo, MI: Blue Mountain,
         1977

JONG, Erica
  2336. Half-lives. New York: Holt, Rinehart and Winston,
         1973
  2337. Here comes and other poems. New York: New Ameri-
         can Library, 1975
  2338. Loveroot. New York: Holt, Rinehart and Winston,
         1975
  2339. Selected poems. London: Panther, 1977
  2340. At the edge of the body. New York: Holt, Rinehart
         and Winston, 1979
  2341. Ordinary miracles. New York: New American Library,
         1983

JORDAN, June
  2342. New days; poems of exile and return. New York:
         Emerson Hall, 1974
  2343. Things I do in the dark. New York: Random House,
         1977
  2344. Passion. Boston: Beacon, 1981

JOSELOW, Beth
  2345. Ice Fishing. Washington: Some of Us, 1974
  2346. Gypsies. Washington: Washington Writers', 1979
  2347. The April wars. Washington: S.O.S., 1983

JOSEPH, Lawrence
  2348. Shouting at no one. Pittsburgh: University of Pittsburgh
         Press, 1983

JOSEPHS, Laurence
  2349. Six elegies. Greenfield Center, NY: Greenfield Re-
         view, 1973
  2350. Poems. Saratoga Springs, NY: Skidmore College,
         1975

JUDSON, John
  2351. Finding words in winter. New Rochelle, NY: Elizabeth,
         1973

2352. Ash in the candle's wick. La Crosse, WI: Juniper, 1975
2353. Routes from the onion's dark. Milwaukee: Pentagram, 1976
2354. Surreal songs. La Crosse, WI: Juniper, 1976
2355. A purple tale. New York: New Rivers, 1978
2356. North of Athens. Peoria, IL: Spoon River, 1980
2357. Reasons why I am not perfect. West Lafayette, IN: Sparrow, 1982

JUERGENSEN, Hans
2358. Journey toward the roots. St. Petersburg, FL: Valkyrie, 1976
2359. California frescoes. Tampa, FL: American Studies, 1980
2360. The record of a green planet. Baltimore: Linden, 1982
2361. Fire-tested. Baltimore: Linden, 1983

JUERGENSEN, Ilse
2362. I don't want to be a thunderbird anymore. Homestead, FL: Olivant, 1977

JUHASZ, Suzanne
2363. Love affair. Berkeley: Samisdat, 1975

JUNKINS, Donald
2364. Crossing by ferry: poems new and selected. Amherst: University of Massachusetts Press, 1978
2365. The Agamenticus poems. Chester, MA: Hollow Spring, 1983

JUSTICE, Donald
2366. Departures. New York: Atheneum, 1973
2367. Selected poems. New York: Atheneum, 1979
2368. Night light. Middletown, CT: Wesleyan University Press, 1981
2369. The summer anniversaries. Middletown, CT: Wesleyan University Press, 1981

KACHMAR, Jessie
2370. Snow quiet. Chicago: Snow, 1976

KAESBERG, Harold
2371. Meadows of my mind. Reseda, CA: Mojave, 1975

KAHN, Hannah
2372. Time, wait. Orlando: University Presses of Florida, 1983

KAHN, Paul
2373. Heart of the world. Carrboro, NC: Truck, 1975
2374. January. Berkeley: Tuumba, 1978

KALLEN, Leo A.
    2375. The flame behind the eye. New York: Ram, 1976

KALLET, Marilyn
    2376. Devils live so near. Ithaca, NY: Ithaca House, 1977
    2377. In the great night. Ithaca, NY: Ithaca House, 1981

KALLSEN, T. J.
    2378. Making. Houston: Houston Writers Guild, 1981

KAMENETZ, Rodger
    2379. The missing Jew. Washington: Dryad, 1980

KAMINSKI, Margaret
    2380. Martinis. Detroit: White Light, 1975
    2381. La vida de la mujer. Highland Park, MI: Fallen
          Angel, 1976
    2382. El Canon and other poems. Eau Claire, WI: Rhiannon,
          1979

KAMINSKY, Daniel
    2383. Snout to snout. Cleveland: Cleveland State University
          Poetry Center, 1974
    2384. Canto the last. Cleveland: Pranayama, 1976

KAMINSKY, Marc
    2385. A new house. New York: Inwood, 1974
    2386. A table with people. New York: Sun, 1981

KANABUS, Henry
    2387. Carapace. Chicago: Yellow, 1978

KAPLAN, Edward
    2388. Hard acts. Boulder Creek, CA: Triton, 1976

KAPLAN, Milton
    2389. In a time between wars. New York: Norton, 1973

KASNER, Sam
    2390. Driving at night. Brooklyn: Hanging Loose, 1976

KASTMILER, Peter
    2391. When the creature is silent. San Francisco: Mother's
          Hen, 1973

KATROVAS, Richard
    2392. Green dragons. Middletown, CT: Wesleyan University
          Press, 1983

KATZ, Menke
    2393. Burning village. New York: Horizon, 1973

KATZ, Steve
   2394. Cheyenne River wild track. Ithaca, NY: Ithaca House,
        1973

KAUFFMAN, Janet
   2395. The weather book. Lubbock: Texas Tech, 1981

KAUFMAN, Bob
   2396. The ancient rain. New York: New Directions, 1981

KAUFMAN, Shirley
   2397. Gold country. Pittsburgh: University of Pittsburgh
        Press, 1973
   2398. Looking at Henry Moore's elephant skull etchings in
        Jerusalem during the war. Greensboro, NC: Uni-
        corn, 1977
   2399. From one life to another. Pittsburgh: University of
        Pittsburgh Press, 1979

KAUFMANN, Walt
   2400. Traveling mind. Reseda, CA: Mojave Books, 1976

KAVANAUGH, James J.
   2401. Sunshine days and foggy nights. New York: Dutton,
        1975
   2402. Winter has lasted too long. New York: Dutton, 1977
   2403. Walk easy on the earth. New York: Dutton, 1979
   2404. Maybe if I loved you more. New York: Dutton, 1982
   2405. Who will love me in my madness? New York: Dutton,
        1983

KEARNEY, Lawrence
   2406. Five. Bolinas, CA: Tombouctou, 1976
   2407. Kingdom come. Middletown, CT: Wesleyan University
        Press, 1980

KEENAN, Deborah
   2408. Household wounds. St. Paul: New Rivers, 1981

KEENS, William
   2409. Dear anyone. Lisbon, IA: Penumbra, 1976

KEES, Weldon
   2410. The collected poems of Weldon Kees. Lincoln: Univer-
        sity of Nebraska Press, 1975

KEITHLEY, George
   2411. Song in a strange land. New York: Braziller, 1974

KELLY, Arnold J.
   2412. The future unscratched. Bigfork, MN: Northwoods,
        1975

KELLY, Dave
2413.   At a time; a dance for voices. Fredonia, NY: Basil-
        isk, 1973
2414.   Did you know they're beheading Bill Johnson today? San
        Francisco: Stone, 1974
2415.   In these rooms. Fairfax, CA: Red Hill, 1976
2416.   Poems in season. Texas City, TX: Texas Portfolio,
        1976
2417.   Filming assassinations. Ithaca, NY: Ithaca House,
        1979
2418.   Great Lakes cycle. Rochester, NY: Steps Inside, 1980

KELLY, Dennis
2419.   Chicken. San Francisco: Gay Sunshine, 1979
2420.   Size queen and other poems. San Francisco: Gay Sun-
        shine, 1981

KELLY, Robert
2421.   The mill of particulars. Los Angeles: Black Sparrow,
        1973
2422.   The tears of Edmund Burke. Annandale-on-Hudson, NY:
        Salitter, 1973
2423.   Whaler frigate clippership. Lawrence, KS: Tansy, 1973
2424.   A line of sight. Los Angeles: Black Sparrow, 1974
2425.   The loom. Los Angeles: Black Sparrow, 1975
2426.   Sixteen odes. Santa Barbara: Black Sparrow, 1976
2427.   The lady of. Santa Barbara: Black Sparrow, 1977
2428.   The book of Persephone. New Paltz, NY: Treacle,
        1978
2429.   The convections. Santa Barbara: Black Sparrow, 1978
2430.   The cruise of the Pnyx. Barrytown, NY: Station Hill, 1979
2431.   Kill the messenger who brings bad news. Santa Barbara:
        Black Sparrow, 1979
2432.   Sentence. Barrytown, NY: Station Hill, 1980
2433.   The alchemist to Mercury. Richmond, CA: North At-
        lantic, 1981
2434.   Spiritual exercises. Santa Barbara: Black Sparrow,
        1981
2435.   Under words. Santa Barbara: Black Sparrow, 1983

KENNEDY, Mary
2436.   New green over old green. New York: Gotham Book
        Mart, 1979

KENNEDY, Rigg
2437.   Riggwords. Beverly Hills, CA: Leprechaun, 1976

KENNEDY, Terry
2438.   Durango. New York: The Smith, 1978
2439.   Heart organ part of the body. San Francisco: Second
        Coming, 1981
2440.   Ludlow fugue. Green Harbor, MA: Wampeter, 1981

KENNEDY, X. J.
- 2441. Emily Dickinson in Southern California. Boston: God-ine, 1973
- 2442. Celebrations after the death of John Brennan. Lincoln, MA: Penmaen, 1974
- 2443. Emily Dickinson in Southern California. Boston: God-ine. 1974

KENNY, Maurice
- 2444. North. Marvin, SD: Blue Cloud Quarterly, 1977
- 2445. Dancing back strong the nation. Marvin, SD: Blue Cloud Quarterly, 1979
- 2446. I am the sun. Buffalo, NY: White Pine, 1979
- 2447. Only as far as Brooklyn. Boston: Good Gay Poets, 1979
- 2448. Kneading the blood. New York: Strawberry, 1981
- 2449. Greyhounding this America. Chico, CA: Heidelberg Graphics, 1983

KENYON, Jane
- 2450. From room to room. Cambridge, MA: Alice James, 1978

KERMAN, Judith
- 2451. Obsessions. Buffalo, NY: Intrepid, 1974
- 2452. Jakoba poems. Buffalo, NY: White Pine, 1976

KERN, W. Bliem
- 2453. Meditationsmeditationsmeditations. New York: New Rivers, 1973

KEROUAC, Jack
- 2454. Heaven & other poems. Bolinas, CA: Grey Fox, 1977

KESSLER, Jascha
- 2455. In memory of the future. Santa Cruz, CA: Kayak, 1976

KESSLER, Milton
- 2456. Sailing too far. New York: Harper & Row, 1973
- 2457. Sweet dreams. Hamlin, NY: Black Bird, 1979

KESSLER, Stephen
- 2458. Nostalgia of the fortune teller. Santa Cruz, CA: Kay-ak, 1975
- 2459. Winter of the fortune teller. Santa Cruz, CA: Kayak, 1976
- 2460. Poems to Walt Disney. San Francisco: Manroot, 1977
- 2461. Thirteen ways of deranging an angel. Santa Cruz, CA: Greenhouse Review, 1977
- 2462. Two. Santa Barbara: Mudborn, 1978
- 2463. Living expenses. Santa Cruz, CA: Alcatraz Editions, 1980

KHERDIAN, David
    2464. The nonny poems. New York: Macmillan, 1974
    2465. Any day of your life. New York: Viking, 1975
    2466. Place of birth. Portland: Breitenbush, 1983

KICKNOSWAY, Faye
    2467. A man is a hook. Trouble. Santa Barbara: Capra, 1974
    2468. Capricorn. San Francisco: Golden Mountain, 1976
    2469. The cat approaches. New York: Alternative, 1978
    2470. Asparagus, asparagus. West Branch, IA: Toothpaste, 1982
    2471. She wears him fancy in her night braid. West Branch, IA: Toothpaste, 1983

KILGORE, James C.
    2472. Let it pass. Beachwood, OH: Sharaqua, 1976
    2473. African violet: poems for a black woman. Detroit: Lotus, 1982

KING, Martha
    2474. Weather. New York: New Rivers, 1978

KING, Nancy
    2475. Traveling. Bellingham, WA: Signpost, 1982

KING, Thomas J.
    2476. Touching. Dubuque, IA: Kendall/Hunt, 1976

KINNELL, Galway
    2477. The avenue bearing the initial of Christ into the new world. Boston: Houghton Mifflin, 1974
    2478. Three poems. New York: Phoenix Book Shop, 1976
    2479. Fergus falling. Newark, VT: Janus, 1979
    2480. Two poems. Newark, VT: Janus, 1979
    2481. Mortal acts, mortal words. Boston: Houghton Mifflin, 1980
    2482. Selected poems. Boston: Houghton Mifflin, 1982

KINZIE, Mary
    2483. The threshold of the year. Columbia: University of Missouri Press, 1982

KIRBY, David
    2484. The opera lover. Tallahassee: Anhinga, 1977
    2485. Sarah Bernhardt's leg. Cleveland: Cleveland State University Poetry Center, 1983

KITRILAKIS, Thalia
    2486. Biting Sun. Berkeley: Kelsey Street, 1983

KLAPPERT, Peter
  2487. Non sequitur O'Connor. Cleveland: Bits, 1977
  2488. After the rhymer's guild. Sarasota, FL: New Collage,
          n. d.

KLAUCK, Daniel L.
  2489. Everything else. Washington: King, 1976

KLEIS, David John
  2490. Lion under the sun. Detroit: Harlo, 1976

KLEPFISZ, Irena
  2491. Periods of stress. Brooklyn: Out & Out, 1975
  2492. Keeper of accounts. Watertown, MA: Persephone, 1982

KLOEFKORN, William
  2493. Uncertain the final run to winter. Lincoln, NE: Wind-
          flower, 1973
  2494. Alvin Turner as farmer. Lincoln, NE: Windflower,
          1974
  2495. Loony. Springfield, IL: Apple, 1975
  2496. Ludi Jr. Milwaukee: Pentagram, 1976
  2497. Not such a bad place to be. Port Townsend, WA:
          Copper Canyon, 1980
  2498. Let the dance begin. Pittsford, NY: State Street, 1981

KLOSS, Phillips Wray
  2499. The great kiva. Santa Fe, NM: Sunstone, 1980

KNAUTH, Stephen
  2500. Night-fishing on Irish Buffalo Creek. Ithaca, NY: Itha-
          ca House, 1982

KNIES, Elizabeth
  2501. Streets after rain. Cambridge, MA: Alice James,
          1980

KNIFE, Jack
  2502. The perfect man. New York: Poet's, 1974

KNIGHT, Ethridge
  2503. Belly song. Detroit: Broadside, 1973
  2504. Born of a woman. Boston: Houghton Mifflin, 1980

KNOEPFLE, John
  2505. Thinking of offerings: poems. La Crosse, WI: Juniper,
          1975
  2506. A box of sandalwood. La Crosse, WI: Juniper, 1979
  2507. Poems for the hours. Mount Carroll, IL: Uzzano,
          1979

KNOEPFLE, Peg
  2508. Sparks from your hoofs. Springfield, IL: Sangamon
          State University, 1977

KNOTT, Bill
  2509. Love poems to myself. Boston: Barn Dream, 1973
  2510. Rome in Rome. Brooklyn: Release, 1976
  2511. Selected and collected poems. New York: Sun, 1977
  2512. Becos. New York: Random House, 1983

KNOX, Caroline
  2513. The house party. Athens: University of Georgia Press,
          1983

KNOX, Hugh
  2514. The queen of snakes. Omaha: Abattoir, 1978

KNOX, Wendy
  2515. A message for the recluse. Minneapolis: Vanilla,
          1975

KOCH, Kenneth
  2516. The art of love. New York: Random House, 1975
  2517. The duplications. New York: Random House, 1977
  2518. The burning mystery of Anna in 1951. New York: Ran-
          dom House, 1979
  2519. Days and nights. New York: Random House, 1982

KOCH, Peter
  2520. Magnus annus. Salt Lake City: Litmus, 1974

KOERTGE, Ronald
  2521. The father poems. Fremont, MI: Sumac, 1973
  2522. Cheapthrills. Stockton, CA: Wormwood Review, 1976
  2523. Men under fire. Fallon, NV: Duck Down, 1976
  2523a. 12 photographs of Yellowstone. Fairfax, CA: Red Hill,
          1976
  2524. The jockey poems. Cape Elizabeth, ME: Maelstrom,
          1980
  2525. Sex object. New York: Little Caesar, 1980
  2526. Life on the edge of the continent: selected poems.
          Fayetteville: University of Arkansas Press, 1982

KOESTENBAUM, Phyllis
  2527. Crazy face. Santa Barbara: Mudborn, 1980
  2528. Hunger food. Fairfax, CA: Jungle Garden, 1980
  2529. Oh I can't say she says. Oakland, CA: Christopher's,
          1980

KOLLER, Alice
  2530. An unknown woman: a journey to self-discovery. New
          York: Holt, Rinehart and Winston, 1981

KOLLER, James
  2531. The tracks run together. Santa Fe, NM: Fourwing,
          1974

2532. Poems for the blue sky. Santa Barbara: Black Sparrow, 1976

KONNER, Mel
2533. Nonrequiem. New York: Inwood, 1976

KOOSER, Ted
2534. How to. Crete, NE: Best Cellar, 1973
2535. Twenty poems. Crete, NE: Best Cellar, 1973
2536. A local habitation & a name. San Luis Obispo, CA: Solo, 1974
2537. Shooting a framhouse. Denver: Ally, 1975
2538. Not coming to be barked at. Milwaukee: Pentagram, 1976
2539. Old marriage and new. Austin, TX: Cold Mountain, 1978
2540. Sure signs. Pittsburgh: University of Pittsburgh Press, 1980

KOPP, Karl
2541. Tarot poems. Three Rivers, MI: Three Herons, 1974
2542. Yarbrough Mountain. Phoenix, AZ: Baleen, 1977

KORAN, Dennis
2543. Vacancies. San Francisco: Mother's Hen, 1975
2544. [No entry]

KORNBLUM, Allan
2545. Threshold. West Branch, IA: Toothpaste, 1976
2546. Awkward song. West Branch, Iowa: Toothpaste, 1980

KORNBLUM, Cinda
2547. Bandwagon. West Branch, IA: Toothpaste, 1976

KOSTELANETZ, Richard
2548. Obliterate. Livermore, CA: Ironwhorse/Ironhores, 1974
2549. Portraits from memory. Ann Arbor, MI: Ardis, 1975
2550. Rain rains rain. Brooklyn: Assembling, 1976
2551. Illuminations. Woodinville, WA: Laughing Bear, 1977
2552. Turfs, fields, pitches, arenas. Battleground, IN: High/Coo, 1980

KOSTINER, Eileen
2553. Love's other face. Willimantic, CT: Curbstone, 1982

KOTZWINKLE, William
2554. Great world circus. New York: Putnam, 1983

KOWIT, Steve
2555. The dirty old man's guide to young girls. Brooklyn: Proexistence, 1975

2556. 10, 000 corpses. Brooklyn: Proexistence, 1975
2557. That salome she sure cd dance. Brooklyn: Proexist-
        ence, 1975
2558. Cutting our losses. New York: Contact II, 1982
2559. Heart in utter confusion. Harpswell, ME: Dog Ear,
        1982
2560. Lurid confessions. Pomery, OH: Carpenter, 1983

KRAMER, Aaron
2561. On the way to Palermo. New York: A. S. Barnes,
        1973

KRANIDAS, Kathleen
2562. The mountain, the stone. Orono, ME: Puckerbrush,
        1976

KRAPF, Norbert
2563. The Playfair book of hours. Denver: Ally, 1976
2564. Arriving on Paumanok. Port Jefferson, NY: Street,
        1980

KRAUSS, Ruth
2565. This breast gothic. Lenox, MA: Lenox Bookstore,
        1973
2566. Little boat lighter than a cork. Weston, CT: Circle,
        1976
2567. When I walk I change the earth. Providence: Burning
        Deck, 1978

KRECH, Richard
2568. The incompleat works of Richard Krech, poems 1966-
        1974. Salt Lake City: Litmus, 1976

KRIEGER, Robert
2569. Headlands, rising. Boise, ID: Ahsahta, 1977

KROLL, Judith
2570. In the temperate zone. New York: Scribner, 1973

KROUSE, Charles
2571. A fool's bubble. Holland, MI: Windmill, 1977

KRUCHKOW, Diane
2572. Odd jobs. E. Lansing, MI: Ghost Dance, 1975

KRUGER, Mollee
2573. Yankee shoes. Bethesda, MD: Maryben, 1975

KRYSL, Marilyn
2574. More palomino, please, more fuchsia. Cleveland:
        Cleveland State University Poetry Center, 1980

KRYSS, T. L.
2575. Music in the winepress, parrots in the flames. Ellens-
       burg, WA: Vagabond, 1976

KUBACH, David
2576. First things. Alamo, CA: Holmgangers, 1979

KUBY, Lolette
2577. In enormous water. Cleveland: Cleveland State Univer-
       sity Poetry Center, 1981

KUDAKA, Geraldine
2578. Numerous avalanches at the point of intersection.
       Greenfield Center, NY: Greenfield Review, 1979

KUMIN, Maxine
2579. House, bridge, fountain, gate. New York: Viking,
       1975

KUMIN, Maxine
2580. The retrieval system. New York: Viking, 1978
2581. Our ground time here will be brief. New York: Viking,
       1982

KUNITZ, Stanley
2582. The coat without a seam; sixty poems 1930-1972.
       Northampton, MA: Gehenna, 1974
2583. The poems of Stanley Kunitz, 1928-1978. Boston:
       Little, Brown, 1979
2584. A kind of order, a kind of folly. Boston: Little,
       Brown, 1982
2585. The Wellfleet whale and companion poems. New York:
       Sheep Meadow, 1983

KUO, Alexander
2586. New letters from Hiroshima and other poems. Green-
       field, NY: Greenfield Review, 1974

KUSHNER, William
2587. Night fishing. New York: Midnight Sun, 1976

KUZMA, Greg
2588. Good news. New York: Viking, 1973
2589. A problem of high water. Reno, NV: West Coast
       Poetry Review, 1973
2590. What friends are for. Crete, NE: Best Cellar, 1973
2591. The buffalo shoot. Fredonia, NY: Basilisk, 1974
2592. The obedience school. Pittsburgh: Three Rivers, 1974
2593. A day in the world. Omaha: Abattoir, 1976
2594. Village journal. Crete, NE: Best Cellar, 1978
2595. Adirondacks. Hanover, NH: Bear Claw, 1979
2596. For my brother. Omaha: Abattoir, 1981

2597. A horse of a different color. Los Angeles: Illuminati, 1982
2598. Everyday life. Peoria, IL: Spoon River, 1983

KYGER, Joanne
    2599. Trip out and fall back. Berkeley: Arif, 1974
    2600. All this every day. Bolinas, CA: Big Sky, 1975
    2601. The wonderful focus of you. Calais, VT: Z Press, 1979
    2602. Up my coast. Point Reyes, CA: Floating Island, 1981
    2603. Going on: selected poems, 1958-1980. New York: Dutton, 1983

La BELLE, Christie
    2604. Our own green confusion. New Rochelle, NY: Eliza-beth, 1974

La GATTUTA, Margo
    2605. Diversion Road. Pittsford, NY: State Street, 1983

LAGIER, Gary G.
    2606. Even dozen. Sunnyvale, CA: Commentators, 1976

LAING, Alexander
    2607. Brant Point. Hanover, NH: University Press of New England, 1975

LAIRD, Mary
    2608. The eggplant skin pants, and poems. Mt. Horeb, WS: Perishable, 1973

LALLY, Michael
    2609. Dues. Iowa City: Stone Wall, 1975
    2610. Mentally, he's a sick man. Lincoln, NE: Salt Lick, 1975
    2611. Rocky dies yellow: poems 1964-1972. Berkeley: Blue Wind, 1975
    2612. Charisma. New York: O Press, 1976
    2613. In the mood. Washington: Titanic, 1978
    2614. Attitude: uncollected poems of the seventies. Brooklyn: Hanging Loose, 1982

LAMANTIA, Philip
    2615. Touch of the marvelous. Bolinas, CA: Four Seasons, 1974
    2616. Becoming visible. San Francisco: City Lights, 1981

LAND, E. Waverly
    2617. Painful entry. Laurinburg, NC: St. Andrews, 1974

LANDERS, John Poindexter
    2618. Perpetuae magnaliz vitae. Houston: Rice University Press, 1980

LANE, Ronnie M.
    2619.   The greatest show on earth.   Grand Rapids, MI: Pilot,
            1975

LANE, William
    2620.   Moonlight standing in as Cordelia.   Brooklyn: Hanging
            Loose, 1980

LANGE, Art
    2621.   On impulse.   Chicago: Ommation, 1976

LANGE, Gerald
    2622.   Starless & Bible black.   Poynette, WI: Bieler, 1975
    2623.   [No entry]

LANGLAND, Joseph
    2624.   Adlai Stevenson.   Iowa City: Stone Wall, 1975
    2625.   The sacrifice poems.   Cedar Falls, IA: North American
            Review, 1975
    2626.   Any body's song.   Garden City, NY: Doubleday, 1980

LANGTON, Daniel J.
    2627.   Querencia.   Columbia: University of Missouri Press, 1975

LAPIDUS, Jacqueline
    2628.   Ready to survive.   Brooklyn: Hanging Loose, 1975

LAPPIN, Linda
    2628.   Twelve poems for Cezanne's black clock.   Gulfport, FL:
            Konglomerati, 1975
    2629.   Wintering with the abominable snowman.   Santa Cruz,
            CA: Kayak, 1976

LARCOMBE, Sam
    2630.   First poems.   Santa Fe, NM: Lightning Tree, 1976

LARKIN, Joan
    2631.   Housework.   Brooklyn: Out & Out, 1975

LARSEN, Jeanne
    2632.   James Cook in search of terra incognita.   Charlottes-
            ville: University Press of Virginia, 1979

LARSON, Clinton F.
    2633.   Centennial portraits.   Provo, UT: Brigham Young
            University Press, 1976

LARSON, Kathryn
    2634.   Night's dead letters.   Bridgeport, CT: University of
            Bridgeport, 1977

LARSON, Kris
    2635.   Ground work.   Dennis, MA: Salt-Works, 1976
    2636.   Second thoughts.   Dennis, MA: Salt-Works, 1976

LASKA, P. J.
    2637. Images and other poems. Beckley, WV: Mountain
        Union, 1975

LATTA, John
    2638. Rubbing torsos. Ithaca, NY: Ithaca House, 1979

LAUGHLIN, James
    2639. In another country; poems 1935-1975. San Francisco:
        City Lights, 1978

LAURSEN, Ross
    2670. Sweet tomorrow. San Francisco: Peace & Pieces,
        1975

LAUTER, Kenneth
    2671. The other side. Shawnee Mission, KS: BkMk, 1973

LAUTERBACH, Ann
    2672. Many times, but then. Austin: University of Texas
        Press, 1979

LAVIERA, Tato
    2673. La carreta made a u-turn. Gary, IN: Arte Publico,
        1979

LAVIN, Stuart R.
    2674. Cambodian spring. Deerfield, MA: Heron, 1973
    2675. Some want for saving. Ware, MA: Four Zoas, 1976
    2676. Look for me in your dreams. Ware, MA: Four Zoas,
        1977
    2677. Let myself shine. New York: Kulchur Foundation,
        1979

LAWDER, Douglas
    2678. Trolling. Boston: Little, Brown, 1977

LAWLESS, Gary
    2679. Full flower moon. Brunswick, ME: Blackberry, 1975
    2680. Wintering. Dennis, MA: Salt-Works, 1975
    2681. Two owls. Buffalo, NY: White Pine, 1976

LAWRENCE, David E.
    2682. The natural lean. Reseda, CA: Mojave, 1974

LAWSON, Todd
    2683. Pacific sun poems. San Francisco: Peace & Pieces,
        1973
    2684. Patriotic poems of Amerikka. San Francisco: Peace
        and Pieces, 1974

LAX, Robert
    2685. Circus black, circus white. New York: Journeyman,
        1974

2686. 13 poems, New York: Journeyman, 1974
2687. Black earth, blue sky. New York: Journeyman, 1975

LAYNE, McAvoy
2688. How Audie Murphy died in Vietnam. Garden City, NY:
         Anchor Books, 1973

LAZARD, Naomi
2689. The moonlit upper deckerina. New York: Sheep
         Meadow, 1977
2690. Ordinances. Ann Arbor, MI: Ardis, 1978

LEA, Sydney
2691. Searching the drowned man. Urbana: University of
         Illinois Press, 1980

LEARY, Tim
2692. Curse of the oval Room. New York: High Times,
         1974

LEAX, John
2693. Reaching into silence. Wheaton, IL: H. Shaw, 1974

LECKEY, Hugo
2694. A set for Edwin Honig. Providence: Hellcoal, 1973

LEE, Al
2695. Time. New York: Ecco, 1974

LEE, David
2696. The porcine legacy. Port Townsend, WA: Copper
         Canyon, 1978
2697. Driving and drinking. Port Townsend, WA: Copper
         Canyon, 1982

LEE, Don L.
2698. From planet to planet. Detroit: Broadside, 1973

LEE, Lawrence
2699. Between the morning and the evening star. Pacific
         Grove, CA: Boxwood, 1973

LEE, Robert Edson
2700. The dialogues of Lewis and Clark. Boulder: Colorado
         Associated University Press, 1979

LEEPER, Robert
2701. The brindle mule. Boone, NC: Appalachian Consortium,
         1983

LEET, Judith
2702. Pleasure seeker's guide. Boston: Houghton Mifflin,
         1976

LEFCOWITZ, Barbara F.
    2703. A risk of green. Washington: Gallimaufry, 1978
    2704. The wild piano. Washington: Dryad Press, 1981

LeFERRE, Adam
    2705. Everything all at once. Middletown, CT: Wesleyan
          University Press, 1978

LEFFLER, Merrill
    2706. Partly pandemonium, partly love. Washington: Dryad,
          1982

LeGUIN, Ursula
    2707. Wild angels. Santa Barbara: Capra, 1975

LEHMAN, David
    2708. Some nerve. New York: Columbia Review, 1973
    2709. Poems by David Lehman. Lansing, NY: Nobodaddy,
          1979

LEITER, Sharon
    2710. The lady and the bailiff of time. New York: Ecco,
          1974

LEITHAUSER, Brad
    2711. Hundreds of fireflies. New York: Knopf, 1982

Le MAN, Dona
    2712. Echoes in the wind. St. Petersburg, FL: Valkyrie,
          1975
    2713. Whispering leaves. St. Petersburg, FL: Valkyrie,
          1977

LeMEADOWS, Fay
    2714. Little silver cloud/one bird flying. St. Petersburg,
          FL: Valkyrie, 1974

LENGYEL, Cornel
    2715. Four dozen songs. Georgetown, CA: Dragon's Teeth,
          1973

LENSON, David
    2716. The gambler. Amherst, MA: Lynx House, 1977
    2717. Ride the shadow. Fort Collins, CO: L'Epervier, 1979

LEONTIEF, Estelle
    2718. Whatever happens. West Burke, VT: Janus, 1975

LEPERGER, Emil
    2719. The figure of fulfillment. University Center, MI:
          Green River, 1975

LEPSON, Ruth
　　2720.　Dreaming in color.　Cambridge, MA:　Alice James,
　　　　　　1980

LERMAN, Eleanor
　　2721.　Armed love.　Middletown, CT:　Wesleyan University
　　　　　　Press, 1973
　　2722.　Come the sweet by and by.　Amherst:　University of
　　　　　　Massachusetts Press, 1975

LESNIAK, Rose
　　2723.　76 Sexuality.　Chicago:　Ommation, 1976
　　2724.　Younger anger.　West Branch, IA:　Toothpaste, 1979
　　2725.　Throwing spitballs at the nuns.　West Branch, IA:
　　　　　　Toothpaste, 1982

LESSER, Rika
　　2726.　Etruscan things.　New York:　Braziller, 1983

LESTER, Julius
　　2727.　Who I am.　New York:　Dial, 1974

LEVENBERG, Diane
　　2728.　Out of the desert.　Garden City, NY:　Doubleday, 1980

LEVENDOSKY, Charles
　　2729.　Aspects of the vertical.　Norman, OK:　Point Riders,
　　　　　　1978
　　2730.　Nocturnes.　Story, WY:　Dooryard, 1982

LEVENSON, Christopher
　　2731.　Stills.　Middletown, CT:　Wesleyan University Press,
　　　　　　1973

LEVERTOV, Denise
　　2732.　The freeing of the dust.　New York:　New Directions,
　　　　　　1975
　　2733.　Chekov on the West Heath.　Andes, NY:　Woolmer/
　　　　　　Brotherton, 1977
　　2734.　Modulations for solo voice.　San Francisco:　Five Trees,
　　　　　　1977
　　2735.　Life in the forest.　New York:　New Directions, 1978
　　2736.　Collected earlier poems, 1940-1960.　New York:　New
　　　　　　Directions, 1979
　　2737.　Wanderer's daysong.　Port Townsend, WA:　Copper
　　　　　　Canyon, 1981
　　2738.　Candles in Babylon.　New York:　New Directions, 1982
　　2739.　Poems, 1960-1967.　New York:　New Directions, 1983

LEVIN, Stuart R.　see　LAVIN, Stuart R.
　　2740.　[No entry]

LEVINE, Miriam
  2741. Friends dreaming. Tucson, AZ: Ironwood, 1974
  2742. To know we are living. Washington: Decatur, 1976
  2743. The graves of Delawanna. Cambridge, MA: Apple-
          wood, 1981

LEVINE, Philip
  2744. 1933. New York: Atheneum, 1974
  2745. New season. Port Townsend, WA: Graywolf, 1975
  2746. The names of the lost. Iowa City: Windhover, 1976;
          New York: Atheneum, 1976
  2747. On the edge & over. Oakland, CA: Cloud Marauder,
          1976
  2748. Ashes; poems new and old. New York: Atheneum,
          1979
  2749. 7 years from somewhere. New York: Atheneum, 1979
  2750. One for the rose. New York: Atheneum, 1981

LEVINE, Steve
  2751. A blue tongue. West Branch, IA: Toothpaste, 1976
  2752. Pure notations. West Branch, IA: Toothpaste, 1982

LEVIS, Larry
  2753. The rain's witness. Iowa City: Southwick, 1975
  2754. The afterlife. Iowa City: University of Iowa Press,
          1977
  2755. The dollmaker's ghost. New York: Dutton, 1981

LEVITT, Peter
  2756. Two bodies dark/velvet. Los Angeles: Momentum,
          1975

LEVY, Lyn
  2757. Singing happy sad. Detroit: Broadside, 1973

LEWANDOWSKI, Stephen
  2758. Visitor. Buffalo, NY: White Pine, 1976
  2759. Inside & out. Trumansburg, NY: Crossing, 1978
  2760. Water. Olean, NY: Allegany Mountain, 1978

LEWIN, Renate
  2761. Intermittent release. Chicago: Ommation, 1976

LEWIS, Betsy
  2762. Animal snackers. New York: Dodd, Mead, 1980

LEWIS, Grover
  2763. I'll be there in the morning if I live. San Francisco:
          Straight Arrow, 1973

LEWIS, Harry
  2764. Home cooking. Northampton, MA: Mulch, 1975
  2765. Hudson. New York: # Magazine, 1980

2766. The wellsprings; poems, 1975-1980. San Francisco:
       Momo's, 1981

LEWIS, Roger
2767. The carbon gang. Wheaton, MD: Cherry Valley, 1983

LEWIS, Steven
2768. Exits off a toll road. Milwaukee: Pentagram, 1975

LEWISOHN, James
2769. Golgotha: letters from prison. Greenfield Center, NY:
       Greenfield Review, 1976
2770. Lead us forth from prison. Greenfield Center, NY:
       Greenfield Review, 1977

LIEBERMAN, Laurence
2771. The osprey suicides. New York: Macmillan, 1973
2772. God's measurements. New York: Macmillan, 1980
2773. Eros at the world kite pageant: poems 1979-1982. New
       York: Macmillan, 1983

LIETZ, Robert
2774. Running in place. Fort Collins, CO: L'Epervier, 1979
2775. At Park and East Division. Seattle: L'Epervier, 1981

LIFSHIN, Lyn
2776. The old house on the Croton. San Lorenzo, CA:
       Shameless Hussy, 1973
2777. 40 days, apple nights. Milwaukee: Morgan, 1974
2778. Poems. Gulfport, FL: Konglomerati, 1974
2779. Shaker poems. Chatham, NY: Omphalos, 1974
2780. Old house poems. Santa Barbara: Capra, 1975
2781. Paper apples. Stockton, CA: Wormwood Review, 1975
2782. Upstate Madonna. Trumansburg, NY: Crossing, 1975
2783. North poems. Milwaukee: Morgan, 1976
2784. Shaker House poems. Chatham, NY: Sagarin, 1976
2785. Some madonna poems. Buffalo, NY: White Pine, 1976
2786. Crazy arms. Chicago: Ommation, 1977
2787. More waters. Cincinnati: Waters, 1977
2788. Early Plymouth women. Milwaukee: Morgan, 1978
2789. Glass. Milwaukee: Morgan, 1978
2790. Leaning South. New York: Red Dust, 1978
2791. Offered by owner. Cambridge, NY: Natalie Slohm,
       1978
2792. 35 Sundays. Chicago: Ommation, 1979
2793. Naked charm. Los Angeles: Illuminati, 1982
2794. Blue Dust, New Mexico. Fredonia, NY: Basilisk,
       1983
2795. Lobster & oatmeal. Sacramento, CA: Pinchpenny,
       1983
2796. The mad girl. Augusta, GA: Blue Horse, 1983
2797. Madonna who shifts for herself. Long Beach, CA:
       Applezaba, 1983

LIGHTS, Rikki
 2798. Dog moon. Bronx, NY: Sunbury, 1976

LIGI, Gary E.
 2799. Stinking and full of eels. Rock Hill, SC: Peaceweed,
   1975

LILLIE, Mary Prentice
 2800. A decade of dreams. Georgetown, CA: Dragon's
   Teeth, 1979

LIMA, Frank
 2801. Angel. New York: Liveright, 1976

LINCOLN, Doris Brandt
 2802. Greening twig. Milwaukee: Membrane, 1975

LINDSAY, Elizabeth Conner
 2803. Angel at the gate. Monterey, CA: Peters Gate, 1975

LINDSAY, Frannie
 2804. Refusal to break. Boston: Stone Soup, 1976
 2805. The house we lie down in. Normal, IL: Pikestaff,
   1980
 2806. The aerial tide coming in. Amherst, MA: Swamp,
   1981

LINDSAY, Jim
 2807. In lieu of Mecca. Pittsburgh: University of Pittsburgh
   Press, 1976

LINDSAY, Karen
 2808. Falling off the roof. Cambridge, MA: Alice James,
   1975

LINEBARGER, J. M.
 2809. Five faces. Denton, TX: Trilobite, 1976

LINER, Amon
 2810. Chrome grass. Carrboro, NC: Carolina Wren, 1975
 2811. Rose, a color of darkness. Chapel Hill, NC: Carolina
   Wren, 1981
 2812. The far journey and final end of Dr. Faustwitz, space-
   man. Chapel Hill, NC: Carolina Wren, 1983
 2813. Faustwitz Part I. Chapel Hill, NC: Carolina Wren,
   1983

LIPMAN, Ed
 2814. No capital crime. San Francisco: Second Coming,
   1975

LIPPE, Jane
 2815. Silent partner. St. Paul: New Rivers, 1980

LIPSITZ, Lou
    2816. Reflections of Samson. Santa Cruz, CA: Kayak, 1977

LITTLE, Geraldine
    2817. Contrasts in keening: Ireland. Hainesport, NJ: Silver
           Apples, 1982
    2818. Hakugai. Austin, TX: Curbstone, 1983

LITTLE, Janet
    2819. Hecate the bandicoot. New York: Dodd Mead, 1980

LIVINGSTON, Jay C.
    2820. The fount of dreams. Milwaukee: Metatron, 1977
    2821. The romantic muse. Milwaukee: Metatron, 1978
    2822. Poetics, prosody & passion. Milwaukee: Metatron,
           1979

LOCKE, Duane
    2823. Meadow 8 - immanentist sutras. Ann Arbor, MI: 1973

LOCKLIN, Gerald
    2824. Toad's Europe. Long Beach, CA: California State,
           1973
    2825. The criminal mentality. Fairfax, CA: Red Hill, 1976
    2826. Pronouncing Borges. Stockton, CA: Wormwood Review,
           1977
    2827. Frisco epic. Cape Elizabeth, ME: Maelstrom, 1978
    2828. Two summer sequences. Long Beach, CA: Maelstrom,
           1979
    2829. Clear & present danger to society. Ashuelot, NH:
           Four Zoas Night House, 1980
    2830. Two for the seesaw/One for the road. Stafford, VA:
           Northwoods, 1980
    2831. Scenes from a second adolescence. Long Beach, CA:
           Applezaba, 1981
    2832. [No entry]

LOEWINSOHN, Ron
    2833. The leaves. Los Angeles: Black Sparrow, 1973
    2834. Eight fairy tales. Los Angeles: Black Sparrow,
           1975
    2835. Goat dances. Santa Barbara: Black Sparrow, 1976

LOFTIS, N. J.
    2836. Black cinema. New York: Liveright, 1973

LOGAN, John
    2837. The anonymous lover. New York: Liveright, 1973
    2838. Poem in progress. San Francisco: Dryad, 1975
    2839. The bridge of change. Brockport, NY: BOA Editions,
           1978
    2840. Only the dreamer can change the dream. Honolulu:
           Petronium, 1975; New York: Ecco, 1981

2841. The transformation poems: January to March, 1981.
San Francisco: Pancake, 1983

LOGAN, William
2842. Sad-faced men. Boston: Godine, 1982

LOMAX, Deane Ritch
2843. Pine ridge poems. Durham, NC: Moore, 1975

LONDON, Jonathan
2844. In a season of birds: poems for Maureen. Santa
Barbara: Mudborn, 1979

LONERGAN, Leonard
2845. The iron road. New York: The Smith, 1981

LONG WOLF, Tony
2846. Long Wolf poems. Marvin, SD: Blue Cloud Quarterly,
1979

LOPATE, Phillip
2847. The daily round. New York: Sun, 1976
2848. The eyes don't always want to stay open. New York:
Sun, 1976

LOPES, Michael
2849. Mr. & Mrs. Mephistopheles and son. Paradise, CA:
Dustbooks, 1975

LORD, May
2850. On a high hill. Winston-Salem, NC: J. F. Blair,
1973

LORDE, Audre
2851. From a land where other people live. Detroit: Broad-
side, 1973
2852. New York head shop and museum. Detroit: Broadside,
1975
2853. Between our selves. San Francisco: Eidolon, 1976
2854. Coal. New York: Norton, 1976
2855. The black unicorn. New York: Norton, 1978
2856. Chosen poems: old and new. New York: Norton, 1982

LOSSY, Rella
2857. Audible dawn. Diablo, CA: Holmgangers, 1975

LOUIS, Adrian C.
2858. The Indian cheap wine seance. Providence: Gray
Flannel, 1974
2859. Muted war drums. Marvin, SD: Blue Cloud Quarterly,
1977
2860. Sweets for the dancing bears. Marvin, SD: Blue
Cloud, 1979

LOURIE, Dick
    2861. Stumbling. Trumansburg, NY: Crossing, 1973
    2862. Anima. Brooklyn: Hanging Loose, 1977

LOUTHAN, Robert
    2863. Shrunken planets. Cambridge, MA: Alice James, 1980
    2864. Living in code. Pittsburgh: University of Pittsburgh
          Press, 1983

LOVE, John
    2865. The touch code. Brooklyn: Release, 1977

LOVENSTEIN, Meno
    2866. Against a garden wall. Boston: Simmons College
          Press, 1974

LOWELL, Robert
    2867. History. New York: Farrar, Straus and Giroux, 1973
    2868. Selected poems. New York: Farrar, Straus and Giroux,
          1976
    2869. Day by day. New York: Farrar, Straus and Giroux,
          1977
    2870. Selected poems. New York: Farrar, Straus and Gir-
          oux, 1977

LOWERY, Mike
    2871. Masks of the dreamer. Middletown, CT: Wesleyan
          University Press, 1979

LUCAS, John
    2872. Leap year choice. Northfield, MN: Carleton College,
          1976

LUCHENBACH, Lucky
    2873. Who knows some of this might be real. Providence:
          Hellcoal, 1975

LUDVIGSON, Susan
    2874. Northern lights. Baton Rouge: Louisiana State Univer-
          sity Press, 1981

LUNCH, Lydia
    2875. Adulterers anonymous. New York: Grove, 1982

LURIA-SUKENICK, Lynn
    2876. Houdini, Houdini. Cleveland: Cleveland State Univer-
          sity Poetry Center, 1982

LUSCHEI, Glenna
    2877. Back into my body. Berkeley: Thorp Springs, 1974

LUSK, Daniel
    2878. Wild onions. Kansas City, MO: Book Mark, 1975

LUSTER, Helen
    2879. The book of rose. San Rafael, CA: Fur Line, 1976
    2880. Year of the hare poems. San Francisco: Manroot,
           1976
    2881. Crystal. San Francisco: Manroot, 1981

LUX, Thomas
    2882. The glassblower's breath: Chico: California State Uni-
           versity Poetry Center, 1975
    2883. Sunday. Boston: Houghton Mifflin, 1979
    2884. Tarantulas on the lifebuoy. Bristol, RI: Ampersand,
           1983

LUYTEN, Meredith
    2885. Prayer wheels. Woods Hole, MA: Pourboire, 1976

LUZI, Mario
    2886. In the dark body of metamorphosis. New York: Norton,
           1975

LYALL, Ione W.
    2887. After the rain. Old Tappan, NJ: Revel, 1975

LYLES, Peggy Willis
    2888. Red leaves in the air. Battleground, IN: High/Coo,
           1979
    2889. Still at the edge. Amherst, MA: Swamp, 1979

LYNCH, Dell Ryan
    2890. Bright orbits. Reseda, CA: Mojave, 1974

LYONS, Richard
    2891. Racer and lame. Moorhead, MN: Territorial, 1975

MacADAMS, Lewis
    2892. Now let us eat of this pollen and place some on our
           heads, for we are to talk of it. New York: Harper
           & Row, 1973
    2893. The population explodes. Storrs: University of Con-
           necticut Library, 1973
    2894. News from Niman farm. Bolinas, CA: Tombouctou,
           1976
    2895. Live at the church. New York: Kulchur Foundation,
           1977

McAFEE, Thomas
    2896. The body & the body's guest. Kansas City, MO: BkMk,
           1975

McALEAVEY, David
    2897. The forty days. Ithaca, NY: Ithaca House, 1975
    2898. Shrine, shelter, cave. Ithaca, NY: Ithaca House, 1980

McAULEY, John
     2899. Hazardous renaissance. Flushing, NY: Cross Country,
              1978
     2900. Mattress testing. Flushing, NY: Cross Country, 1978

McBRIDE, Dick
     2901. Cometh with clouds. Rochester, NY: Cherry Valley,
              1983

McBRIDE, Mekeel
     2902. A change in the weather. Milton, MA: Chowder, 1979
     2903. No ordinary world. Pittsburgh: Carnegie-Mellon Uni-
              versity Press, 1979
     2904. The going under of the evening land. Pittsburgh:
              Carnegie-Mellon University Press, 1983

McCABE, Angela
     2905. The keeper of height. New York: Barlenmir, 1974

McCAFFREY, Phillip
     2906. Cold frames. Richford, VT: Samisdat, 1976

McCANN, David
     2907. Keeping time. Chicago: Troubadour, 1980

McCANN, Richard
     2908. Dream of the traveler. Ithaca, NY: Ithaca House,
              1976

McCARTHY, Eugene J.
     2909. Ground fog and night. New York: Harcourt Brace Jo-
              vanovich, 1979

McCARTHY, Gerald
     2910. War story, Vietnam War poems. Trumansburg, NY:
              Crossing, 1977

McCARTY, Tom
     2911. Dreams of state. Berkeley: Samisdat, 1974

McCAWLEY, Chris
     2912. The first thing in the field. Whitehorn, CA: Holm-
              gangers, 1982

McCLANE, Kenneth A.
     2913. Out beyond the bay. Ithaca, NY: Ithaca House, 1975
     2914. Moons and low times. Ithaca, NY: Ithaca House,
              1978
     2915. - [No entry]
     2919.
     2920. Three halves are whole. Norristown, PA: Black
              Willow, 1983

McCLATCHY, J. D.
    2921. Scenes from another life. New York: G. Braziller,
        1981

McCLELLAND, Bruce
    2922. The Dracula poems. New York: Sixpack, 1978
    2923. The maerchen cycle. Barrytown, NY: Station Hill,
        1980

McCLELLAND, Jeanette
    2924. In the middle way. Laurinburg, NC: Curveship, 1975

McCLINTOCK, Michael
    2925. Seven dead fleas. Los Angeles: Seer Ox, 1975
    2926. Jesus leaving Vegas. Milwaukee: Pentagram, 1976

McCLURE, Michael
    2927. The book of Joanna. Berkeley: Sand Dollar, 1973
    2928. Rare angel. Los Angeles: Black Sparrow, 1973
    2929. Transfiguration. Cambridge, MA: Pomegranate, 1973
    2930. A fist full (1956-1957). Los Angeles: Black Sparrow,
        1974
    2931. Fleas 189-195. New York: Aloe, 1974
    2932. Hail thee who play. Albany, CA: Sand Dollar, 1974
    2933. On organism. Buffalo, NY: Institute of Further Studies,
        1974
    2934. Rare angel (writ with raven's blood). Los Angeles:
        Black Sparrow, 1974
    2935. September blackberries. New York: New Directions,
        1974
    2936. Solstice blossom. Berkeley: Arif, 1974
    2937. Jaguar skies. New York: New Directions, 1975
    2938. Man of moderation. New York: F. Hallman, 1975
    2939. Antechamber & other poems. New York: New Directions,
        1978
    2940. Hymns to St. Geryon/Dark brown, San Francisco: Grey
        Fox, 1980
    2941. Fragments of Perseus. New York: J. Davies, 1978;
        New York: New Directions, 1983

McCOMBS, Judith
    2942. Sisters and other selves. Detroit: Glass Bell, 1976
    2943. Against nature: wildness poems. Paradise, CA: Dust-
        books, 1979

McCORD, Fletcher
    2944. For rent or for sale. Tulsa, OK: Knight's Gambit,
        1973

McCORD, Howard
    2945. Friend. New York: New Rivers, 1974
    2946. The old beast. Port Townsend, WA: Copper Canyon,
        1975

2947. The selected poems of Howard McCord; 1955-1971.
   Trumansburg, NY: Crossing, 1975
2948. Peach Mt. smoke out. Dennis, MA: Salt-Works, 1978
2949. The great toad hunt and other expeditions. Trumans-
   burg, NY: Crossing, 1980

McCOWN, Clint
2950. Sidetracks. Winston-Salem, NC: Jackpine, 1977

McCRORIE, Ted
2951. After a cremation. Berkeley: Thorp Springs, 1974

McCURRY, Jim
2952. CTA. East Lansing, MI: Ghost Dance, 1976

McDANIEL, Judith
2953. November woman. Glens Falls, NY: Loft, 1983

McDANIEL, Wilma Elizabeth
2954. The fish hook. Big Timber, MT: Seven Buffaloes,
   1978
2955. Tollbridge. New York: Contact II, 1980
2956. Sister Vayda's song. Brooklyn: Hanging Loose, 1982

MACDONALD, Cynthia
2957. Transplants. New York: Braziller, 1976
2958. (W)holes. New York: Knopf, 1980

MacDONALD, Douglas
2959. Spirals. Chicago: Ommation, 1979

McDONALD, Shel
2960. Living paradox dying. Reseda, CA: Mojave, 1975

McDONALD, Walter
2961. Caliban in blue, and other poems. Lubbock: Texas
   Tech, 1976
2962. Anything, anything. Seattle: L'Epervier, 1980
2963. Working against time. Glenview, IL: Calliope, 1981

McDONOUGH, George E.
2964. A long perspective. Seattle: Seattle Pacific University,
   1980

McDOWELL, Robert
2965. At the house of the tin man. Milton, MA: Chowder,
   1983

McELROY, Colleen J.
2966. Music from home: selected poems. Carbondale:
   Southern Illinois University Press, 1976
2967. Winters without snow. Berkeley: I. Reed, 1980

McELROY, David
2968. Making it simple. New York: Ecco, 1975

McFARLAND, Ronald E.
2969. Certain women. Lewiston, ID: Confluence, 1977

McFEE, Michael
2970. Plain air. Orlando: University Presses of Florida, 1983

McGRATH, Mary
1971. Trespassing stoplights and attitudes. Santa Barbara: Mudborn, 1980

McGRATH, Thomas
2972. Voices from beyond the wall. Moorhead, MN: Territorial, 1974
2973. A sound of one hand. St. Peter: Minnesota Writers', 1975
2974. Letters to Tomasito. Minneapolis: Holy Cow!, 1977
2975. Open songs; sixty short poems. Mt. Carroll, IL: Uzzano, 1977
2976. Passages toward the dark. Port Townsend, WA: Copper Canyon, 1982
2977. Echoes inside the labyrinth. New York: Thunder's Mouth, 1983

McHUGH, Heather
2978. Dangers. Boston: Houghton Mifflin, 1977
2979. A world of difference. Boston: Houghton Mifflin, 1981

McKAIN, David
2980. In touch. Ann Arbor, MI: Ardis, 1975
2981. The common life. Cambridge, MA: Alice James, 1982

McKEON, Ken
2982. Winter man. Berkeley: Thorp Springs, 1975

McKEOWN, Tom
2983. The luminous revolver. Fremont, MI: Sumac, 1973
2984. Driving to New Mexico. Sante Fe, NM: Sunstone, 1974
2985. The house of water: early poems. Fredonia, NY: Basilisk, 1974
2986. Certain minutes. Stevens Point, WI: Scopcraeft, 1978

McKERMAN, John
2987. Walking along the Missouri River. Fayetteville, AR: Lost Roads, 1977

MACKEY, Mary
2988. Split ends. Berkeley: Ariel, 1974

2989. One night stand. Emeryville, CA: Effie's, 1977
2990. Skin deep. Arlington, VA: Gallimaufry, 1978

McKIM, Elizabeth
2991. Family salt. Green Harbor, MA: Wampeter, 1981
2992. Body India. Brighton, MA: Yellow Moon, 1982

McKINNEY, Virginia
2993. Sudden Ripples. North Babylon, NY: J. Mark, 1974

McKINNON, Karen
2994. Stereoscopic. San Luis Obispo, CA: Solo, 1975

McLAUGHLIN, Daniel
2995. Where the warm wind blows. N. Babylon, NY: J.
Mark, 1976

McLAUGHLIN, Joseph
2996. Infidelities. Bigfork, MN: Northwoods, 1973

McLAUGHLIN, Lissa
2997. Approached by fur. Providence: Burning Deck, 1976

McLAUGHLIN, William
2998. At rest in the Midwest. Cleveland: Cleveland State
University Poetry Center, 1981

MACLEOD, Norman
2999. Selected poems. Boise, ID: Ahsahta, 1975
3000. The distance. Pembroke, NC: Pembroke, 1977

MAC LOW, Jackson
3001. Four trains, 4-5 December, 1964. Providence: Burn-
ing Deck, 1974
3002. 36th light poem; in memoriam Buster Keaton. London:
Permanent, 1975
3003. 3 light poems for 3 women. Barrytown, NY: Station
Hill, 1977
3004. First book of gathas. Milwaukee: Membrane, 1978
3005. 21 matched asymmetries. London: Aloes, 1978
3006. Phone. Barrytown, NY: Printed Editions, 1979
3007. The pronouns. Barrytown, NY: Station Hill, 1979
3008. Asymmetries 1-260. Barrytown, NY: Printed Editions,
1980
3009. Is that wool hat my hat? Milwaukee: Membrane, 1982

McMAHON, Michael
3010. A day's work. Orono, ME: Puckerbrush, 1976
3011. Dead of winter. Orono, ME: Puckerbrush, 1982

McMICHAEL, James
3012. Four good things. Boston: Houghton Mifflin, 1980

McMULLEN, Richard E.
    3013. Chicken beacon. Ann Arbor, MI: Street Fiction, 1975

McNAIR, Wesley
    3014. The faces of Americans in 1853. Columbia: University
        of Missouri Press, 1983

McNALLY, John
    3015. Northern lights. Washington: Washington Writers',
        1977

McNEILL, Louise
    3016. Elderberry flood. Charleston, WV: Elderberry, 1979

McNICOLL, Ron
    3017. Sail away, silvery moon. Diablo, CA: Holmganger,
        1975

McNULTY, Tim
    3018. Pawtracks. Port Townsend, WA: Copper Canyon, 1978

McPHERSON, Sandra
    3019. Radiation. New York: Ecco, 1973
    3020. The year of our birth. New York: Ecco, 1978
    3021. Sensing. San Francisco: Meadow, 1979
    3022. Patron happiness. New York: Ecco, 1983

McROBERTS, Robert L.
    3023. Lip service. Ithaca, NY: Ithaca House, 1976

McWHINNEY, Norman
    3024. Advice to a vampire at puberty. Derry, PA: Rook,
        1976
    3025. The night still in your kiss. Derry, PA: Rook, 1976

McWILLIAMS, Peter
    3026. Love and all the other verbs of life. Garden City, NY:
        Doubleday, 1973

MADGETT, Naomi Long
    3027. Exits and entrances. Detroit: Lotus, 1978

MADHUBUTI, Mwalimu Haki
    3028. Book of life. Detroit: Broadside, 1973

MADOFF, Mark
    3029. Paper nautilus. Vancouver, BC: Pulp, 1973

MADSON, Jerry
    3030. Race Horse Station. Bemidji, MN: Truly Fine, 1974

MAGORIAN, James
    3031. The red, white, & blue bus. Berkeley: Samisdat, 1975

3032. Alphabetical order. San Francisco: Amphion, 1976
3033. Two hundred push-ups at the YMCA. Chicago: Specific
       Gravity, 1977
3034. Phases of the moon. Lincoln, NE: Black Oak, 1978
3035. Night shift at the poetry factory. Chicago: Broken
       Whisker, 1979
3036. Piano tuning at midnight. Woodinville, WA: Laughing
       Bear, 1979
3037. Revenge. Richford, VT: Samisdat, 1979
3038. Safe passage. Menemesha, MA: Stone Country, 1979
3039. Spiritual rodeo. West Branch, Iowa: Toothpaste, 1980
3040. Tap dancing on a tightrope. San Jose, CA: Laughing
       Bear, 1981
3041. Taxidermy lessons. Lincoln, NE: Black Oak, 1982
3042. Selected poetry. Urbana, IL: Peradam, 1983

MAGOWAN, Robin
3043. Looking for binoculars. Santa Cruz, CA: Kayak, 1976

MAHAN, Kent
3044. Cornflakes. Bowling Green, OH: Newedi, 1975

MAISEL, Carolyn
3045. Witnessing. Fort Collins, CO: L'Epervier, 1978

MALAKI
3046. Tracks. Gulfport, FL: Konglomerati, 1979

MALANGA, Gerard
3047. Poetry on film. Norwood, PA: Telegraph, 1973
3048. Wheels of light. Los Angeles: Black Sparrow, 1973
3049. Nine poems for Cesar Vallejo. New York: Vanishing
       Triangle, 1974
3050. 7 poems for Pilar Crespi. Kenosha, WI: Del Sol,
       1974
3051. Ten years after. Los Angeles: Black Sparrow, 1974
3052. 22. Los Angeles: Black Sparrow, 1974
3053. Incarnations. Los Angeles: Black Sparrow, 1975
3054. Rosebud. Lincoln, MA: Penmaen, 1975
3055. Leaping over gravestones. Ashuelot, NH: Four Zoas
       Night House, 1976
3056. Leaping over gravestones. Hardwicks, MA: Four Zoas,
       1978
3057. 100 years have passed. New York: Little Caesar,
       1978
3058. This will kill that. Santa Barbara: Black Sparrow,
       1978

MALLOY, Merrit
3059. Things I meant to say to you when we were old. Gar-
       den City, NY: Dolphin, 1977

MALONEY, Frank R.
 3060. How to eat a slug. Port Townsend, WA: Copper Canyon, 1976

MALONEY, J. J.
 3061. Beyond the wall. Greenfield Center, NY: Greenfield Review, 1973

MANDEL, Tom
 3062. Ency. Berkeley: Tuumba, 1978
 3063. Erat. Providence: Burning Deck, 1981
 3064. Ready to go: poems, 1972-1977. Ithaca, NY: Ithaca House, 1981

MANDELBAUM, Allen
 3065. Chiemaxions. Boston: Godine, 1977

MANFRED, Frederick
 3066. Winter count. Berkeley: Thorp Springs, 1977

MANFRED, Freya
 3067. Yellow squash woman. Berkeley: Thorp Springs, 1976

MANLEY, Frank
 3068. Resultances. Columbia: University of Missouri Press, 1980

MARANO, Russell
 3069. Poems from a mountain ghetto. Webster Springs, WV: Back Fork, 1979

MARCUS, Aaron
 3070. Soft where, inc.. Reno, NV: West Coast Poetry Review, 1975

MARCUS, Adrianne
 3071. Faced with love. Providence: Copper Beech, 1978

MARCUS, Mordecai
 3072. Return from the desert. Bowling Green, OH: Newedi, 1977

MARCUS, Morton
 3073. Big winds, glass mornings, shadows cast by stars. Los Angeles: Jazz, 1982

MARIAH, Paul
 3074. Electric holding company. San Francisco: Manroot, 1974
 3075. Letter to Robert Duncan while bending the bow. South San Francisco: Manroot, 1974
 3076. Apparitions of a black pauper's suit: 13 eulogies. San Francisco: Hoddypoll, 1976

3077. Personae non gratae. San Lorenzo, CA: Shameless
          Hussy, 1976
3078. Selected poems, 1960-1975. South San Francisco:
          Manroot, 1977

MARIANI, Paul L.
   3079. Timing devices. Boston, MA: Godine, 1979
   3080. Crossing Cocytus. New York: Grove, 1982

MARIN, Sutter
   3081. 113 simple-minded poems for the semi-simple minded.
          San Francisco: Peace & Pieces, 1973

MARION, Jeff Daniel
   3082. Out in the country, back home. Winston-Salem, NC:
          Jackpine, 1976
   3083. Watering places. Knoxville, TN: Puddingstone, 1976
   3084. Tight lines. Emory, VA: Iron Mountain, 1981

MARKS, S. J.
   3085. Lines. Iowa City: Cummington, 1973

MARSH, Michael
   3086. Gemini. Berkeley: Samisdat, 1975

MARSHALL, Jack
   3087. Arriving on the playing fields of paradise. Iowa City:
          Cedar Creek, 1974
   3088. Bits of thirst. Iowa City: Cedar Creek, 1974
   3089. Bits of thirst & other poems & translations. Berkeley:
          Blue Wind, 1976

MARTIN, Charles
   3090. Room for error. Athens: University of Georgia Press,
          1977
   3091. Four for Roethke. Port Jefferson, NY: Street, 1978

MARTIN, Herbert Woodward
   3092. The shit-storm poems. Grand Rapids, MI: Pilot, 1973
   3093. The persistence of the flesh. Detroit: Lotus, 1976
   3094. The forms of silence. Detroit: Lotus, 1980

MARTIN, James
   3095. A reunion. Providence: Copper Beech, 1975

MARTINSON, David
   3096. Bleeding the radiator. Moorhead, MN: Territorial,
          1974

MARTONE, John
   3097. In the course of the real. Providence: Copper Beech,
          1978
   3098. Ocean vows. Providence: Copper Beech, 1983

MARTONE, Michael
   3099. At a loss. Fort Wayne, IN: The Windless Orchard,
          1977

MARVELLE, James
   3100. Wallflowers and wayfarers. San Diego: Realities, 1976
   3101. Howling at the wind. San Jose, CA: Realities, 1977
   3102. Standing on my head. San Jose, CA: Realities, 1978
   3103. No title yet. San Jose, CA: Realities, 1983

MARX, Anne
   3104. A time to mend. Georgetown, CA: Dragon's Teeth,
          1973

MARZ, Roy
   3105. The island-maker. Ithaca, NY: Ithaca House, 1982

MASARIK, Al
   3106. An end to pinball. Ellensburg, WA: Vagabond, 1973
   3107. A post card from Europe. Ellensburg, WA: Vagabond,
          1975
   3108. Red Mountain, Agatha Christie & love. Ellensburg, WA:
          Vagabond, 1976
   3109. Nonesuch Creek. Fallon, NV: Duck Down, 1980

MASON, Anneke
   3110. A handful of bubbles: Pensees. Tacoma, WA: Univer-
          sity of Puget Sound, 1981
   3111. Journey. Tacoma, WA: University of Puget Sound,
          1981

MASON, Madeline
   3112. Sonnets in a new form. Georgetown, CA: Dragon's
          Teeth, 1975

MASON, Scott
   3113. No dogs in heaven. Cleveland: Cleveland State Univer-
          sity Poetry Center, 1980

MASTERN, Ric
   3114. Speaking poems. Boston: Beacon, 1977

MASTERSON, Dan
   3115. On earth as it is. Urbana: University of Illinois
          Press, 1978

MATHEWS, Harry
   3116. The planisphere. Providence: Burning Deck, 1974
   3117. Tial impressions. Providence: Burning Deck, 1977

MATHIS, Cleopatra
   3118. Aerial view of Louisiana. New York: Sheep Meadow,
          1979
   3119. The bottom land. New York: Sheep Meadow, 1983

MATOS, Luis Pales
    3120. Obras completas. Rio Piedras: University of Puerto
          Rico Press, 1977

MATSON, Clive
    3121. On the inside. Silver Spring, MD: Cherry Valley,
          1982

MATTHEWS, Jack
    3122. Private landscapes. Athens, OH: Croissant, 1975

MATTHEWS, William
    3123. An oar in old water; poems in one line. Ithaca, NY:
          Stone, 1973
    3124. Sticks and stones. Milwaukee: Pentagram, 1975
    3125. An oar in the old water. San Francisco: The Stone,
          1976
    3126. Rising and falling. Boston: Little, Brown, 1979
    3127. Flood. Boston: Little, Brown, 1982

MATTHIAS, John
    3128. Double derivation, association, and cliche from the
          Great Tournament Roll of Westminster. Chicago:
          Wine, 1975
    3129. Turns. Chicago: Swallow, 1975
    3130. Crossing. Chicago: Swallow, 1978

MATTINGLY, George
    3131. Breathing space. Berkeley: Blue Wind, 1975

MATTISON, Alice
    3132. Animals. Cambridge, MA: Alice James, 1979

MAURA, Sister
    3133. What we women know. West Lafayette, IN: Sparrow,
          1980

MAXSON, H. A.
    3134. Turning the wood. Stillwater, OK: Cedar Creek, 1976

MAYER, Bernadette
    3135. Ceremony Latin. Lenox, MA: Angel Hair, 1975
    3136. Studying hunger. Bolinas, CA: Big Sky, 1975
    3137. Poetry. New York: Kulchur Foundation, 1976
    3138. The golden book of words. New York: United Artists,
          1978

MAYO, E. L.
    3139. Selected poems. Iowa City: Prairie, 1973
    3140. Collected poems. Kansas City, MO: New Letters, 1981

MAZUR, Gail
    3141. Nightfire. Boston: Godine, 1978

MAZZARO, Jerome
  3142. Grailing. Pittsburgh: Slow Loris, 1976

MAZZOCCO, Robert
  3143. Trader. New York: Knopf, 1980

MAZZOLINI, Michael
  3144. Hot knoves, greasy spoons, & all night diners. Elkins,
          WV: Cheat Mountain, 1979

MEAGHER, Kathleen
  3145. Going outside. Bronx, NY: Sunbury, 1974

MEDARY, Marjorie
  3146. Under many a star. Mount Vernon, NY: Peter Pauper,
          1975

MEEK, Jay
  3147. The week the dirigible came. Pittsburgh: Carnegie-
          Mellon University Press, 1976

MEIER, Judith
  3148. Hickory and a smooth dime. Santa Fe, NM: Sunstone,
          1975

MEINERS, R. K.
  3149. Journeying back to the world. Columbia: University
          of Missouri Press, 1975

MEINKE, Peter
  3150. Lines from Neuchatel. Gulfport, FL: Konglomerati,
          1974
  3151. The night train & The golden bird. Pittsburgh: Univer-
          sity of Pittsburgh Press, 1977
  3152. The rat poems. Cleveland: Bits, 1978
  3153. Trying to surprise God. Pittsburgh: University of
          Pittsburgh Press, 1981

MEISSNER, William
  3154. Learning to breathe underwater. Athens: Ohio Univer-
          sity Press, 1979

MELHEM, D. H.
  3155. Rest in love. New York: Dovetail, 1975

MELTZER, David
  3156. Bark, a polemic. Santa Barbara: Capra, 1973
  3157. The eyes, the blood. San Francisco: Mudra, 1973
  3158. French broom. Berkeley: Oyez, 1973
  3159. Tens; selected poems 1961-1971. New York: McGraw-
          Hill, 1973
  3160. Blue rags. Berkeley: Oyez, 1974

3161. Harps. Berkeley: Oyez, 1975
3162. Bolero. Berkeley: Oyez, 1976
3163. Six. Santa Barbara: Black Sparrow, 1976
3164. The art/the veil. Milwaukee: Membrane, 1981
3165. The name. Santa Barbara: Black Sparrow, 1983

MENASHE, Samuel
3166. To open. New York: Viking, 1974

MENDOZA, George
3167. Fishing the morning lonely. Rockville Center, NY:
      Freshet, 1974

MEREDITH, William
3167a. Hazard, the painter. New York: Knopf, 1975
3168. The cheer. New York: Knopf, 1980

MERRILL, Boynton
3169. A bestiary. Lexington: University Press of Kentucky,
      1976

MERRILL, James
3170. Yannina. New York: Phoenix Book Shop, 1973
3171. The yellow pages; 59 poems. Cambridge, MA: Temple
      Bar, 1974
3172. Divine/comedies. New York: Atheneum, 1976
3173. Metamorphosis of 741. Pawlet, VT: Banyan, 1977
3174. Mirabell, books of number. New York: Atheneum,
      1978
3175. Scripts for the pageant. New York: Atheneum, 1980
3176. The changing light at Sandover. New York: Atheneum,
      1982
3177. Santorini: stopping the leak. Worcester, MA: Meta-
      com, 1982
3178. From the first nine: poems, 1946-1976. New York:
      Atheneum, 1983

MERRILL, Joe
3179. Waterweed. Salt Lake City: Litmus, 1976

MERTON, Thomas
3180. He is risen. Niles, IL: Argus, 1975
3181. The collected poems of Thomas Merton. New York:
      New Directions, 1977

MERTZ, Jerred
3182. The temperate voluptuaries. Santa Barbara: Capra,
      1975

MERWIN, W. S.
3183. Asian figures. New York: Atheneum, 1973
3184. Writings to an unfinished accompaniment. New York:
      Atheneum, 1973

3185. The first four books of poems: A mask for Janus; The
       dancing bear; Green with beasts; The drunk in the
       furnace. New York: Atheneum, 1975
3186. Three poems. Honolulu: Petronium, 1975
3187. The compass flower. New York: Atheneum, 1977
3188. Feathers from the hill. Iowa City: Windhover, 1978
3189. Finding the islands. San Francisco: North Point, 1982
3190. Opening the hand. New York: Atheneum, 1983

METCALF, Jim
3191. In some quiet place. Gretna, LA: Pelican, 1975

METCALF, Paul
3192. The middle passage. Millerton, NY: Jargon, 1976

METIVER, Marion
3193. Should anyone listen? Willimantic, CT: Curbstone,
       1976

METRAS, Gary
3194. Roses in lyric light. Easthampton, MA: Adastra, 1974
3195. A room full of walls. Easthampton, MA: Adastra,
       1978
3196. The yearnings. Richford, VT: Samisdat, 1979
3197. The necessities. Easthampton, MA: Adastra, 1979
3198. The night watches. Easthampton, MA: Adastra, 1981

METZ, Roberta
3199. Private parts. Chicago: Ommation, 1978
3200. Women, the children, the men. Woodinville, WA:
       Laughing Bear, 1979

MEYER, Tom
3201. Staves calends legends. Highlands, NC: Jargon, 1979

MEYERS, Bert
3202. Sunlight on the wall. Santa Cruz, CA: Kayak, 1976
3203. The wild olive tree. Reno, NV: West Coast Poetry
       Review, 1979
3204. Windowsills. New Haven, CT: Common Table, 1979

MEZEY, Robert
3205. Small song. Kalamazoo, MI: Practices of the Wind,
       1979

MICHELINE, Jack
3206. Last house in America. San Francisco: Second
       Coming, 1976
3207. North of Manhattan: collected poems, ballads and songs,
       1954-1975. San Francisco: Manroot, 1976

MICHELSON, Peter
3208. Pacific plainsong I-XIII. Boulder, CO: Brillig, 1978

MICHELSON, Richard
    3209. The head of the family. Urbana, IL: Red Herring,
          1979

MIKOLOWSKI, Ken
    3210. Thank you call again. Mt. Horeb, WI: Perishable,
          1973
    3211. Little mysteries. West Branch, IA: Toothpaste, 1979

MILES, Josephine
    3212. To all appearances. Urbana: University of Illinois
          Press, 1974
    3213. Coming to terms. Urbana: University of Illinois Press,
          1979
    3214. Collected poems, 1930-1983. Urbana: University of
          Illinois Press, 1983

MILLER, Brown
    3215. The liquid child's son. Cleveland: Black Rabbit,
          1975
    3216. Hiroshima flows through us. Cherry Valley, NY:
          Cherry Valley, 1977

MILLER, Carol
    3217. Vari-ari-ations. Oyster Bay, NY: Panther, 1976
    3218. Bone china beliefs. Oyster Bay, NY: Press on Regard-
          less, 1977
    3219. Articulation in blue. Oyster Bay, NY: Press on Re-
          gardless, 1978

MILLER, David
    3220. Areas. Santa Cruz, CA: Green Horse, 1976
    3221. Primavera. Providence: Burning Deck, 1979

MILLER, Jane
    3222. Many junipers, heartbeats. Providence: Copper Beech,
          1980
    3223. The greater leisures. Garden City, NY: Doubleday,
          1983

MILLER, Jim Wayne
    3224. Dialogue with a dead man. Athens: University of
          Georgia Press, 1974
    3225. The mountains have come closer. Boone, NC: Appa-
          lachian Consortium, 1980

MILLER, Marcie Muth
    3226. Postcard view and other views. Santa Fe, NM: Sun-
          stone, 1973

MILLER, May
    3227. Not that far. San Luis Obispo, CA: Solo, 1973

3228. Dust of uncertain journey. Detroit: Lotus, 1975
3229. Halfway to the sun. Washington: Washington Writers',
       1981
3230. The ransomed wait. Detroit: Lotus, 1983

MILLER, Rob Hollis
3231. Shanghai Creek fire. Laurinburg, NC: St. Andrews,
       1979
3232. Shanghai Creek. Laurinburg, NC: St. Andrews, 1980

MILLER, Steve
3233. Wild night irises. Madison, WI: Red Ozier, 1976

MILLER, Vassar
3234. If I could sleep deeply enough. New York: Liveright,
       1974
3235. Small change. Houston: Wings, 1977
3236. Selected and new poems. Austin, TX: Latitudes, 1982

MILLER, Walter James
3237. Making an angel. New York: Pylon, 1977

MILLER, Wayne
3238. Shadows of remembered ancestors. San Francisco:
       Smoking Mirror, 1973
3239. From Mesoamerica. San Francisco: Smoking Mirror,
       1976

MILLING, Chapman J.
3240. Singing arrows. Hancock, MD: Trunk, 1976
3241. Singing Arrows. Hancock, MD: Trunk, 1977

MILLS, Barriss
3242. Roughened roundnesses. New Rochelle, NY: Elizabeth,
       1976

MILLS, Ralph J. Jr.
3243. Door to the sun. Phoenix: Baleen, 1974
3244. A man to his shadow. La Crosse, WI: Juniper, 1975
3245. Night road. Ruffsdale, PA: Rook, 1978
3246. With no answer. La Crosse, WI: Juniper, 1980
3247. March light. West Lafayette, IN: Sparrow, 1983

MILLS, Robert
3248. Brown bag. Peoria, IL: Spoon River, 1979
3249. Toward sunset, at a great height. Peoria, IL: Spoon
       River, 1983

MILLS, William
3250. Watch for the fox. Baton Rouge: Louisiana State
       University Press, 1974
3251. Stained glass. Baton Rouge: Louisiana University
       Press, 1979

MILTON, John R.
    3252.   The tree of bones and other poems. Vermillion: University of South Dakota Press, 1973
    3253.   The blue belly of the world. Vermillion, SD: Spirit Mount, 1974

MINTY, Judith
    3254.   Lake songs and other fears. Pittsburgh: University of Pittsburgh Press, 1974
    3255.   Yellow dog journal. Los Angeles: Center, 1979
    3256.   In the presence of mothers. Pittsburgh: University of Pittsburgh Press, 1981
    3257.   Letters to my daughters. Kent, OH: Mayapple, 1981

MINTZER, Yvette
    3258.   Dreamline express. New York: Inwood, 1975

MIRANDA, Gary
    3259.   Listeners at the breathing place. Princeton: Princeton University Press, 1978
    3260.   Grace period. Princeton: Princeton University Press, 1983

MITCHELL, David
    3261.   Wrecks and other poems. Binghamton, NY: Bellevue, 1973

MITCHELL, Irene
    3262.   I don't own you so I can't give you away. Evanston, IL: Abstract, 1975

MITCHELL, James
    3263.   Buddhist poems. San Francisco: Hoddypoll, 1975
    3264.   New poems. San Francisco: Hoddypoll, 1975
    3265.   Various poems. San Francisco: Hoddypoll, 1977

MITCHELL, Joe H.
    3266.   Lovin' you. Markham, IL: Natural Resources Unlimited, 1974

MITCHELL, Susan
    3267.   The water inside the water. Middletown, CT: Wesleyan University Press, 1983

MITSUI, James Masao
    3268.   Journal of the sun. Port Townsend, WA: Copper Canyon, 1974
    3269.   Crossing the Phantom River. Port Townsend, WA: Graywolf, 1978

MIZEJEWSKI, Linda
    3270.   The other woman. Bellingham, WA: Signpost, 1983

MOFFETT, Judith
3271.   Keeping time.   Baton Rouge: Louisiana State University
        Press, 1976

MOFFI, Larry
3272.   A simple progression.   Bristol, RI: Ampersand, 1982

MOFFITT, John
3273.   Escape of the leopard.   New York: Harcourt, Brace,
        1974

MOMADAY, N. Scott
3274.   Angle of geese and other poems.   Boston: Godine, 1974
3275.   The gourd dancer.   New York: Harper & Row, 1976

MONALES, Jorge Luis
3276.   Poesia afroantillana y negrista.   Rio Piedras: Univer-
        sity of Puerto Rico Press, 1977

MONETTE, Paul
3277.   The carpenter at the asylum.   Boston: Little, Brown,
        1975
3278.   No witnesses.   New York: Avon, 1981
3279.   Musical comedy.   Los Angeles: Illuminati, 1983

MONTAG, Tom
3280.   Making hay and other poems.   Milwaukee: Pentagram,
        1975
3281.   Naming the creeks.   Milwaukee: Morgan, 1976
3282.   Ninety notes towards partial images & lovers' prints.
        Milwaukee: Pentagram, 1976
3283.   This gathering season.   La Crosse, WI: Juniper, 1980

MONTESI, A. J.
3284.   Windows and mirrors.   Fenton, MO: Cornerstone,
        1977

MOORE, James
3285.   The new body.   Pittsburgh: University of Pittsburgh
        Press, 1975
3286.   What the bird sees.   Santa Monica, CA: Momentum,
        1978

MOORE, Prentiss
3287.   The garden in winter and other poems.   Austin: Uni-
        versity of Texas Press, 1981

MOORE, Stewart
3288.   Dandelions have their own gold standard.   Detroit:
        Orion, 1975

MOORE, Todd
3289.   The man in the black chevrolet.   Fallon, NV: Duck
        Down, 1976

3290.   The Dillinger poems.   Menomonie, WI: Uzzano,
        1977
3291.   The dark and bloody ground.   Browns Mills, NJ:
        Ptolemy/Browns Mills Review, 1981

MOOS, Michael
3292.   Hawk hover.   Moorhead, MN: Territorial, 1974
3293.   Morning windows.   St. Paul: New Rivers, 1983

MORANDA, Harold
3294.   The hands of time.   Reseda, CA: Mojave, 1976

MORENO, Leonides
3295.   Of stone and tears.   Greenfield Center, NY: Greenfield
        Review, 1975
3296.   [No entry]

MORGAN, Frederick
3297.   Poems of the two worlds.   Urbana: University of
        Illinois Press, 1977
3298.   The tarot of Cornelius Agrippa.   New York: Hudson
        Review, 1978
3299.   Death mother and other poems.   Urbana: University
        of Illinois Press, 1979
3300.   Northbook: poems.   Urbana: University of Illinois
        Press, 1982

MORGAN, Robert
3301.   Land diving.   Baton Rouge: Louisiana State University
        Press, 1976
3302.   Trunk & thicket.   Ft. Collins, CO: L'Epervier, 1978
3303.   Groundwork.   Frankfort, KY: Gnomen, 1979
3304.   Bronze age.   Emory, VA: Iron Mountain, 1981

MORGAN, Robin
3305.   Monster.   New York: Random House, 1973
3306.   Lady of the beasts.   New York: Random House, 1976
3307.   Death perception: new poems and a masque.   Garden
        City, NY: Doubleday, 1982

MORGENSTERN, Christian
3308.   The daynight lamp.   Boston: Houghton Mifflin, 1973

MORICE, Dave
3309.   Snapshots from Europe. West Branch, IA: Toothpaste,
        1974
3310.   Quicksand through the hourglass.   West Branch, IA:
        Toothpaste, 1979
3311.   A visit from St. Alphabet.   West Branch, IA: Tooth-
        paste, 1980
3312.   Dot town.   West Branch, IA: Toothpaste, 1982

MORLEY, Hilda
  3313. A blessing outside us. Woods Hole, MA: Pourboire,
         1976

MORREL, Jane
  3314. Wordings like love. Springfield, IL: Sangamon, 1975
  3315. This paradox shadow. Peoria, IL: Ellis, 1982

MORRIS, Herbert
  3316. Afghanistan. Los Angeles: Illuminati, 1983
  3317. Intimate letters. Los Angeles: Illuminati, 1983
  3318. Peru. New York: Harper & Row, 1983

MORRIS, James Cliftonne
  3319. Love poems for a remembered Black-Indian grandma.
         Detroit: Harlo, 1976

MORRIS, John N.
  3320. The life beside this one. New York: Atheneum, 1975
  3321. The glass houses. New York: Atheneum, 1980

MORRIS, John S.
  3322. Bean Street. Rogers, AR: Lost Roads, 1975

MORRIS, Phyllis Franklin
  3323. Time to close the cottage. Seattle: Mill Mountain,
         1975

MORRIS, Richard
  3324. Poetry is a kind of writing. Berkeley: Thorp Springs,
         1975
  3325. The board of directors. East Lansing, MI: Ghost
         Dance, 1976

MORRIS, Wright
  3326. The cat's meow. Los Angeles: Black Sparrow, 1975

MOSBY, George
  3327. Population. Brooklyn: Hanging Loose, 1983

MOSER, Norman
  3328. A shaman's songbook. Berkeley: Thorp Springs, 1975
  3329. Open season. Berkeley: Illuminations, 1980

MOSES, W. R.
  3330. Passage. Middletown, CT: Wesleyan University Press,
         1976
  3331. Not native. La Crosse, WI: Juniper, 1980

MOSS, Howard
  3332. Buried city. New York: Atheneum, 1975
  3333. A swim off the rocks. New York: Atheneum, 1976
  3334. Notes from the castle. New York: Atheneum, 1979

MOSS, Stanley
  3335. Skull of Adam. New York: Horizon, 1979

MOTT, Michael
  3336. Absence of unicorns, presence of lions. Boston:
          Little, Brown, 1976

MOULDER, John
  3337. Infinity at Euclid Avenue. Boulder, CO: Lodestar,
          1975
  3338. Metal. Cherry Valley, NY: Cherry Valley, 1975

MUDFOOT, Judyl
  3339. Presents. Santa Barbara: Mudborn, 1977

MUELLER, Lisel
  3340. The private life. Baton Rouge: Louisiana State Univer-
          sity Press, 1976
  3341. Voices from the forest. La Crosse, WI: Juniper,
          1977
  3342. The need to hold still. Baton Rouge: Louisiana State
          University Press, 1980

MUELLER, Melinda
  3343. Private gallery. Seattle: Seal, 1976
  3344. Asleep in another country. Waldron Island, WA: Jaw-
          bone, 1979

MUJAHADA, Sayif
  3345. Get back insanity. Boston: Afrikan Heritage, 1975

MURPHY, Joseph Francis
  3346. Spellbound, and other poems. Old Greenwich, CT:
          Devin-Adair, 1977

MURRAY, Dan
  3347. Short circuits. Mastic, NY: Street, 1975

MURRAY, G. E.
  3348. American gasoline dreams. San Francisco: Red Hill,
          1978
  3349. Repairs. Columbia: University of Missouri Press,
          1979

MURRAY, Joan
  3350. Egg tooth. Bronx, NY: Sunbury, 1975

MURRAY, Michele
  3351. The great mother and other poems. New York: Sheed
          and Ward, 1974

MUSKE, Carol
  3352. Camouflage. Pittsburgh: University of Pittsburgh
          Press, 1975

3353.   We drive through Tyndall's theory of sight.   Emory,
        VA: Iron Mountain, 1982

MYCUE, Edward
  3354.   Chronicle.   San Francisco.   Mother's Hen, 1974
  3355.   Damage within the community.   San Francisco: Pan-
           jandrum, 1976
  3356.   Root, route & range.   Albany, CA: Holmgangers, 1977
  3357.   The singing man my father gave me.   London: Menard,
           1980

MYERS, Jack
  3358.   The family war.   Fort Collins, CO: L'Epervier, 1977
  3359.   I'm amazed that you're still singing.   Seattle: L'Eper-
           vier, 1981

MYERS, Neil
  3360.   All that, so simple.   West Lafayette, IN: Purdue Uni-
           versity Press, 1980

NASH, Valery
  3361.   The narrows.   Cleveland: Cleveland State University
           Poetry Center, 1980

NASON, Richard
  3362.   The wedding at Touisset.   New York: The Smith, 1975
  3363.   A modern Dunciad.   New York: The Smith, 1978

NATHAN, Leonard
  3364.   Without wishing.   Berkeley: Thorp Springs, 1973
  3365.   Coup.   Lincoln, NE: Windflower, 1975
  3366.   The likeness.   Berkeley: Thorp Springs, 1975
  3367.   Returning your call.   Princeton, NJ: Princeton Univer-
           sity Press, 1975
  3368.   The teachings of Grandfather Fox.   Ithaca, NY: Ithaca
           House, 1976
  3369.   Lost distance.   Milton, MA: Chowder, 1978
  3370.   Dear blood.   Pittsburgh: University of Pittsburgh
           Press, 1980
  3371.   Holding patterns.   Pittsburgh: University of Pittsburgh
           Press, 1982

NATHAN, Robert
  3372.   Evening song; selected poems 1950-1973.   San Francisco:
           Capra, 1973

NATHANSON, Tenney
  3373.   The book of death.   Milwaukee: Membrane, 1975

NAVRATIL, Patricia E.
  3374.   Trails through the Northwoods.   Bigfork, MN: North-
           woods, 1976

NEAL, Larry
    3375.   Hoodoo hollerin' bebop ghosts. Washington: Howard
           University Press, 1974

NEIDERBACH, Shelley
    3376.   Lovestalk. Bronx, NY: Sunbury, 1976

NELSON, Bill
    3377.   Implementing standards of good behavior. Fort Collins,
           CO: L'Epervier, 1979

NELSON, Harry W.
    3378.   Wolf stone, wolf stone, and other poems. New London,
           CT: Blue Leaf, 1976

NELSON, Howard
    3379.   Creatures. Cleveland: Cleveland State University
           Poetry Center, 1983

NELSON, Nils
    3380.   Chicago. Tucson, AZ: Ironwood, 1976

NELSON, Paul
    3381.   Ice. Kalamazoo, MI: Blue Mountain, 1974
    3382.   Average nights. Fort Collins, CO: L'Epervier, 1977
    3383.   Days off. Charlottesville: University Press of Virginia,
           1982

NELSON, Peter
    3384.   Between lives. Tucson, AZ: Ironwood, 1974

NELSON, Rodney
    3385.   The burning of Bilskirnir. Diablo, CA: Holmgangers,
           1976
    3386.   Thor's home. Whitehorn, CA: Holmgangers, 1983

NELSON, Stanley
    3387.   The travels of Ben Sira. New York: The Smith, 1978

NELSON, Yvette
    3388.   We'll come when it rains. St. Paul: New Rivers, 1983

NEMEROV, Howard
    3389.   Gnomes and occasions. Chicago: University of Chicago
           Press, 1973
    3390.   The Western approaches. Chicago: University of
           Chicago Press, 1975
    3391.   The collected poems of Howard Nemerov. Chicago:
           University of Chicago Press, 1977
    3392.   Sentences. Chicago: University of Chicago Press, 1980

NETTELBECK, F. A.
    3393.   Destroy all monsters. Gulfport, FL: Konglomerati,
           1976

3394. No place fast. Inglewood, CA: Rough Life, 1976
3395. Americruiser. Los Angeles: Illuminati, 1983

NEWLIN, Margaret
3396. The snow falls upward. Ann Arbor, MI: Ardis, 1976

NEWMAN, Louis
3397. Pebbles & sand. New York: The Smith, 1973
3398. Tear Down the walls. New York: The Poets, 1973

NEWMAN, Paul Baker
3399. Paula. Georgetown, CA: Dragon's Teeth, 1974
3400. The house on the Saco. Dublin, NH: Bauhan, 1977
3401. The light of the red horse. Chapel Hill, NC: Carolina
       Wren, 1981

NEWPORT, Jiri
3402. Lonely Battle. Syracuse, NY: Pulp Artforms United,
       1974

NEWTH, Rebecca
3403. A journey whose bones are mine. St. Paul: Truck,
       1978
3404. Finding the lamb. Barrytown, NY: Open Book, 1981

NEWTON, Huey P.
3405. Insights & poems. San Francisco: City Lights, 1975

NEWTON, S. A.
3406. Whitlathe walrus. New York: New Rivers, 1976

NEY, Peggy
3407. Hangups. Roslyn Heights, NY: Libra, 1975

NIATUM, Duane
3408. Taos Pueblo. Greenfield Center, NY: Greenfield
       Review, 1973
3409. Ascending red cedar moon. New York: Harper & Row,
       1974
3410. The death of an elder Klallam. Phoenix, AZ: Baleen,
       1974
3411. Digging out the roots. New York: Harper & Row,
       1977
3412. Songs for the harvester of dreams. Seattle: University
       of Washington Press, 1981

NIBBELINK, Cynthia
3413. Gypsies, including animals. University Center, MI:
       Green River, 1978

NICKERSON, Sheila
3414. To the waters and the wild. Berkeley: Thorp Springs,
       1975

3415. Songs of the pine -wife. Port Townsend, WA: Copper
        Canyon, 1979

NICKSON, Richard
3416. Staves. New York: Moretus, 1977

NIEDECKER, Lorine
3417. Blue chicory. New Rochelle, NY: Elizabeth, 1976

NIELSEN, Veneta
3418. Familiar as a sparrow. Provo, UT: Brigham Young
        University Press, 1978

NIMMO, Kurt
3419. Confederate jasmine. Richford, VT: Samisdat, 1976
3420. Midnight shift in Detroit. Richfort, VT: Samisdat,
        1979

NIMNICHT, Nona
3421. In the museum naked. San Francisco: Second Coming,
        1978

NIMOY, Leonard
3422. We are all children searching for love. Boulder, CO:
        Blue Mountain Arts, 1977
3423. Warmed by love. Boulder, CO: Blue Mountain, 1983

NIMS, John Frederick
3424. The kiss: a jambalaya. Boston: Houghton Mifflin,
        1982
3425. Selected poems. Chicago: University of Chicago Press,
        1982

NIXON, Sallie
3426. Second grace. Durham, NC: Moore, 1977

NOCERINO, Kathryn
3427. Wax lips. St. Paul: New Rivers, 1980

NOLAN, James
3428. Why I live in the forest. Middletown, CT: Wesleyan
        University Press, 1974

NOLAN, Pat
3429. The Chinese quartet: poems. San Francisco: Cranium,
        1973
3430. Fast asleep. Calais, VT: Z Press, 1977
3431. Drastic measures. New York: Telephone, 1981

NOLAND, Jeannetta
3432. Intimations. Portland: Out of the Ashes, 1974

NORMAN, Charles
  3433. The portents of the air. Indianapolis: Bobbs-Merril,
         1973

NORRIS, Harold
  3434. You are this nation. Detroit: Harlo, 1976

NORRIS, Kathleen
  3435. The middle of the world. Pittsburgh: University of
         Pittsburgh Press, 1981

NORSE, Harold
  3436. Karma circuit. San Francisco: Panjandrum, 1973
  3437. Hotel Nirvana; selected poems 1953-1973. San Francis-
         co: City Lights, 1974
  3438. I see America daily. San Francisco: Mother's Hen,
         1974
  3439. The Roman sonnets of G. G. Belli. Van Nuys, CA:
         Perivale, 1974
  3440. Carnivorous saint; gay poems, 1941-1976. San Fran-
         cisco: Gay Sunshine, 1977

NORTH, Charles
  3441. Six buildings. Putnam Valley, NY: Swollen Magpie,
         1977
  3442. Leap year; poems, 1968-1978. New York: Kulchur
         Foundation, 1978

NORTH, Susan
  3443. All that is left. Tucson, AZ: Desert First Works,
         1976

NORTH SUN, Nila
  3444. Diet Pepsi & nacho cheese. Fallon, NV: Duck Down,
         1978
  3445. Small bones, little eyes. Fallon, NV: Duck Down, 1982

NORTON, Joshua
  3446. The Blue and the Gray. Cherry Valley, NY: Cherry
         Valley, 1975
  3447. Pool. New York: Telephone, 1975

NOTELY, Alice
  3448. Incidentals in the day world. Lenox, MA: Angel Hair,
         1973
  3449. Phoebe light. Bolinas, CA: Big Sky, 1974
  3450. Alice ordered me to be made. Chicago: Yellow, 1976
  3451. Songs for the unborn second baby. New York: United
         Artists, 1979
  3452. How spring comes. West Branch, IA: Toothpaste, 1981
  3453. Waltzing Matilda. New York: Kulchur Foundation, 1981

NOVAK, Robert
    3454.   Shoes.   Ft. Wayne, IN: Windless Orchard, 1975

NOVOTNAK, Paula
    3455.   Circle of hearts.   Washington: Some of Us, 1974

NOWER, Joyce
    3456.   Year of the fires.   San Diego: Center for Women's
            Studies, 1983

NOYES, Stanley
    3457.   Faces and spirits.   Santa Fe, NM: Sunstone, 1974

NYE, Naomi Shihab
    3458.   Different ways to pray.   Portland: Breitenbush, 1980
    3459.   Hugging the jukebox.   New York: Dutton, 1982

NYE, Peter
    3460.   Enough cordwood for a hundred years.   Okemos, MI:
            Stone, 1973

NYHART, Lockwood
    3461.   Temper.   Cambridge, MA: Alice James, 1979

NYHART, Nina
    3462.   Openers.   Cambridge, MA: Alice James, 1979

NYUKA
    3463.   Pleasure boat: poems and block cuts.   Easthampton,
            MA: Adastra, 1981

OANDASAN, William
    3464.   A branch of California redwood.   Los Angeles: Ameri-
            can Indian Studies Center, University of California,
            1980

OATES, Joyce Carol
    3465.   Angel fire.   Baton Rouge: Louisiana State University
            Press, 1973
    3466.   A posthumous sketch.   Los Angeles: Black Sparrow,
            1973
    3467.   Plagiarized material by Fernandes.   Los Angeles:
            Black Sparrow, 1974
    3468.   The fabulous beasts.   Baton Rouge: Louisiana State
            University Press, 1975
    3469.   Women whose lives are food, men whose lives are
            money.   Baton Rouge: Louisiana State University
            Press, 1978
    3470.   Invisible woman: new & selected poems, 1970-1982.
            Princeton, NJ: Ontario Review, 1982

0159 Oberg

OBERG, Arthur
   3471. Anna's song. Seattle: University of Washington Press, 1980

O'BRIEN, Michael
   3472. Blue springs. New York: Sun, 1976
   3473. To a dark moon. St. Petersburg, FL: Valkyrie, 1979

O'BRIEN, Muriel
   3474. Ghost wind. Bigfork, MN: Northwoods, 1974

OCHESTER, Ed
   3475. Dancing on the edges of knives: Columbia, MO: University of Missouri, 1973
   3476. The end of the ice age. Pittsburgh: Slow Loris, 1976
   3477. A drift of swine. Birmingham, AL: Thunder City, 1981

O'DALY, Bill
   3478. The whale in the web. Port Townsend, WA: Copper Canyon, 1979

ODAM, Joyce
   3479. Lemon center for hot buttered roll. Sacramento: Hibiscus, 1975

O'GRADY, Tom
   3480. Establishing a vineyard. Farmville, VA: Rose Bower, 1977

O'HARA, Frank
   3481. The selected poems of Frank O'Hara. New York: Knopf, 1974
   3482. Poems retrieved. Bolinas, CA: Grey Fox, 1977

O'HEHIR, Diana
   3483. Summoned. Columbia: University of Missouri Press, 1976
   3484. The power to change geography. Princeton: Princeton University Press, 1979

OLDER, Julia
   3485. Oonts and others. Greensboro, NC: Unicorn, 1982

OLDKNOW, Antony
   3486. Anthem for rusty saw and blue sky. Moorhead, MN: Territorial, 1975

OLDS, Sharon
   3487. Satan says. Pittsburgh: University of Pittsburgh Press, 1980
   3488. The dead and the living. New York: Knopf, 1983

O'LEARY, Thomas
    3489. Fool at the funeral. Amherst, MA: Lynx House, 1975

OLES, Carole
    3490. The loneliness factor. Lubbock: Texas Tech Press,
         1979
    3491. Quarry. Salt Lake City: University of Utah Press,
         1983

OLIPHANT, David
    3492. Lines and mounds. Berkeley: Thorp Springs, 1976

OLIVER, Mary
    3493. Twelve moons. Boston: Little, Brown, 1979
    3494. American primitive. Boston: Little, Brown, 1983

OLIVER, Raymond
    3495. Entries. Boston: Godine, 1982

OLSON, Charles
    3496. Spearmint & rosemary. Berkeley: Turtle Island, 1975
    3497. Some early poems. Iowa City: Windhover, 1978
    3498. The Maximus poems. Berkeley: University of California
         Press, 1983

OLSON, Elder
    3499. Olson's penny arcade. Chicago: University of Chicago
         Press, 1975

OLSON, Toby
    3500. Fishing. Mt. Horeb, WI: Perishable, 1973
    3501. City. Milwaukee: Membrane, 1974
    3502. A kind of psychology. Milwaukee: Lionhead, 1974
    3503. The wrestlers & other poems. New York: Barlenmir,
         1974
    3504. Changing appearance. Milwaukee: Membrane, 1975
    3505. A moral proposition. New York: Aviator, 1975
    3506. Priorities. Milwaukee: Lionhead, 1975
    3507. Seeds. Milwaukee: Membrane, 1975
    3508. Standard-4. New York: Aviator, 1975
    3509. Home. Milwaukee: Membrane, 1976
    3510. Three & one. Perry Township, WI: Perishable, 1976
    3511. Doctor Miriam. Perry Township, WI: Perishable, 1977
    3512. Aesthetics. Milwaukee: Perishable, 1978
    3513. The Florence poems. Sag Harbor, NY: Permanent,
         1978

OLUMO
    3514. The blue narrator. Chicago: Third World, 1974

O'NEILL, Catherine
    3515. The daffodil farmer. Washington: Washington Writers',
         1979

ONTKEAN, Michael
   3516. Long pants. Pacific Palisades, CA: Membrane Music,
          1975

OPPEN, George
   3517. Collected poems. London: Fulcrum, 1973
   3518. The collected poems of George Oppen; 1929-1975. New
          York: New Directions, 1975
   3519. Primitive. Santa Barbara: Black Sparrow, 1978

OPPENHEIMER, Joel
   3520. On occasion. Indianapolis: Bobbs-Merrill, 1973
   3521. The woman poems. Indianapolis: Bobbs-Merrill, 1975
   3522. Acts. Mt. Horeb, WI: Perishable, 1976
   3523. Names, dates, and places. Laurinburg, NC: St. An-
          drews, 1979
   3524. Just friends/friends and lovers: poems, 1959-1962.
          Highlands, NC: Jargon, 1980
   3525. The progression begins. New York: # Magazine, 1980
   3526. Houses. Buffalo, NY: White Pine, 1981
   3527. At fifty. Laurinburg, NC: St. Andrews, 1982
   3528. Poetry, the ecology of the soul. Buffalo, NY: White
          Pine, 1983
   3529. Talks & selected poems. Buffalo, NY: White Pine,
          1983

ORLEN, Steve
   3530. Sleeping on doors. Lisbon, IA: Penumbra, 1975
   3531. Separate creatures. Tucson, AZ: Ironwood, 1976
   3532. Permission to speak. Middletown, CT: Wesleyan Uni-
          versity Press, 1978
   3533. A place at the table. New York: Holt, Rinehart, and
          Winston, 1982

ORLOVSKY, Peter
   3534. Clean asshole poems & smiling vegetable songs. San
          Francisco: City Lights, 1978

ORR, Gregory
   3535. Burning the empty nests. New York: Harper & Row,
          1973
   3536. Gathering the bones together. New York: Harper &
          Row, 1975
   3537. The red house. New York: Harper & Row, 1980

ORR, Linda
   3538. That certain x. Seattle: L'Epervier, 1980

ORTH, Ghita
   3539. The music of what happens. Upper Montclair, NJ:
          Saturday, 1983

ORTIZ, Simon J.
    3540. Going for the rain. New York: Harper & Row, 1976
    3541. A good journey. Berkeley: Turtle Island, 1977
    3542. The people shall continue. San Francisco: Children's, 1977
    3543. Song, poetry, language. Tsaile, AZ: Navajo Community College Press, 1978
    3544. From Sand Creek: rising in this heart which is our America. New York: Thunder's Mouth, 1981

ORTNER-ZIMMERMAN, Toni
    3545. I dream now of the sun. Gulfport, FL: Konglomerati, 1977
    3546. As if anything could grow back perfect. Kent, OH: Mayapple, 1979
    3547. Dream in Pienza and other poems: selected poems 1963-1977. Fulton, MO: Timberline, 1979

OSBURN, Timothy
    3548. Outtakes. Springfield, IL: Sangamon, 1974

OSGOOD, Charles
    3549. There's nothing I wouldn't do if you would be my POSSLQ. New York: Holt, Rinehart, and Winston, 1981

OSING, Gordon
    3550. From the boundary waters. Memphis: Memphis State University Press, 1981

OSTERLUND, Steven
    3551. Twenty love poems. Lincoln, NE: Windflower, 1976

OSTRIKER, Alicia
    3552. Once more out of darkness. Berkeley: Poets Cooperative, 1974
    3553. A dream of springtime; poems 1970-1978. New York: The Smith, 1979
    3554. A woman under the surface. Princeton: Princeton University Press, 1982

OTT, Gil
    3555. Maize. Markesan, WI: Pentagon, 1980
    3556. The children. Philadelphia: Tamarisk, 1981
    3557. For the salamander. Philadelphia: Tamarisk, 1983

OTTENSEN, Carol Clark
    3558. Line upon line. Salt Lake City: Bookcraft, 1975

OVERTON, Ron
    3559. Dead reckoning. Port Jefferson, NY: Street, 1980

OWEN, Maureen
    3560. The no traveling journal. Cherry Valley, NY: Cherry

Valley, 1975
3561. Hearts in space.　New York:　Kulchur Foundation, 1980

OWEN, Sue
　　3562. Nursery rhymes for the dead.　Ithaca, NY:　Ithaca
　　　　　House, 1980

OWENS, Rochelle
　　3563. Poems from Joe's garage.　Providence:　Burning Deck,
　　　　　1973
　　3564. The Joe 82 creation poems.　Santa Barbara:　Black
　　　　　Sparrow, 1974
　　3565. Selected poems.　New York:　Seabury, 1974
　　3566. The Joe chronicles, part 2.　Santa Barbara:　Black
　　　　　Sparrow, 1979
　　3567. Shemuel.　St. Paul.　New Rivers, 1979

OWER, John
　　3568. Legendary acts.　Athens:　University of Georgia Press,
　　　　　1977

PACK, Robert
　　3569. Keeping watch.　New Brunswick, NJ:　Rutgers Univer-
　　　　　sity Press, 1976
　　3570. Waking to my name.　Baltimore:　Johns Hopkins Uni-
　　　　　versity Press, 1980

PACKARD, William
　　3571. First selected poems.　New York:　Pylon, 1977

PADDOCK, Nancy
　　3572. A dark light.　Minneapolis:　Vanilla, 1978

PADGETT, Ron
　　3573. Crazy compositions.　Bolinas, CA:　Big Sky, 1974
　　3574. Toujours l'amour.　New York:　Sun, 1976
　　3575. Tulsa kid.　Calais, VT:　Z Press, 1979
　　3576. Triangles in the afternoon.　New York:　Sun, 1980

PAGOULATOU, Regina
　　3577. Transplants.　New York:　Pella, 1983

PALLISTER, Jan
　　3578. Green balloon.　Bigfork, MN:　Northwoods, 1974
　　3579. Mon autre lyre.　Lawrence, KS:　Presse Orphique,
　　　　　1974

PALMER, Doug
　　3580. In quire.　Berkeley:　Oyez, 1973

PALMER, Michael
　　3581. C's songs.　Albany, CA:　Sand Dollar, 1973

3582. Six poems. Los Angeles: Black Sparrow, 1973
3583. The circular gates. Santa Barbara: Black Sparrow,
       1974
3584. Without music. Santa Barbara: Black Sparrow, 1977

PAPE, Greg
3585. Little America. Tucson, AZ: Maguey, 1976
3586. Border crossings. Pittsburgh: University of Pittsburgh
       Press, 1978

PARCELLI, Carlo
3587. Pillow book. Takoma Park, MD: Aleph, 1976

PARINI, Jay
3588. Anthracite country. New York: Random House, 1982

PARKER, Elinor Minor
3589. Four seasons five senses. New York: Scribner, 1974

PARKER, Linda
3590. Graphite, BK 1. St. Paul: Truck, 1976

PARKER, Pat
3591. Pit stop. Oakland, CA: Women's Press, 1975
3592. Movement in Black. Oakland, CA: Diana, 1978

PARKINSON, Thomas
3593. The canters of Thomas Parkinson. Berkeley: Thorp
       Springs, 1978
3594. Centers; chiefly concerning John Wayne and his horse
       and many incredibilities. Berkeley: Thorp Springs,
       1978

PARLATORE, Anselm
3595. Hybrid Inoculum. Ithaca, NY: Ithaca House, 1974
3596. The circa poems. Cincinnati: Stone-Marrow, 1975

PARMAN, Frank
3597. The daybook of Western heroes. Norman, OK: Point
       Riders, 1978

PARRISH, Wendy
3598. Conversations in the gallery. St. Paul: New Rivers,
       1977
3599. In the gallery. New York: New Rivers, 1978
3600. Blenheim Palace. St. Paul: New Rivers, 1983

PARTON, Dolly
3601. Just the way I am. Boulder, CO: Blue Mountain, 1979

PASAMANIK, Luisa
3602. The exiled angel. Fairfax, CA: Red Hill, 1973

PASTAN, Linda
  3603. Aspects of Eve. New York: Liveright, 1975
  3604. On the way to the zoo. Washington: Dryad, 1975
  3605. The five stages of grief. New York: Norton, 1978
  3606. Selected poems of Linda Pastan. London: J. Murray, 1979
  3607. Even as we sleep. Athens, OH: Croissant, 1980
  3608. Setting the table. Washington: Dryad, 1980
  3609. Waiting for my life. New York: Norton, 1981
  3610. PM/AM; new and selected poems. New York: Norton, 1982

PATANO, Clare
  3611. Clarifications. Chicago: Ommation, 1977

PATCHEN, Kenneth
  3612. Still another pelican in the breadbox. Youngstown, OH: Pig Iron, 1981

PATRICK, W. B.
  3613. Letter to the ghosts. Ithaca, NY: Ithaca House, 1977

PATTON, Rob
  3614. Dare. Ithaca, NY: Ithaca House, 1977

PAU-LLOSA, Ricardo
  3615. Sorting metaphors. Tallahassee, FL: Anhinga, 1983

PAUKER, John
  3616. Angry candy. Youngstown, OH: Pig Iron, 1976
  3617. In solitary and other imaginations. Washington: Word Works, 1977

PAULSON, James
  3618. A note for the flowers I didn't send. Texas City, TX: Poetry Texas, 1977

PAYACK, Paul
  3619. Solstice. Berkeley: Samisdat, 1975
  3620. Solstice II. Richford, VT: Samisdat, 1976
  3621. The evolution of death. Richford, VT: Samisdat, 1977

PAYACK, Peter
  3622. Cornucopia. New York: New York Culture Review, 1975
  3623. The white line. New York: New York Culture Review, 1975
  3624. Solstice III. Richford, VT: Samisdat, 1976

PEABODY, Richard
  3625. I'm in love with the Morton salt girl echt and ersatz. Washington: Paycock, 1983

PEACOCK, Molly
    3626. And live apart. Columbia: University of Missouri
           Press, 1980

PEARCE, T. M.
    3627. Spoon River on campus. Peoria, IL: Spoon River,
           1976

PEARSON, Carol Lynn
    3628. The growing season. Salt Lake City: Bookcraft, 1976

PECK, John
    3629. Shagbark. Indianapolis: Bobbs-Merrill, 1974
    3630. The broken blockhouse wall. Boston: Godine, 1978

PECK, Richard
    3631. Pictures that storm inside my head. New York: Holt,
           Rinehart and Winston, 1973

PEDRICK, Jean
    3632. Wolf Moon. Cambridge, MA: Alice James, 1974
    3633. Pride & splendor. Cambridge, MA: Alice James, 1976
    3634. The gaudy book. La Crosse, WI: Juniper, 1980
    3635. Greenfellow. St. Paul: New Rivers, 1982

PELHAM, Philip
    3636. Larry lost. St. Paul: Trunk, 1977

PENNANT, Edmund
    3637. Dream's navel. Staten Island, NY: Lintel, 1979

PENNINGTON, Lee
    3638. Songs of bloody harlan. Fennimore, WI: Westburg,
           1975
    3639. Wildflower, poems for Joy. Louisville, KY: Love
           Street, 1975
    3640. Spring of violets. Louisville, KY: Love Street, 1976
    3641. I knew a woman. Louisville, KY: Love Street, 1977

PENZI, James
    3642. Salt fever. San Francisco: Isthmus, 1976
    3643. SCENE/s in bk & wh. New York: Contact II, 1982

PERCHIK, Simon
    3644. Both hands screaming. New Rochelle, NY: Elizabeth,
           1975
    3645. The club fits either hand. New Rochelle, NY: Eliza-
           beth, 1979
    3646. The snowcat poems. North Charleston, SC: Linwood,
           1983

PEREIRA, Sam
    3647. The marriage of the Portuguese. Fort Collins, CO:
           L'Epervier, 1978

PERELMAN, Bob
   3648. Braille. Ithaca, NY: Ithaca House, 1975
   3649. a. k. a. Berkeley: Tuumba, 1979
   3650. Primer. Berkeley: This, 1981

PEREZ, Tony
   3651. Soundscape with humans. Hollywood, CA: Pygmalion,
       1974
   3652. On Earth. Los Angeles: Illuminati, 1980

PERIMAN, John
   3653. Swath. New Rochelle, NY: Elizabeth, 1978

PERISH, Melanie
   3654. Notes of a daughter from the old country. Pittsburgh:
       Motheroot, 1979

PERKINS, David
   3655. License to kill. Shawnee Mission, KS: BkMk, 1973

PERKOFF, Stuart Z.
   3656. Alphabet poems. Fairfax, CA: Red Hill, 1973
   3657. Love is the silence; poems, 1948-1974. Los Angeles:
       Red Hill, 1975

PERLBERG, Mark
   3658. The feel of the sun. Chicago: Swallow, 1981

PERLMAN, Anne S.
   3659. Sorting it out. Pittsburgh: Carnegie-Mellon, 1983

PERLMAN, Jess
   3660. Poems past eighty. Georgetown, CA: Dragon's Teeth,
       1979

PERLMAN, John
   3661. Dinner 650 Warburton Avenue Yonkers. New Rochelle,
       NY: Elizabeth, 1974
   3662. Notes toward a family. New Rochelle, NY: Elizabeth,
       1975
   3663. Nicole. New Rochelle, NY: Elizabeth, 1976
   3664. Homing. New Rochelle, NY: Elizabeth, 1981

PERRY, Connie
   3665. The small emptiness in our bodies. St. Paul: Truck,
       1977

PERRY, Ronald
   3666. Denizens. New York: Random House, 1980

PESEROFF, Joyce
   3667. The hardness scale. Cambridge, MA: Alice James,
       1977

PETERFREUND, Stuart
    3668. Harder than rain. Ithaca, NY: Ithaca House, 1977

PETERS, Robert
    3669. Cool zebras of light. Santa Barbara: Christopher's,
           1973
    3670. Bronchial tangle, heart system: Hanover, NH: Granite,
           1974
    3671. Holy Cow: parable poems. Fairfax, CA: Red Hill,
           1974
    3672. The gift to be simple. New York: Liveright, 1975
    3673. Shaker light. Milwaukee: Pentagram, 1975
    3674. Gauguin's chair, poems 1964-1974. Trumansburg, NY:
           Crossing, 1977
    3675. The drowned man to the fish. St. Paul: New Rivers,
           1979
    3676. The picnic in the snow: Ludwig of Bavaria. St. Paul:
           New Rivers, 1982
    3677. What Dillinger meant to me. New York: Sea Horse,
           1983

PETERSON, Carl
    3678. For Anna Akhmatova and other poems. Ithaca, NY:
           Ithaca House, 1977

PETERSON, Nils
    3679. Here is no ordinary rejoicing. Portola Valley, CA:
           Red Hill, 1974

PETERSON, Robert
    3680. Under sealed orders. Berkeley: Cloud Marauder, 1976
    3681. Leaving Taos. New York: Harper & Row, 1981

PETRIE, Paul
    3682. The idol. Kingston, RI: Biscuit City, 1973
    3683. The academy of goodbye. Hanover, NH: University
           Press of New England, 1974
    3684. Light from the furnace rising. Providence: Copper
           Beech, 1978
    3685. Not seeing is believing. La Crosse, WI: Juniper,
           1983

PETROSKY, Tony
    3686. Waiting out the rain. Tucson, AZ: Ironwood, 1974
    3687. Finding the day. Binghamton, NY: Bellevue, 1976
    3688. Stoutes Creek Road. Bloomington, IN: Raintree, 1976
    3689. Jurgis Petraskas. Baton Rouge: Louisiana State Uni-
           versity Press, 1983

PETT, Stephen
    3690. Pulpit of bones. New York: Morrow, 1975

PETTIT, Michael
3691. American light. Athens: University of Georgia Press,
1983

PEVEAR, Richard
3692. Night talk and other poems. Princeton, NJ: Princeton
University Press, 1977

PFLUM, Richard
3693. Moving into the light. Bloomington, IN: Raintree,
1975

PHELPS, Dean
3694. Shoshoni River witching hour. Diablo, CA: Holmgang-
ers, 1975
3695. The serum of the water. Livermore, CA: Holmgangers,
1978

PHILBRICK, Charles
3696. Nobody laughs, nobody cries. New York: The Smith,
1976

PHILLIPS, Frances
3697. The celebrated running horse messenger. Berkeley:
Kelsey St., 1979
3698. For a living. Brooklyn: Hanging Loose, 1981

PHILLIPS, Jayne Anne
3699. Sweethearts. Carrboro, NC: Truck, 1976

PHILLIPS, Robert S.
3700. The pregnant man. Garden City, NY: Doubleday, 1978
3701. Running on empty. Garden City, NY: Doubleday, 1981

PIASECKI, Bruce
3702. Stray prayers. Ithaca, NY: Ithaca House, 1976

PICCIONE, Anthony
3703. Nearing land. Port Townsend, WA: Graywolf, 1975
3704. In a gorge with a friend. Syracuse, NY: Tamarack,
1979

PICCIONE, Sandi
3705. Polar sun. Pittsburgh: Slow Loris, 1979

PICHASKE, David R.
3706. Beowulf to Beatles & beyond. New York: Macmillan,
1981

PICK, Michael Robert
3707. Childhood, Namhood, manhood. San Gabriel, CA:
Pizzuto, 1982

PICKEL, Norman
    3708. Re-up. Cleveland: Pranayama, 1975

PIERCE, David
    3709. Ballads of a bench warmer. San Jose, CA: Caislan, 1982

PIERCE, Rosanne Knight
    3710. Over the Fence. Bigfork, MN: Northwoods, 1973

PIERCY, Marge
    3711. To be of use. Garden City, NY: Doubleday, 1973
    3712. Living in the open. New York: Knopf, 1976
    3713. The twelve-spoked wheel flashing. New York: Knopf, 1978
    3714. The moon is always female. New York: Knopf, 1980
    3715. Circles on the water; selected poems. New York: Knopf, 1982
    3716. Stone, paper, knife. New York: Knopf, 1982

PIERSON, Philip
    3717. See Rock City. Washington: Gallimaufry, 1978
    3718. Natives. Milton, MA: Chowder, 1979

PIJEWSKI, John
    3719. Dinner with Uncle Jozef. Middletown, CT: Wesleyan University Press, 1982

PILLIN, William
    3720. The abandoned music room. Santa Cruz, CA: Kayak, 1975

PINSKER, Sanford
    3721. Still-life and other poems. Greenfield Center, NY: Greenfield Review, 1975

PINSKY, Robert
    3722. Sadness and happiness. Princeton, NJ: Princeton University Press, 1975
    3723. An explanation of America. Princeton, NJ: Princeton University Press, 1979

PIPKIN, John Moses
    3724. Half-after love. Durham, NC: Moore, 1976

PITCHFORD, Kenneth
    3725. Color photos of the atrocities. Boston: Atlantic Monthly, 1973
    3726. The contraband poems. New York: Templar, 1976

PIZZARELLI, Alan
    3727. Karma poems. Paterson, NJ: From Here, 1974

3728. Kika-da raga. Los Angeles: Seer Ox, 1975
3729. Zenryu and other works, 1974. Fanwood, NJ: From
       Here, 1975

PLANZ, Allen
   3730. Wild-craft. Chicago: Swallow, 1973
   3731. Wild craft. New York: Living Poets, 1975
   3732. Chunder Hara. Port Jefferson, NY: Street Magazine,
          1976

PLATH, Sylvia
   3733. Pursuit. London: Rainbow, 1973
   3734. The collected poems. New York: Harper & Row, 1981

PLATOR, Maraquita
   3735. 17 Sonnets. Tannersville, NY: Tideline, 1975

PLATTHY, Jeno
   3736. Winter tunes. Washington: Poetry Society, 1974

PLUMB, David
   3737. Drugs and all that. San Francisco: Smoking Mirror,
          1975

PLUMLY, Stanley
   3738. Giraffe. Baton Rouge: Louisiana State University
          Press, 1973
   3739. How the Plains Indians got horses. Crete, NE: Best
          Cellar, 1973
   3740. Out-of-the-body travel. New York: Ecco, 1976
   3741. Summer celestial. New York: Ecco, 1983

PLUMPP, Sterling
   3742. Steps to break the circle. Chicago: Third World, 1974
   3743. The Mojo hands call, I must go. New York: Thunder's
          Mouth, 1982

PLYMELL, Charles
   3744. Over the stage of Kansas. New York: Telephone, 1973
   3745. Blue orchid numero uno. New York: Telephone, 1975
   3746. The trashing of America. New York: Kulchur Founda-
          tion, 1975
   3747. Are you a kid? Cherry Valley, NY: Cherry Valley,
          1977

POAGE, Michael
   3748. Born. Missoula, MT: Black Stone, 1975

POLK, Brigid
   3749. Scars. Norwood, PA: Telegraph, 1973

POLLAK, Felix
   3750. Ginkgo. New Rochelle, NY: Elizabeth, 1973
   3751. Subject to change. La Crosse, WI: Juniper, 1978

POLLER, Nidra
    3752. African journals. Cherry Valley, NY: Cherry Valley,
           1975

POLLITT, Katha
    3753. Antarctic traveller. New York: Knopf, 1982

POMMY-VEGA, Janine
    3754. Morning passage. New York: Telephone, 1976
    3755. Hermit. Cherry Valley, NY: Cherry Valley, 1977
    3756. Here at the door. Brooklyn: Zonepress, 1979
    3757. Journal of a hermit. Cherry Valley, NY: Cherry
           Valley, 1979
    3758. The bard owl. New York: Kulchur Foundation, 1980

PONSOT, Marie
    3759. Admit impediment. New York: Knopf, 1981

POPE, Robert
    3760. Imagine a moment. Iowa City, IA: Meadow, 1976

PORCHE, Verandah
    3761. The body's symmetry. New York: Harper & Row,
           1974

PORTER, Bern
    3762. Selected founds. Athens, OH: Croissant & Company,
           1975
    3763. Found poems. Belfast, ME: Bern Porter Books, 1976

POSNER, David
    3764. The sandpipers; selected poems, 1965-1975. Gaines-
           ville: University Presses of Florida, 1976

POTTS, Charles
    3765. Charle Kiot. Salt Lake City: Litmus, 1975
    3766. The golden calf. Salt Lake City: Litmus, 1975
    3767. The opium must go thru. Salt Lake City: Litmus,
           1976
    3768. Rocky Mountain man. New York: The Smith, 1978

POULIN, A., Jr.
    3769. Catawba; omens, prayers and songs. Port Townsend,
           WA: Graywolf, 1977
    3770. The widow's taboo; poems after Catawba. Tokyo: Mush-
           insha, 1977
    3771. The nameless garden. Athens, OH: Croissant, 1978

POULTER, S. L.
    3772. Distant thunder. Milwaukee: Peacock, 1974

POWELL, Roxie
    3773. Dreams of straw. Cherry Valley, NY: Cherry Valley,
           1974

3774.   Kansas collateral.   Cherry Valley, NY: Cherry Valley,
        1978

POWER, Marjorie
3775.   Living with it.   Green Harbor, MA: Wampeter, 1983

POWERS, Jeffrey
3776.   Thrones and dominions.   Hollywood, CA: Pygmalion
        Press, 1974

PRADO, Holly
3777.   Nothing breaks off at the edge.   New York: New Rivers
        1976

PRESS, Simone Juda
3778.   Thaw.   New York: Inwood, 1974

PRICE, Bren
3779.   Inside the wind.   Santa Fe, NM: Sunstone, 1983

PRICE, Reynolds
3780.   Lessons learned.   New York: Albondocani, 1977
3781.   Nine mysteries (four joyful, four sorrowful, one glori-
        ous).   Winston-Salem, NC: Palaemon, 1979
3782.   Vital provisions.   New York: Atheneum, 1982

PRICE, Vincent Barrett
3783.   Semblances, 1962-1971.   Santa Fe, NM: Sunstone, 1976

PRIVETT, Katharine H.
3784.   The dreams of exiles.   Whitehorn, CA: Holmgangers,
        1982

PROPPER, Dan
3785.   The tale of the amazing tramp.   Cherry Valley, NY:
        Cherry Valley, 1977

PRUITT, Bill
3786.   Ravine Street.   Buffalo, NY: White Pine, 1977

PRUNTY, Wyatt
3787.   The times between.   Baltimore: Johns Hopkins Univer-
        sity Press, 1982

PRYOR, Mary Anne
3788.   No metaphysics.   Moorhead, MN: Territorial, 1974
3789.   The bicycle in the snowbank.   Moorhead, MN: Dacotah
        Territory, 1980

PUMPHREY, Jean
3790.   Sheltered at the edge.   Alascadero, CA: Solo, 1981

QUAGLIANO, Tony
    3791. Language drawn & quartered. Lansing, MI: Ghost
        Dance, 1975
    3792. Fierce meadows. Honolulu: Petronium, 1979

QUASHA, George
    3793. Somapoetics. Fremont, MI: Sumac, 1973
    3794. Giving the lily back her hands. Barrytown, NY: Station
        Hill, 1979
    3795. Traveling in the castle. Barrytown, NY: Station Hill,
        1983

QUATRALE, Don
    3796. Factory dances. Ware, MA: Four Zoas, 1977

QUINN, John
    3797. The wolf last seen. Omah: Abattoir, 1980

QUIRK, Cathleen
    3798. Rue and grace. Trumansburg, NY: Crossing, 1981

RAAB, Lawrence
    3799. The collector of cold weather. New York: Ecco, 1976

RABBITT, Thomas
    3800. Exile. Pittsburgh: University of Pittsburgh Press,
        1975
    3801. The Booth interstate. New York: Knopf, 1981

RABE, David
    3802. In the boom boom room. New York: Knopf, 1975

RAESCHILD, Sheila
    3803. Lessons in leaving. Pittsburgh: Know, 1974

RAFFEL, Burton
    3804. Evenly distributed rubble. Miami: Moonsquilt, 1983

RAGOSTA, Ray
    3805. The act proves untenable. Woods Hole, MA: Pourboire,
        1976
    3806. Sherds. Providence: Burning Deck, 1982

RAIZISS, Sonia
    3807. Bucks County blues. New York: New Rivers, 1977

RAKOSI, Carl
    3808. Ex cranium, night. Los Angeles: Black Sparrow, 1975
    3809. My experiences in Parnassus. Santa Barbara: Black
        Sparrow, 1977
    3810. Droles de journal. West Branch, IA: Toothpaste, 1981

RAMKE, Bin
    3811. The difference between night and day. New Haven, CT:
          Yale University Press, 1977
    3812. White monkeys. Athens: University of Georgia Press,
          1981

RAMSEY, Jarold
    3813. Love in an earthquake. Seattle: University of Washing-
          ton Press, 1973
    3814. No running on the boardwalk. Athens: University of
          Georgia Press, 1975
    3815. Eve, singing. Easthampton, MA: Pennyroyal, 1976

RANDALL, Belle
    3816. 101 different ways of playing solitaire. Pittsburgh:
          University of Pittsburgh Press, 1973

RANDALL, Dudley
    3817. After the killing. Detroit: Broadside, 1973
    3818. A litany of friends. Detroit: Lotus, 1981

RANDALL, James
    3819. Cities and other disasters. Detroit: Broadside, 1973

RANDALL, Jon C.
    3820. Indigoes. Detroit: Broadside, 1975

RANDALL, Margaret
    3821. Part of the solution; portrait of a revolutionary. New
          York: New Directions, 1973
    3822. With our hands. Vancouver, BC: New Star Books, 1974
    3823. Carlota. Vancouver, BC: New Star, 1978
    3824. We. Brooklyn: Smyrna, 1978

RANDOLPH, Leonard
    3825. Wind over ashes: selected poems. Chapel Hill, NC:
          Carolina Wren, 1982

RANE, Bill
    3826. Talfulano. New York: The Smith, 1976

RANKIN, Paula
    3827. By the wreckmaster's cottage. Pittsburgh: Carnegie-
          Mellon University Press, 1977

RANSOM, W. M.
    3828. Finding true north. Denver: Copper Canyon, 1973
    3829. Waving arms at the blind. Port Townsend, WA: Copper
          Canyon, 1975
    3830. Last rites. Waldron Island, WA: Jawbone, 1978

RANSON, Nicholas
    3831. Track made good. Cleveland: Bits, 1977

RAPHAEL, Dan
    3832. Energumen. Cherry Valley, NY: Cherry Valley, 1976

RATCH, Jerry
    3833. Puppet X: a lamentable tragedie. San Lorenzo, CA:
          Shameless Hussy, 1974
    3834. Clown birth. San Lorenzo, CA: Shameless Hussy,
          1975
    3835. Hot weather: poems selected and new. Metuchen, NJ:
          Scarecrow, 1982

RATCLIFF, Carter
    3836. Fever coast. New York: Kulchur Foundation, 1973

RATNER, Rochelle
    3837. False trees. New York: New Rivers, 1973
    3838. The mysteries. Holly Springs, MS: Ragnarok, 1976
    3839. Pirate's song. New York: Jordan Davies, 1976
    3840. The tightrope walker. Calgary, Alta.: Pennyworth, 1976
    3841. Quarry. St. Paul: New Rivers, 1978
    3842. Combing the waves. Brooklyn: Hanging Loose, 1979
    3843. Hide and seek. Chicago: Ommation, 1979
    3844. Sea air in a grave ground hog turns toward. Brooklyn:
          Gull, 1980
    3845. Practicing to be a woman: new and selected poems.
          Metuchen, NJ: Scarecrow, 1982

RAWLS, Isetta Crawford
    3846. Flashbacks. Detroit: Lotus, 1977

RAY, David
    3847. Gathering firewood, new poems and selected. Middletown,
          CT: Wesleyan University Press, 1974
    3848. Enough of flying. Calcutta: Writers Workshop,
          1977
    3849. The tramp's cup. Kirksville: Northeast Missouri State
          University Press, 1978
    3850. The farm in Calabria and other poems. Iowa City:
          Spirit That Moves Us, 1980
    3851. The touched life. Metuchen, NJ: Scarecrow, 1982

RAY, Grayce
    3852. The river is always straight ahead. Moorhead, MN:
          Territorial, 1974

RAY, Michael see RYAN, Michael
    3853. [No entry]

RAY, Shreela
    3854. Night conversations with none other. Paradise, CA:
          Dustbooks, 1977

RAYNARD, John
    3855. Dog's breakfast. Springfield, IL: Sangamon State Uni-
          versity, 1977

READ, Hadley
    3856. Morning chores and other times remembered. Urbana:
          University of Illinois Press, 1977

RED HAWK
    3857. Journey of the medicine man. Little Rock, AR: August
          House, 1983

REDDY, T. J.
    3858. Less than a score, but a point. New York: Random
          House, 1974
    3859. Poems in one part harmony. Chapel Hill, NC: Caro-
          lina Wren, 1980

REED, Ishmael
    3860. Chattanooga. New York: Random House, 1973
    3861. Secretary to the spirits. New York: Nok, 1977

REEDE, Jo Ann
    3862. To the far side of somewhere. New York: William
          Frederick, 1973

REESE, Sarah Carolyn
    3863. Songs of freedom. Detroit: Lotus, 1983

REINHOLD, Robert
    3864. Teak. New York: The Smith, 1976

REISS, James
    3865. The breathers. New York: Ecco, 1974
    3866. Express. Pittsburgh: University of Pittsburgh Press,
          1983

REITER, Thomas
    3867. Starting from bloodroot. Milton, MA: Chowder, 1982

RELLA, Ettore
    3868. The scenery for a play & other poems. New York:
          Braziller, 1981

RENDLEMAN, Danny L.
    3869. The winter rooms. Ithaca, NY: Ithaca House, 1975

RENNER, Bruce
    3870. Wakefulness. Fort Collins, CO: L'Epervier, 1978
    3871. Song made out of pale smoke. Seattle, WA: L'Eper-
          vier, 1982

REPS, Paul
    3872. Sit in: what is it like. San Francisco, CA: Zen
          Center, 1975
    3873. Juicing. Garden City, NY: Anchor, 1978

REVELL, Donald
    3874. The broken juke. Binghamton, NY: Iris, 1975
    3875. From the abandoned cities. New York: Harper & Row,
          1983

REXROTH, Kenneth
    3876. Sky sea birds trees earth house beasts flowers. Greens-
          boro, NC: Unicorn, 1973
    3877. New Poems. New York: New Directions, 1974
    3878. On Flower Wreath Hill. Burnaby, BC: Blackfish, 1976
    3879. The silver swan. Port Townsend, WA: Copper Canyon,
          1976
    3880. The morning star. New York: New Directions, 1979

REYES, Carlos
    3881. The prisoner. Santa Barbara: Capra, 1973
    3882. The shingle weaver's journal. Amherst, MA: Lynx
          House, 1980

REYNOLDS, Tim
    3883. The women poem. New York: Phoenix Book Shop, 1973
    3884. Dawn chorus. Ithaca, NY: Ithaca House, 1980

REZMERSKI, John C.
    3885. An American gallery. Pittsburgh: Three Rivers, 1977

REZNIKOFF, Charles
    3886. Holocaust. Santa Barbara: Black Sparrow, 1975
    3887. By the well of living and seeing: Poems 1918-1973.
          Santa Barbara: Black Sparrow, 1976
    3888. The complete poems of Charles Reznikoff; vol. I, poems
          1918-1936. Santa Barbara: Black Sparrow, 1976
    3889. The complete poems of Charles Reznikoff; vol. II, poems
          1937-1975. Santa Barbara: Black Sparrow, 1977
    3890. The manner music. Santa Barbara: Black Sparrow,
          1977
    3891. Testimony: The United States (1885-1915). Santa Bar-
          bara: Black Sparrow, vol. I, 1978; vol. II, 1979

RICE, David L.
    3892. Erogenous zone. Washington: King, 1975
    3893. Lock this man up. Detroit: Lotus, 1978

RICE, Stan
    3894. Some lamb. Berkeley: The Figures, 1975
    3895. Whiteboy. Berkeley: Mudra, 1976
    3896. Body of work. Fayetteville, AR: Lost Roads, 1983

RICH, Adrienne
    3897. Diving into the wreck. New York: Norton, 1973
    3898. Poems: selected and new, 1950-1974. New York:
          Norton, 1975
    3899. Twenty-one love poems. Emeryville, CA: Effie's,
          1976
    3900. On lies, secrets, and silence. New York: Norton,
          1979
    3901. The dream of a common language: poems 1974-1977.
          New York: Norton, 1981
    3902. A wild patience has taken me this far; poems, 1978-
          1981. New York: Norton, 1981

RICHARDS, Stan
    3903. Hobo signs. New York: Barlenmir, 1976

RICHARDSON, James E.
    3904. Reservations. Princeton, NJ: Princeton University
          Press, 1977

RIDGWAY, Earl
    3905. Twist of lemon. Wichita, KS: Latch String, 1975

RIDING, Laura
    3906. Selected poems in five sets. New York: Norton, 1973

RIDLAND, John
    3907. In the shadowless light. Omaha: Abattoir, 1978
    3908. In the tangled grass. La Crosse, WI: Juniper, 1978
    3909. The lazy man comes back. Oakland, CA: Christopher's,
          1979

RIGSBEE, David
    3910. Stamping ground. Ann Arbor, MI: Ardis, 1976

RIGSBY, Mike
    3911. Milky Way poems. Carrboro, NC: Carolina Wren,
          1976

RILEY, Peter
    3912. Strange family. Providence: Burning Deck, 1973

RINALDI, Nicholas
    3913. The resurrection of the snails. Winston-Salem, NC:
          Blair, 1977
    3914. We have lost our fathers. Orlando: University Presses
          of Florida, 1982

RINDE, John MacDonald
    3915. Wit or without. Milwaukee: Peacock, 1975

RIOS, Alberto
    3916. Sleeping on fists. Story, WY: Dooryard, 1981

3917. Whispering to fool the wind. New York: Sheep Meadow, 1982

RISSEEUW, John
    3918. I nearly died laughing. Tempe, AZ: Cabbagehead, 1974
    3919. Found in space. Vermillion, SD: Headbone Productions, 1976

RITCHIE, Elisavietta
    3920. Tightening the circle over eel country. Washington: Acropolis, 1974
    3921. A sheath of dreams, and other games. Arlington, VA: Proteus, 1976
    3922. Raking the snow. Washington: Washington Writers', 1982

RITCHIE, Michael Karl
    3923. Night blindness. Lakeville, NY: La Huerta, 1976

RIVERO, Isel
    3924. Night rained her. Birmingham, AL: Ragnarok, 1976
    3925. [No entry]

RIVERS, J. W.
    3926. From the Chicago notebook. Peoria, IL: Spoon River, 1979

RO, Emmanuel
    3927. Rocks. San Francisco: Peace & Pieces, 1973
    3928. Antares. San Francisco: Peace & Pieces, 1974

ROBBINS, Richard
    3929. Toward new weather. Missoula: University of Montana, 1979

ROBERSON, Ed
    3930. Etai-eken. Pittsburgh: University of Pittsburgh Press, 1975

ROBERTS, George
    3931. The blessing of winter rain. Moorhead, MN: Territorial, 1976
    3932. Scrut. Minneapolis: Holy Cow!, 1983

ROBERTS, Joseph Boxley
    3933. Of time and love. Troy, AL: Troy State University Press, 1980

ROBERTSON, Foster
    3934. The wood path. Berkeley: Thorp Springs, 1975

ROBERTSON, Kell
    3935.   All the bar room poetry in this world can't mend this
          heart of mine, dear. Salt Lake City: Litmus, 1974

ROBERTSON, Kirk
    3936.   Drinking beer at 22 below. Long Beach, CA: Russ
          Haas, 1976
    3937.   Shooting at shadows, killing crows. Marvin, SD: Blue
          Cloud Quarterly, 1976
    3938.   Under the weight of the sky. Cherry Valley, NY:
          Cherry Valley, 1978

ROBINS, Natalie S.
    3939.   Eclipse. Chicago: Swallow, 1981

RODEFER, Stephen
    3940.   After Lucretius. Storrs: University of Connecticut
          Press, 1973
    3941.   One or two love poems from the white world. San
          Francisco: Pick Pocket, 1976
    3942.   Safety. San Francisco: Miam, 1977
    3943.   The bell clerk's tears keep flowing. Berkeley: The
          Figures, 1978
    3944.   Plane debris. Berkeley: Tuumba, 1981
    3945.   Four lectures. Berkeley: The Figures, 1982

RODGERS, Carolyn M.
    3946.   How I got ovah: new and selected poems. Garden City,
          NY: Anchor, 1975
    3947.   The heart as ever green. Garden City, NY: Double-
          day, 1978

RODITI, Edouard
    3948.   Emperor of midnight. Los Angeles: Black Sparrow,
          1974
    3949.   Meetings with Conrad. Los Angeles: Pegacycle Lady,
          1977
    3950.   In a lost world. Santa Barbara: Black Sparrow, 1978
    3951.   Thrice chosen. Santa Barbara: Black Sparrow, 1981

RODNEY, Janet
    3952.   Crystals. Richmond, CA: North Atlantic, 1979

RODRIGUEZ, Ron
    3953.   The captains that dogs aren't. Washington: Washington
          Writers', 1977

ROECKER, W. A.
    3954.   You know me. Fremont, MI: Sumac, 1973

ROETHKE, Theodore
    3955.   Collected poems. Garden City, NY: Doubleday, 1975

3956. The collected poems of Theodore Roethke. Seattle:
       University of Washington Press, 1982

ROGERS, Pattiann
3957. The expectations of light. Princeton, NJ: Princeton
       University Press, 1981

ROMERO, Leo
3958. During the growing season. Tucson, AZ: Maguey,
       1979
3959. Agua Negra. Boise, ID: Ahsahta, 1981

RONAN, Richard
3960. Kindred. Buffalo: State University of New York at
       Buffalo, 1978
3961. Buddha's kisses and other poems. San Francisco: Gay
       Sunshine, 1980
3962. Narratives from America. Port Townsend: WA: Drag-
       on Gate, 1982

ROOT, Judith, C.
3963. Little mysteries. Okemos, MI: Stone, 1974

ROOT, William Pitt
3964. Striking the air for music. New York: Atheneum, 1973
3965. The port of Galveston. Galveston, TX: Galveston Arts
       Center, 1974
3966. Coot and other characters. Lewiston, ID: Confluence,
       1977
3967. A journey south. Port Townsend, WA: Graywolf, 1977
3968. 7 Mendocino songs. Portland: Mississippi Mud, 1977
3969. Fireclock. Ashuelot, NH: Four Zoas Night House,
       1979
3970. Reasons for going it on foot. New York: Atheneum,
       1981

RORIPAUGH, Robert
3971. Learn to love the haze. Vermillion, SD: Spirit Mound,
       1977

ROSE, Wendy
3972. Hopi roadrunner dancing. Greenfield, NY: Greenfield
       Review, 1973
3973. Lost copper. Banning, CA: Malki Museum, 1980
3974. Long Division: a tribal history. New York: Strawberry,
       1981
3975. What happened when the Hopi hit New York. New York:
       Contact II, 1982

ROSELIEP, Raymond
3976. Flute over Walden. West Lafayette, IN: Sparrow, 1975
3977. A beautiful woman moves with grace. Derry, PA:
       Rook, 1976

3978. Light footsteps. La Crosse, WI: Juniper, 1976
3979. Dusk and ocean. Derry, PA: Rook, 1977
3980. Step on the rain. Derry, PA: Rook, 1977
3981. Sun in his belly. West Lafayette, IN: High/Coo, 1977
3982. Wake to the bell. Derry, PA: Rook, 1977
3983. Walk in love. La Crosse, WI: Juniper, 1977
3984. A day in the life of Sobi-Shi. Ruffsdale, PA: Rook, 1978
3985. Sailing bones. Ruffsdale, PA: Rook, 1978
3986. Firefly in my eyecup. Battleground, IN: High/Coo, 1979
3987. Sky in my legs. La Crosse, WI: Juniper, 1979
3988. The still point. Menomonie, WI: Uzzano, 1979
3989. A Roseliep retrospective. Plainfield, IN: Alembic, 1981
3990. Swish of cow tail. Amherst, MA: Swamp, 1982
3991. Rabbit in the moon: haiku. Plainfield, NJ: Alembic, 1983

ROSEN, Kenneth
3992. Black leaves. St. Paul: New Rivers, 1980

ROSENBERG, David
3993. Some psalms. New York: Angel Hair, 1973
3994. Blues of the sky. New York: Angel Hair, 1974

ROSENBERGER, Francis Coleman
3995. An alphabet. Charlottesville: University Press of Virginia, 1978

ROSENBLUM, Martin J.
3996. The werewolf sequence. Milwaukee: Membrane, 1975.
3997. As I magic. Milwaukee: Morgan, 1976
3998. Scattered on. Milwaukee: Pentagram, 1976

ROSENTHAL, David
3999. Eyes on the street. New York: Barlenmir House, 1973

ROSENTHAL, M. L.
4000. She; a sequence of poems. Brockport, NY: Boa, 1977
4001. Poems, 1964-1980. New York: Oxford University Press, 1981

ROSENTHAL, Ted
4002. How could I not be among you? New York: Braziller, 1973

ROSS, Dennis
4003. The conservation of strangeness. Alamo, CA: Holm-gangers, 1980

ROSS, Frances
4004. Inside/outside. Hollywood, CA: Pygmalion, 1975
4005. Some special times. Hollywood, CA: Pygmalion, 1976

ROSS, Bob
    4006. Solitary confinement. Omaha: Abattoir, 1977

ROSS, Tom
    4007. Gurgle of little feet. San Francisco: Mother's Hen,
        1974

ROSTEN, Norman
    4008. Selected poems. New York: Braziller, 1979

ROSTON, Ruth
    4009. I live in the watchmakers' town. St. Paul: New Rivers,
        1981

ROTHENBERG, Jerome
    4010. A poem of beavers. Blue Mounds Township, WI: Per-
        ishable, 1973
    4011. The cards. Los Angeles: Black Sparrow, 1974
    4012. Esther K comes to America: 1931. Santa Barbara:
        Unicorn, 1974
    4013. Poland/1931. New York: New Directions, 1974
    4014. Book of palaces: the gatekeepers. Boston: Pomegran-
        ate, 1975
    4015. The pirke and the pearl. Berkeley: Tree, 1975
    4016. A poem to celebrate the spring and Diane Rothenberg's
        birthday. Madison, WI: Perishable, 1975
    4017. Rain events. Milwaukee: Membrane, 1975
    4018. The notebooks. Milwaukee: Membrane, 1976
    4019. A vision of the chariot in heaven. Boston: Hundred
        Flowers, 1976
    4020. A Seneca journal. New York: New Directions, 1978
    4021. Abulafia's circles. Milwaukee: Membrane, 1979
    4022. B*R*M*Tz*V*H. Madison, WI: Perishable, 1979
    4023. Numbers and letters. Madison, WI: Salient Seedling,
        1979
    4024. Vienna blood & other poems. New York: New Direc-
        tions, 1980
    4025. Altar pieces. Barrytown, NY: Station Hill, 1983
    4026. That Dada strain. New York: New Directions, 1983

ROYSTER, Sandra
    4027. Women talk. Chicago: Third World, 1974

RUARK, Gibbons
    4028. Reeds. Lubbock: Texas Tech, 1978
    4029. Keeping company. Baltimore: Johns Hopkins University
        Press, 1983

RUBIN, Larry
    4030. All my mirrors lie. Boston: Godine, 1975

RUDD, Gail
    4031. John danced. Berkeley: Poets Workshop, 1983

RUDDER, Virginia L.
    4032.   After the ifaluk. Berkeley: Thorp Springs, 1975
    4033.   The gallows lord. Winston-Salem, NC: Blair, 1978

RUDINGER, Joel
    4034.   First edition 40 poems. Sandusky, OH: Gull, 1975
    4035.   The human condition. Huron, OH: Cambric, 1976

RUDNIK, Raphael
    4036.   In the heart of our city. New York: Random House,
        1973

RUDOLPH, Lee
    4037.   Curses & songs & poems. Cambridge, MA: Alice
        James, 1974
    4038.   The country changes. Cambridge, MA: Alice James,
        1978

RUFFLE, Mary
    4039.   Memling's veil. University: University of Alabama
        Press, 1982

RUFFIN, Paul
    4040.   Lighting the furnace pilot. Peoria, IL: Spoon River,
        1980

RUGGLES, Eugene
    4041.   The lifeguard in the snow. Pittsburgh: University of
        Pittsburgh Press, 1977

RUGO, Marieve
    4042.   Fields of vision. University: University of Alabama
        Press, 1983

RUHL, Steven
    4043.   No bread without the dance. Amherst, MA: Nocturnal
        Canary, 1979

RUKEYSER, Muriel
    4044.   Breaking open. New York: Random House, 1973
    4045.   Own face diary. New York: Random House, 1973
    4046.   The gates. New York: McGraw-Hill, 1976
    4047.   The collected poems. New York: McGraw-Hill, 1978
    4048.   The outer banks. Greensboro, NC: Unicorn, 1980
    4049.   The collected poems. New York: McGraw-Hill, 1982

RUSSELL, Norman H.
    4050.   Open the flower. Mt. Horeb, WI: Perishable, 1974
    4051.   Russell, the man, the teacher, the Indian. Bigfork,
        MN: Northwoods, 1974

RUTSALA, Vern
    4052.   Lament. New York: New Rivers, 1975

4053. The journey begins. Athens: University of Georgia
        Press, 1976
4054. The new life. Portland: Truck House, 1978
4055. Paragraphs. Middletown, CT: Wesleyan University
        Press, 1978
4056. Walking home from the icehouse. Pittsburgh: Carnegie-
        Mellon University Press, 1981

RYAN, Michael
4057. Threats instead of trees. New Haven, CT: Yale Uni-
        versity Press, 1974
4058. In winter. New York: Holt, Rinehart, and Winston,
        1981

RYAN, Tom
4059. Encephalogeorgics. Providence: Burning Deck, 1973

SADOFF, Ira
4060. Settling down. Boston: Houghton Mifflin, 1975
4061. Palm reading in winter. Boston: Houghton Mifflin,
        1978
4062. A northern calendar. Boston: Godine, 1982

SAFT, Stephen
4063. I will mean. Camden, ME: Meanings, 1975

SAGAN, Miriam
4064. Dangerous body. Richford, VT: Samisdat, 1975

ST. ARMAND, Barton Levi
4065. Hypogeum. Providence: Burning Deck, 1975

ST. JOHN, David
4066. Hush. Boston: Houghton Mifflin, 1976
4067. The shore. Boston: Houghton Mifflin, 1980

ST. JOHN, Primus
4068. Skins on the earth. Port Townsend, WA: Copper Can-
        yon, 1976
4069. Love is not a consolation; it is a light. Pittsburgh:
        Carnegie-Mellon, 1983

SALAMON, Russell
4070. Poems. Los Angeles: Admiral, 1976

SALEH, Dennis
4071. Palmway. Ithaca, NY: Ithaca House, 1975
4072. 100 chameleons. New York: New Rivers, 1978
4073. First z poems. St. Paul: Bieler, 1980

SALINGER, Wendy
4074. Folly River. New York: Dutton, 1980

SALISBURY, Ralph J.
    4075. Pointing at the rainbow: poems from a Cherokee heri-
           tage. Marvin, SD: Blue Cloud Quarterly, 1980
    4076. Spirit beast chant. Marvin, SD: Blue Cloud Quarterly,
           1982

SALTMAN, Benjamin
    4077. The leaves the people. Fairfax, CA: Red Hill, 1974
    4078. Deck. Ithaca, NY: Ithaca House, 1979

SAMPERI, Frank
    4079. The fourth. New Rochelle, NY: Elizabeth, 1973
    4080. Quadrifarian. New York: Grossman, 1973
    4081. Infinitesimals. New Rochelle, NY: Elizabeth, 1974
    4082. Lumen gloriae. New York: Grossman, 1974
    4083. Sanza mezzo. New Rochelle, NY: Elizabeth, 1977
    4084. Letargo. Barrytown, NY: Station Hill, 1980
    4085. The kingdom. Todmorden, Eng.: Arc, 1982

SAMPLER, Mildred V.
    4086. Second chance. Oyster Bay, NY: Press on Regardless,
           1977

SANCHEZ, Sonia
    4087. Love poems. New York: Third, 1973
    4088. A blues book for blue black magical women. Detroit:
           Broadside, 1974
    4089. I've been a woman; new and selected poems. San
           Francisco: Black Scholar, 1979

SANDEEN, Ernest Emanuel
    4090. Like any road anywhere. Notre Dame, IN: University
           of Notre Dame Press, 1976
    4091. Collected poems, 1953-1977. Notre Dame: University
           of Notre Dame Press, 1977

SANDERS, Cliff
    4092. Dispatch DP 163, and other poems. Lemoyne, PA:
           Obadiah Holmes, 1976

SANDERS, Ed
    4093. Egyptian hieroglyphics. Canton, NY: Institute of Further
           Studies, 1973
    4094. Investigative poetry. San Francisco: City Lights, 1976
    4095. 20, 000 A.D. Plainfield, VT: North Atlantic, 1976

SANDERS, Grant
    4096. Solstice. Hollywood, CA: Pygmalion, 1974
    4097. Hollywood, CA: Pygmalion, 1975

SANDY, Stephen
    4098. The Austin tower. San Francisco: Empty Elevator,
           1975

4099. The difficulty. Providence: Burning Deck, 1975
4100. From "Freestone." Binghamton, NY: Bellevue, 1975
4101. Landscapes. Cambridge, NY: White Creek, 1975
4102. End of the picaro. Pawlet, VT: Banyan, 1977
4103. Freestone: sections 25 and 26. Binghamton, NY:
           Bellevue, 1977
4104. The Hawthorne effect. Lawrence, KS: Tansy, 1979
4105. After the hunt. Miami: Moonsquilt, 1982
4106. Riding the Greylock. New York: Knopf, 1983

SANER, Reg
4107. Climbing into the roots. New York: Harper & Row,
           1976
4108. So this is the map. New York: Random House, 1981

SANFIELD, Steve
4109. Water before and water after. Brunswick, ME: Black-
           berry, 1974
4110. A fall from grace. Berkeley: Aldebaran, 1976
4111. A new way. Santa Fe, NM: Tooth of Time, 1983

SANGE, Gary
4112. Sudden around the bend. Kansas City, MO: BkMk, 1981

SANTOS, Sherod
4113. Begin, distance. Santa Cruz, CA: Greenhouse Review,
           1981
4114. Accidental weather. Garden City, NY: Doubleday, 1982

SARGENT, Robert
4115. Now is always the miraculous time. Washington: Wash-
           ington Writers', 1977
4116. A woman from Memphis. Washington: Word Works,
           1979
4117. Aspects of a Southern story. Washington: Word Works,
           1983

SAROYAN, Aram
4118. The rest. Norwood, PA: Telegraph, 1973
4119. The Bolinas book. Lancaster, MA: Other, 1974
4120. O my generation, and other poems. Brunswick, ME:
           Blackberry, 1976

SARTON, May
4121. Collected poems, 1930-1973. New York: Norton, 1974
4122. Selected poems of May Sarton. New York: Norton,
           1978
4123. Halfway to silence. New York: Norton, 1980

SASLOW, Helen
4124. Arctic summer. New York: Barlenmir, 1974

SAVITT, Lynne
4125. Lust in 28 flavors. San Francisco: Second Coming, 1979

4126. Eros unbound. Augusta, GA: Blue Horse, 1981
4127. No apologies. Tulsa, OK: Cardinal, 1981

SAVORY, Teo
4128. Transitions. Santa Barbara: Unicorn, 1973
4129. Dragons of mist and torrent. Greensboro, NC: Uni-
corn, 1974

SAWYER, Paul
4130. Bezerkley sun and rain dance poems. Berkeley: Thorp
Springs, 1973

SCALAPINO, Leslie
4131. O, and other poems. Berkeley: Sand Dollar, 1976
4132. The woman who could read the minds of dogs. Berkeley:
Sand Dollar, 1976
4133. Instead of an animal. Berkeley: Poltroon, 1977
4134. This eating and walking. Bolinas, CA: Tombouctou,
1978

SCALF, Sue
4135. Devils' wine. Troy, AL: Troy State University Press,
1976

SCARBROUGH, George
4136. New and selected poems. Binghamton, NY: Iris, 1977

SCHAAF, Richard
4137. Revolutionary at home. Willimantic, CT: Curbstone,
1975

SCHAEFER, Ted
4138. After drought. Independence, MO: Raindust, 1976

SCHAEFFER, Susan Fromberg
4139. Granite lady. New York: Macmillan, 1973
4140. The rhymes and runes of the toad. New York: Mac-
millan, 1975
4141. Alphabet for the lost years. San Francisco: Galli-
maufry, 1976
4142. The red white & blue poem. Denver: Ally, 1977
4143. The blue man. Birmingham, AL: Thunder City, 1978
4144. Time of the king and queen. San Francisco: Galli-
maufry, 1979
4145. The Bible of the beasts of the little field. New York:
Dutton, 1980

SCHECHTER, Barry
4146. The grand et cet'ra. Chicago: Yellow, 1977

SCHECTER, Ruth Lisa
4147. Offshore. New York: Barlenmir, 1974
4148. Moving closer. Scarborough, ON: Catalyst, 1977

SCHEELE, Roy
    4149. Accompanied. Crete, NE: Best Cellar, 1974
    4150. Noticing. Lincoln, NE: Three Sheets, 1979

SCHEINMAN, Julie
    4151. In passing. Hardwick, MA: Four Zoas, 1976

SCHEVILL, James
    4152. The buddhist car and other characters. Chicago: Swal-
          low, 1973
    4153. Pursuing elegy. Providence: Copper Beech, 1974
    4154. The Mayan poems. Providence: Copper Beech, 1978
    4155. Fire of eyes: A Guatemalan sequence. Providence:
          Copper Beech, 1979
    4156. The American fantasies: collected poems, 1945-1981.
          Chicago: Swallow, 1983

SCHJELDAHL, Peter
    4157. Dreams. New York: Angel Hair, 1973
    4158. Since 1964; new and selected poems. New York: Sun,
          1978

SCHMITT, Gladys
    4159. Sonnets for an analyst. New York: Harcourt Brace,
          1973

SCHMITZ, Dennis
    4160. Goodwill, Inc. New York: Ecco, 1975
    4161. String. New York: Ecco, 1980

SCHNACKENBERG, Gjertrud
    4162. Portraits and elegies. Boston: Godine, 1982

SCHNEIDRE, P.
    4163. Suspended sentences. Hollywood, CA: Pygmalion Press,
          1974

SCHOLL, Betsy see SHOLL, Betsy
    4164. [No entry]

SCHOMAKER, Ric
    4165. Work songs. Gulfport, FL: Konglomerati Press, 1979

SCHORB, E. M.
    4166. The poor boy. Georgetown, CA: Dragon's Teeth, 1975

SCHOTT, Penelope Scambly
    4167. My grandparents were married for sixty-five years.
          Madison, NJ: Fairleigh Dickinson University, 1977

SCHREIBER, Ron
    4168. Living space. Brooklyn: Hanging Loose, 1973
    4169. Moving to a new place. Cambridge, MA: Alice James,
          1974

4170. False clues. Ithaca, NY: Calamus, 1977
4171. Against that time. Cambridge, MA: Alice James, 1978
4172. False clues. Ithaca, NY: Calamus, 1978

SCHULMAN, Grace
4173. Burn down the icons. Princeton, NJ: Princeton University Press, 1976

SCHULTZ, Philip
4174. Like wings. New York: Viking, 1978

SCHULTZ, Susan Polis
4175. Someone else to love. Boulder, CO: Blue Mountain Arts, 1976

SCHUTZMAN, Steve
4176. Smoke the burning body makes. San Francisco: Panjandrum, 1978

SCHUYLER, James
4177. Hymn to life. New York: Random House, 1974
4178. The fireproof floors of Witley Court. Newark, VT: Janus, 1976
4179. Song. Syracuse, NY: Kermani, 1976
4180. The home book. Calais, VT: Z Press, 1977
4181. What's for dinner? Santa Barbara: Black Sparrow, 1978
4182. Freely espousing. New York: Sun, 1979
4183. The morning of the poem. New York: Farrar, Straus, and Giroux, 1980
4184. Early in '71. Berkeley: The Figures, 1982

SCHWARTZ, Barry
4185. The voyeur of our time. New York: Barlenmir House, 1973

SCHWARTZ, Delmore
4186. Last and lost poems of Delmore Schwartz. New York: Vanguard, 1979

SCHWARTZ, Hillel
4187. Phantom children. Pittsford, NY: State Street, 1982

SCHWARTZ, Howard
4188. Lilith's cave. San Francisco: Isthmus, 1975
4189. Vessels. Greensboro, NC: Unicorn, 1977

SCHWARTZ, Jeffrey
4190. Contending with the dark. Cambridge, MA: Alice James, 1978

SCHWARTZ, Jeri
4191. Tiny fingers. Milwaukee: Peacock, 1975

SCHWARTZ, Lloyd
    4192. These people. Middletown, CT: Wesleyan University
          Press, 1981

SCHWERNER, Armand
    4193. Bacchae sonnets. Omaha: Abattoir, 1974
    4194. The tablets, xvi-xviii. Boston: Herron, 1976
    4195. This practice; tablet XIX and other poems. New York:
          Permanent, 1976
    4196. Triumph of the will. Mt. Horeb, WI: Perishable, 1976
    4197. The Bacchae sonnets 1-7. Baltimore: Pod, 1977
    4198. The work, the joy, and the triumph of the will. New
          York: New Rivers, 1977
    4199. Sounds of the River Naranjana & The tablets I-XXIV.
          Barrytown, NY: Station Hill, 1983

SCOTT, Dennis
    4200. Uncle time. Pittsburgh: University of Pittsburgh
          Press, 1973

SCOTT, Herbert
    4201. Disguises. Pittsburgh: University of Pittsburgh Press,
          1974
    4202. The shoplifter's handbook. Kalamazoo: Blue Mountain,
          1974
    4203. Groceries. Pittsburgh: University of Pittsburgh Press,
          1976

SCOTT, Shirley
    4204. The thoughts of giants. Washington: Washington Writ-
          ers', 1981

SCOTT, Virginia
    4205. Poems for a friend in late winter. New York: Sunbury,
          1975

SCULLY, James
    4206. Santiago poems. Willimantic, CT: Curbstone, 1975
    4207. Walking with Deirdre. Willimantic, CT: Curbstone,
          1976
    4208. Scrap book. Willimantic, CT: Ziesing, 1977
    4209. The marches. Willimantic, CT: Ziesing, 1979
    4210. Apollo helmet. Willimantic, CT: Curbstone, 1983

SEARS, Peter
    4211. I want to be a crowd. Portland: Breitenbush, 1978
    4212. The lady who got me to say so long, mom. Portland:
          Truck House, 1979
    4213. Icehouse Beach. Milton, MA: Chowder, 1983

SEAY, James
    4214. Water tables. Middletown, CT: Wesleyan University
          Press, 1974

SECRIST, Margaret
    4215. Women of the revolution.   Peoria, IL: Špoon River,
          1976

SEE, Molly
    4216. Sleeping over.   Amherst, MA: Lynx House, 1978

SEGAL, Edith
    4217. Poems and songs for dreamers who dare.   New York:
          Hill, 1975

SEIBERT, Marianne
    4218. This day's madness.   Detroit: Harlo, 1977

SEIDEL, Frederick
    4219. Sunrise.   New York: Viking, 1980

SEIDMAN, Hugh
    4220. Blood Lord.   Garden City, NY: Doubleday, 1974
    4221. Throne falcon eye: poems.   New York: Vintage Books,
          1982

SEILER, Barry
    4222. Retaining wall.   Fort Collins, CO: L'Epervier, 1979

SERENI, Vittorio
    4223. Sixteen poems of V. S.   Fairfax, CA: Red Hill, 1970

SEVERY, Bruce
    4224. Jackrabbit, North Dakota.   Lubbock, TX: Chawed
          Rawzin, 1977

SEXTON, Anne
    4225. The book of folly.   London: Chatto & Windus, 1974
    4226. The death notebooks.   Boston: Houghton Mifflin, 1974
    4227. The awful rowing toward God.   Boston: Houghton Miff-
          lin, 1975
    4228. 45 Mercy Street.   Boston: Houghton Mifflin, 1976
    4229. The complete poems.   Boston: Houghton Mifflin, 1981

SEXTON, Thomas F.
    4230. Terra Incognita.   San Luis Obispo, CA: Solo, 1974

SHAFER, Margaret
    4231. Sleeping in Damascus.   St. Paul: New Rivers, 1980

SHAKELY, Lauren
    4232. Guilty bystander.   New York: Random House, 1978

SHAMBAUGH, Joan
    4233. Poems given.   Concord, MA: Chthon, 1976
    4234. Book of stones, or, stone songs.   Weston, MA: Acorn,
          1983

SHANGE, Ntosake
    4235.   For colored girls who have considered suicide, when
              the rainbow is enuf. San Lorenzo, CA: Shameless
              Hussy, 1975; New York: Macmillan, 1977
    4236.   Nappy edges. New York: St. Martin's, 1978
    4237.   A daughter's geography. New York: St. Martin's, 1983

SHANKEN, Phyllis
    4238.   Silhouettes of women. Wynnewood, PA: Philmer, 1976

SHANNON, John Kingsley
    4239.   Each soul is where it wishes to be. Milwaukee: Mem-
              brane, 1973
    4240.   Hyde park. Milwaukee: Membrane, 1973
    4241.   W: Tungsten. Milwaukee: Membrane, 1976

SHAPIRO, Alan
    4242.   The courtesy. Chicago: University of Chicago Press,
              1983

SHAPIRO, David
    4243.   The page turner. New York: Liveright, 1973
    4244.   Lateness. Woodstock, NY: Overlook, 1977

SHAPIRO, Harvey
    4245.   Lands. New York: Sun, 1975
    4246.   Lauds & nightsounds. New York: Sun, 1978

SHAPIRO, Karl
    4247.   Auden (1907-1973). Davis, CA: Putah Creek, 1973
    4248.   Adult bookstore. New York: Random House, 1976
    4249.   Collected poems 1940-1978. New York: Random House,
              1978

SHAUGHNESSY, Timothy
    4250.   Becoming. Bigfork, MN: Northwoods, 1975

SHAW, Maxine
    4251.   Beautiful cages. Boston: Stone Soup Poetry, 1974

SHAW, Robert B.
    4252.   Comforting the wilderness. Middletown, CT: Wesleyan
              University Press, 1977

SHAW, Sharon
    4253.   Auctions. Winston-Salem, NC: Blair, 1977

SHEA, Martin
    4254.   Across the loud stream: Los Angeles: Seer Ox, 1974
    4255.   Blackdog in the headlights. Milwaukee: Shelters, 1975

SHECK, Laurie
    4256.   Amaranth. Athens: University of Georgia Press, 1981

SHELLEY, Pat
    4257. As I go. Saratoga, CA: Saratoga Trunk, 1976

SHELTON, Richard
    4258. Among the stones. Pittsburgh: Monument, 1973
    4259. Chosen place. Crete, NE: Best Cellar, 1975
    4260. You can't have everything. Pittsburgh: University of
          Pittsburgh Press, 1975
    4261. The bus to Veracruz. Pittsburgh: University of Pitts-
          burgh Press, 1978
    4262. A kind of glory. Port Townsend, WA: Copper Canyon,
          1982
    4263. Selected poems, 1969-1981. Pittsburgh: University of
          Pittsburgh Press, 1982

SHER, Steven
    4264. Caught in the revolving door. Louisville, KY: Love
          Street, 1980

SHERIDAN, Michael
    4265. Warm spell. Davenport, WA: Peaceweed, 1975
    4266. The fifth season. Athens: Ohio University Press, 1978

SHERRY, Sal
    4267. Cobblestones. Reseda, CA: Mojave, 1976

SHERWIN, Judith Johnson
    4268. Impossible buildings. Garden City, NY: Doubleday,
          1973
    4269. The town scold. Woodstock, VT: Countryman, 1977
    4270. How the dead count. New York: Norton, 1978
    4271. Transparencies. Woodstock, VT: Countryman, 1978
    4272. Dead's good company. Woodstock, VT: Countryman,
          1979

SHEVIN, David
    4273. Expecting Ginger Rogers. Bowling Green, OH: Newedi,
          1975
    4274. Camptown spaces. Southfield, MI: Anti-Ocean, 1978
    4275. The stop book. Gulfport, FL: Konglomerati, 1978

SHIPLEY, Vivian
    4276. Jack tales. Greenfield Center, NY: Greenfield Review,
          1983

SHIVLEY, Charley
    4277. Nuestra Senora de los Dolores. Boston: Good Gay
          Poets, 1975

SHOEMAKER, Lynn
    4278. Curses and blessings. Ithaca, NY: Ithaca House, 1978
    4279. Hands. Amherst, MA: Lynx House, 1982

SHOLL, Betsy
    4280. Changing faces. Cambridge, MA: Alice James, 1974
    4281. Appalachian winter. Cambridge, MA: Alice James, 1978

SHORE, Jane
    4282. Eye level. Amherst: University of Massachusetts Press, 1977

SHORT, Clarice
    4283. The old one and the wind. Salt Lake City: University of Utah Press, 1973

SHUMWAY, Mary
    4284. Time and other birds. Gulfport, FL: Konglomerati, 1977

SHURIN, Aaron
    4285. The night sun. San Francisco: Gay Sunshine, 1976
    4286. Giving up the ghost. San Francisco: Rose Deeprose, 1980
    4287. The graces. San Francisco: Four Seasons Foundation, 1983

SHUSTER, Ronald L.
    4288. The ever increasing dawn. Reseda, CA: Mojave, 1973

SIEGEL, Lee
    4289. Vivisections. Bellingham, WA: Goliards, 1973

SIEGEL, Robert
    4290. The beasts & the elders. Hanover, NH: University Press of New England, 1973
    4291. A tale whose time has come. San Francisco: Panjandrum, 1977
    4292. In a pig's eye. Orlando: University Presses of Florida, 1980

SILVERT, Layle
    4293. Making a baby in Union Park, Chicago. Brooklyn: Downtown Poets, 1983

SILKO, Leslie
    4294. Laguna woman. Greenfield Center, NY: Greenfield Review, 1974

SILLIMAN, Ron
    4295. Nox. Providence: Burning Deck, 1973
    4296. Sitting up, standing, taking steps. Willits, CA: Tuumba, 1978
    4297. Ketjak. San Francisco: This, 1979
    4298. Tjanting. Berkeley: The Figures, 1981

4299. BART. Elmwood, CT: Potes & Poets, 1982
4300. ABC. Berkeley: Tuumba, 1983

SILVER-LILLYWHITE, Eileen
4301. All that autumn. Ithaca, NY: Ithaca House, 1983

SILVERMAN, Maxine
4302. Survival song. Bronx: Sunbury, 1976

SIMIC, Charles
4303. Return to a place lit by a glass of milk. New York:
        Braziller, 1974
4304. Biography and a lament. West Hartford, CT: Bar-
        tholomew's Cobble, 1976
4305. Charon's cosmology. New York: Braziller, 1977
4306. Brooms; selected poems. Barry, Glamorgan, Wales:
        Edge, 1978
4307. School for dark thoughts. Pawlet, VT: Banyan, 1978
4308. Classic ballroom dances. New York: Braziller, 1980
4309. White: a new version. Durango, CO: Logbridge-
        Rhodes, 1980
4310. Austerities. New York: Braziller, 1982
4311. Weather forecast for utopia and vicinity. Barrytown,
        NY: Station Hill, 1983

SIMMERMAN, Jim
4312. Home. Port Townsend, WA: Dragon Gate, 1983

SIMMONS, J. D.
4313. Judith's blues. Detroit: Broadside, 1973

SIMMONS, Ted
4314. Magical Friday. San Rafael, CA: Fur Line, 1975

SIMON, John Oliver
4315. Animal. Berkeley: Aldebaran, 1973
4316. Snake's tooth. Berkeley: Aldebaran, 1974
4317. Living in the boneyard. Oak Park, IL: Cat's Pajamas,
        1975
4318. The panamint city badman ballad. Berkeley: Aldebaran,
        1976
4319. Rattlesnake grass. Brooklyn: Hanging Loose, 1978
4320. Neither of us can break the other's hold. Berkeley:
        Shameless Hussy, 1981

SIMON, Kia
4321. & everybody is a children. San Lorenzo, CA: Shame-
        less Hussy, 1974
4322. Toddler. Berkeley: Aldebaran, 1976

SIMPSON, Louis
4323. The invasion of Italy. Northampton, MA: Main Street,
        1976

4324. Searching for the ox. New York: Morrow, 1976
4325. Caviare at the funeral. New York: F. Watts, 1980
4326. The best hour of the night. New Haven, CT: Ticknor & Fields, 1983
4327. People live here; selected poems, 1949-1983. Brockport, NY: BOA, 1983

SIMPSON, Nancy
4328. Across water. Pittsford, NY: State Street, 1983

SIMPSON, Peter
4329. Keeping open. Shawnee Mission, KS: BkMk, 1973

SIPORIN, Ona
4330. Poems for a primitive mythology. Bloomington, IN: Raintree, 1976

SISSMAN, L. E.
4331. Hello, darkness. Boston: Little, Brown, 1978

SJEVOM, David see SHEVIN, David
4332. [No entry]

SJOBERG, John
4333. Hazel. West Branch, IA: Toothpaste, 1976

SKELLINGS, Edmund
4334. Heart attacks. Gainesville: University Presses of Florida, 1976
4335. Face value. Orlando: University Presses of Florida, 1977
4336. Showing my age. Gainesville: University Presses of Florida, 1978

SKLAR, Morty
4337. Riverside. Iowa City: Spirit That Moves Us, 1974
4338. The night we stood up for our rights; poems, 1969-1975. West Branch, IA: Toothpaste, 1977

SKLAREW, Myra
4339. In the basket of the blind. Cherry Valley, NY: Cherry Valley, 1975
4340. From the backyard of the Diaspora. Washington: Dryad, 1976
4341. Blessed art thou. Milton, MA: Chowder, 1982
4342. The science of goodbyes. Athens: University of Georgia Press, 1982

SKRATZ, G. P.
4343. The gates of disappearance. Gulfport, FL: Konglomerati, 1981

SKY, Gino
    4344. Sweet ass'd angels, pilgrims & boogie woogies. San
           Francisco: Cranium, 1973
    4345. Jonquil rose: jus' one more cowboy. San Francisco:
           Five Trees, 1976

SLATER, Robert
    4346. Survival Kit. Shawnee Mission, KS: BkMk, 1973
    4347. A rumor of inhabitants. Washington: Some of Us, 1974

SLAVITT, David R.
    4348. Vital signs; new and selected poems. Garden City, NY:
           Doubleday, 1975
    4349. Rounding the horn. Baton Rouge: Louisiana State Uni-
           versity Press, 1978
    4350. Dozens. Baton Rouge: Louisiana State University Press,
           1981
    4351. Big nose. Baton Rouge: Louisiana State University
           Press, 1983

SLEIGH, Tom
    4352. After one. Boston: Houghton Mifflin, 1983

SMALLWOOD, Vivian
    4353. And finding no mouse there. Mobile, AL: Negative
           Capability, 1983

SMITH, Bruce
    4354. The common wages. New York: Sheep Meadow, 1983

SMITH, Craig
    4355. Capsule Cranium. Laurinburg, NC: St. Andrews, 1974

SMITH, Dave
    4356. Mean rufus throw down. Fredonia, NY: Basilisk, 1973
    4357. Drunks. Edwardsville, IL: Sou'wester, 1974
    4358. The fisherman's whore. Athens: Ohio University Press,
           1974
    4359. Cumberland Station. Urbana: University of Illinois
           Press, 1976
    4360. In dark, sudden with light. Athens, OH: Croissant,
           1976
    4361. Goshawk, antelope. Urbana: University of Illinois
           Press, 1979
    4362. Men with women. Syracuse, NY: Tamarack, 1979
    4363. Dream flights. Urbana: University of Illinois Press,
           1981
    4364. Homage to Edgar Allan Poe. Baton Rouge: Louisiana
           State University Press, 1981
    4365. In the house of the judge. New York: Harper & Row,
           1983

SMITH, Edward
    4366. The flutes of Gama. Salt Lake City: Litmus, 1976
    4367. Going. Salt Lake City: Litmus, 1976

SMITH, Harry
    4368. Trinity. Lansing, MI: Ghost Dance, 1974; New York:
          Horizon, 1975
    4369. West Battery. New York: The Smith, 1975
    4370. The early poems. East Lansing, MI: Ghost Dance,
          1977
    4371. Me, the people. New York: State of the Culture, 1979

SMITH, Jared
    4372. Song of the blood. New York: The Smith, 1983

SMITH, Jordan
    4373. An apology for loving the old hymns. Princeton, NJ:
          Princeton University Press, 1982

SMITH, Larry R.
    4374. Growth. Bigfork, MN: Northwoods, 1975
    4375. Scissors, paper, rock. Cleveland: Cleveland State
          University Poetry Center, 1982

SMITH, Linwood
    4376. Silence, love, and kids I know. Washington: Internation-
          al Books, 1973

SMITH, Marth N.
    4377. Turning inward, reaching out. New Haven, CT: Pippin,
          1983

SMITH, Milton
    4378. To go on. Shawnee Mission, KS: BkMk, 1973

SMITH, Patti
    4379. Seventh heaven. Norwood, PA: Telegraph, 1973

SMITH, R. T.
    4380. Good water. Syracuse, NY: Tamarack, 1979
    4381. Rural route. Syracuse, NY: Tamarack, 1980
    4382. Beasts did leap. Syracuse, NY: Tamarack, 1982
    4383. From the high dive. Huntington Bay, NY: Water Mark,
          1982
    4384. Finding the path. Norristown, PA: Black Willow, 1983

SMITH, Ray
    4385. The deer on the freeway. Vermillion: University of
          South Dakota Press, 1973
    4386. Weathering. Menomonie, WI: Uzzano, 1980

SMITH, Rick
    4387. Exhibition game. Pasadena, CA: G. Sack, 1973

SMITH, Robert L.
    4388. Refractions. Georgetown, CA: Dragon's Teeth, 1979

SMITH, William
    4389. The traveler's tree. New York: Persea, 1980

SMITH, William Jay
    4390. Venice in the fog. Greensboro, NC: Unicorn, 1976
    4391. Journey to the Dead Sea. Omaha: Abattoir, 1979
    4392. The tall poets. Winston-Salem, NC: Palaemon, 1979

SMYTH, Paul
    4393. Conversions. Athens: University of Georgia Press,
        1974

SNODGRASS, W. D.
    4394. The fuhrer bunker. Brockport, NY: Boa, 1977
    4395. Six troubadour songs. Providence: Burning Deck, 1977
    4396. If birds build with your hair. New York: Nadja, 1979
    4397. Six minnesinger songs. Providence: Burning Deck,
        1983

SNOW, Edith
    4398. Hold your hands to the earth. Newcastle, CA: Blue
        Oak, 1976

SNOW, Karen
    4399. Wonders. New York: Penguin, 1980
    4400. Outsiders. Woodstock, VT: Countryman, 1983

SNYDER, Gary
    4401. Turtle Island. New York: New Directions, 1974
    4402. He who hunted birds in his father's village. San Fran-
        cisco: Grey Fox, 1979
    4403. Songs for Gaia. Port Townsend, WA: Copper Canyon,
        1979
    4404. Axe handles. Berkeley: North Point, 1983

SOBIN, Anthony
    4405. The Sunday naturalist. Athens: Ohio University Press,
        1982

SOLEM, Knute
    4406. The insurrection of Earth in dragon pastures. Bodega
        Bay, CA: Anexis, 1974

SOLHEIM, David R.
    4407. On the ward. Moorhead, MN: Territorial, 1975

SOLOMON, Abba A.
    4408. Of basements & other digs. Portland: Out of the Ashes,
        1973
    4409. Cantos V & VI, chicken mishigas. Portland: Out of

the Ashes, 1974
4410.   The poultry colloquium.   Portland: Out of the Ashes,
        1974

SOLT, Mary Ellen
4411.   The people-mover.   Reno, NV: West Coast Poetry Re-
        view, 1978

SOMOZA, Joseph
4412.   Olive women.   Los Cerrillos, NM: San Marcos, 1976

SONG, Cathy
4413.   Picture bride.   New Haven: Yale University Press,
        1983

SORCIC, Jim
4414.   Human Songbook.   Milwaukee: Morgan, 1974
4415.   Johnnie Panic and his fantastic circus of fear.   New
        York: New Rivers, 1975

SORRELL, John Edward
4416.   Clenched horizon.   Sarasota, FL: New Collage, 1978

SORRENTINO, Gilbert
4417.   Splendite-Hotel.   New York: New Directions, 1973
4418.   A dozen oranges.   Santa Barbara: Black Sparrow, 1976
4419.   White sail.   Santa Barbara: Black Sparrow, 1977
4420.   The orangery.   Austin: University of Texas Press,
        1978
4421.   Selected poems, 1958-1980.   Santa Barbara: Black
        Sparrow, 1981

SOTO, Gary
4422.   The elements of San Joaquin.   Pittsburgh: University
        of Pittsburgh Press, 1977
4423.   The tale of sunlight.   Pittsburgh: University of Pitts-
        burgh Press, 1978
4424.   Father is a pillow tied to a broom.   Pittsburgh: Slow
        Loris, 1980
4425.   Where sparrows work hard.   Pittsburgh: University of
        Pittsburgh Press, 1981

SOUDERS, Bruce
4426.   To a student dying young.   Georgetown, CA: Dragon's
        Teeth, 1978

SOUTHWICK, Marcia
4427.   What the trees go into.   Providence: Burning Deck,
        1977
4428.   The night won't save anyone.   Athens: University of
        Georgia Press, 1980

SPACKS, Barry
  4429. Teaching the penguins to fly. Boston: Godine, 1975
  4430. Imagining a unicorn. Athens: University of Georgia
       Press, 1978
  4431. Spacks Street: new & selected poems. Baltimore:
       Johns Hopkins University Press, 1982

SPEAKES, Richard
  4432. Hannah's travel. Boise, ID: Ahsahta, 1982

SPEAR, Roberta
  4433. Silks. New York: Holt, Rinehart and Winston, 1980

SPEARS, Monroe
  4434. The levitator. Princeton, NJ: Pilgrim, 1975

SPEER, Laurel
  4435. The sitting duck. Chicago: Ommation, 1978
  4436. Don't dress your cat in an apron. Easthampton, MA:
       Adastra, 1981
  4437. The Hobbesian apple. Bellingham, WA: Signpost,
       1982
  4438. Hokum; visions of a gringa. Big Timber, MT: Seven
       Buffaloes, 1982
  4439. Roosevelt tracks the last buffalo. Eau Claire, WI:
       Rhiannon, 1982
  4440. I'm hiding from the cat. Tunnel, NY: Geryon, 1983

SPICER, Jack
  4441. Admonitions. New York: Adventures in Poetry, 1974
  4442. 15 false propositions about God: San Francisco: Man-
       root, 1974
  4443. A lost poem. Verona, Italy: Plain Wrapper, 1974
  4444. The collected books of Jack Spicer. Los Angeles:
       Black Sparrow, 1975
  4445. One-night stand & other poems. San Francisco: Grey
       Fox, 1980

SPINGARN, Lawrence P. The dark playground. Van Nuys, CA:
       Perivale, 1979

SPIRES, Elizabeth
  4447. Boardwalk. Cleveland: Bits, 1980
  4448. Globe. Middletown, CT: Wesleyan University Press,
       1981

SPIVACK, Kathleen
  4449. Flying inland. Garden City, NY: Doubleday, 1973
  4450. The Jane poems. Garden City, NY: Doubleday, 1974

SPROUSE, James
  4451. Methane. Cincinnati: Stone-Marrow, 1974

SPRUNT, William
>   4452.   A sacrifice of dogs.   Laurinburg, NC: St. Andrews
>   College Press, 1976

SQUIRE, Glen
>   4453.   Sounds of silence.   Escondido, CA: Omni, 1975

SQUIRES, Radcliffe
>   4454.   Waiting in the bone and other poems.   Omaha: Abattoir,
>   1973
>   4455.   Gardens of the world.   Baton Rouge: Louisiana State
>   University Press, 1981
>   4456.   Journeys.   New York: Elysian, 1983

STAFF, Susan
>   4457.   From the fire.   Pittsburgh: Know, 1974

STAFFORD, Kim
>   4458.   Braided apart.   Lewiston, ID: Confluence, 1976
>   4459.   A gypsy's history of the world.   Port Townsend, WA:
>   Copper Canyon, 1976

STAFFORD, William
>   4460.   In the clock of reason.   Victoria, BC, Canada: Soft,
>   1973
>   4461.   Someday, maybe.   New York: Harper & Row, 1973
>   4462.   That other alone.   Mt. Horeb, WI: Perishable, 1973
>   4463.   Going places.   Reno, NV: West Coast Poetry Review,
>   1974
>   4464.   Artist, come home.   Pittsburgh: Slow Loris, 1976
>   4465.   Late, passing prairie farm.   Northampton, MA: Main
>   Street, 1976
>   4466.   The design on the oriole.   N. P.:   Night Heron, 1977
>   4467.   Stories that could be true.   New York: Harper & Row,
>   1977
>   4468.   Passing a creche.   Seattle: Sea Pen Press & Paper
>   Mill, 1978
>   4469.   Tuft by puff.   Mt. Horeb, WI: Perishable, 1978
>   4470.   Two about music.   Knotting, Eng.:   Sceptre, 1978
>   4471.   Around you, your house and A catechism.   Knotting,
>   Eng.:   Sceptre, 1979
>   4472.   Things that happen where there aren't any people.
>   Brockport, NY: Boa, 1980
>   4473.   Sometimes like a legend.   Port Townsend, WA: Copper
>   Canyon, 1981
>   4474.   A glass face in the rain.   New York: Harper & Row,
>   1982
>   4475.   Roving across fields.   Daleville, IN: Barnwood, 1983
>   4476.   Smoke's way: poems from limited editions, 1968-1981.
>   Port Townsend, WA: Graywolf, 1983

STAINTON, Albert
>   4477.   The crossing.   Orono, ME: Puckerbrush, 1974

STANFORD, Ann
4478. Climbing up to light. Los Angeles: Magpie, 1973
4479. In Mediterranean air. New York: Viking, 1977

STANFORD, Frank
4480. Arkansas bench stone. Spokane, WA: Mill Mountain, 1975
4481. The battlefield where the moon says I love you. Fayette-
       ville, AR: Lost Roads, 1977
4482. Crib death. Tucson, AZ: Ironwood, 1978
4483. The singing knives. Fayetteville, AR: Lost Roads, 1979
4484. You. Fayetteville, AR: Lost Roads, 1979

STANLEY, George
4485. The stick; poems 1969-73. Vancouver, BC: Talonbooks, 1974
4486. You; poems 1957-67. Vancouver, BC: New Star, 1974

STANSBERGER, Richard
4487. Glass hat. Baton Rouge: Louisiana State University
       Press, 1979

STANTON, Maura
4488. Snow on snow. New Haven, CT: Yale University
       Press, 1975

STARBUCK, George
4489. Elegy in a country church yard. Boston: Pym Randall, 1975
4490. Desperate measures. Boston: Godine, 1978
4491. Talkin' B.A. blues. Roslindale, MA: Pym-Randall, 1980
4492. The argot merchant disaster: poems new and selected.
       Boston: Little, Brown, 1982

STASZKO, Ray
4493. The last fiddler crab. Georgetown, CA: Dragon's Teeth, 1974
4494. Penny Candy. Georgetown, CA: Dragon's Teeth, 1974

STEELE, Nancy
4495. Tracking. Port Townsend, WA: Copper Canyon, 1977

STEELE, Paul Curry
4496. Anse on Island Creek and other poems. Charleston,
       WV: Mountain State, 1981

STEELE, Timothy
4497. Uncertainties and rest. Baton Rouge: Louisiana State
       University Press, 1979

STEFANILE, Felix
    4498.   East River nocturn. New Rochelle, NY: Elizabeth,
          1976

STEFANILE, Selma
    4499.   The poem beyond my reach. West Lafayette, IN: Spar-
          row, 1982

STEFANSON, D. H.
    4500.   Sonnets for women. Birmingham, AL: Ragnarok, 1975

STEIN, Charles
    4501.   Witch-hazel. Albany, CA: Sand Dollar, 1975
    4502.   The river menace. Barrytown, NY: Station Hill, 1979
    4503.   Horse sacrifice. Barrytown, NY: Station Hill, 1980
    4504.   Parts and other parts. Barrytown, NY: Station Hill,
          1982
    4505.   The transcripts. Madison, WI: Xerox Sutra, 1983

STEINBERG, David
    4506.   If I knew the way. Santa Cruz, CA: Red Alder, 1975
    4507.   Welcome, brothers: poems of a changing man's con-
          sciousness. Santa Cruz, CA: Red Alder, 1976
    4508.   Beneath this calm exterior. Santa Cruz, CA: Red
          Alder, 1982

STEINBERGH, Judith W.
    4509.   Motherwriter. Green Harbor, MA: Wampeter, 1983

STEINGASS, David
    4510.   American handbook. Pittsburgh: University of Pitts-
          burgh Press, 1973

STEINMAN, Lisa Malinowski
    4511.   Lost poems. Ithaca, NY: Ithaca House, 1976

STEPANCHEV, Stephen
    4512.   Mining the darkness. Los Angeles: Black Sparrow,
          1974
    4513.   Medusa and others. Los Angeles: Black Sparrow, 1975
    4514.   What I own. Santa Barbara: Black Sparrow, 1978

STEPHENS, Alan
    4515.   White River poems. Chicago: Swallow, 1976
    4516.   In plain air: poems 1958-1980. Chicago: Swallow,
          1982

STEPHENS, Jim
    4517.   Posthumous work. Madison, WI: Abraxas, 1975

STEPHENS, Michael Gregory
    4518.   Paragraphs. Amherst, MA: Mulch, 1974

STERN, Gerald
   4519. Rejoicings; selected poems, 1966-1972. Fredericton,
         NB: Fiddlehead, 1973
   4520. Lucky life. Boston: Houghton Mifflin, 1977
   4521. The red coal. Boston: Houghton Mifflin, 1981

STERN, Robert
   4522. Spirit hand. Gulfport, FL: Konglomerati, 1978

STETTNER, Irving
   4523. If a poet is. New York: Twin Angel, 1974
   4524. Stone-Crazy. La Jolla, CA: Inca, 1974
   4525. On the 2nd Avenue patrol. New York: Home Planet,
         1976
   4526. Hurrah!: selected poems. Brooklyn: Downtown Poets,
         1980

STEVENS, Richard
   4527. Chords & tunings. Laurinburg, NC: Curveship, 1975

STEVENSON, Diane
   4528. Beauty shop monologues. Hardwicke, MA: Four Zoas,
         1976

STEWART, Pamela
   4529. The St. Vlas Elegies. Fort Collins, CO: L'Epervier,
         1977
   4530. Half-tones. Tucson, AZ: Maguey, 1978
   4531. Cascades. Seattle: L'Epervier, 1980
   4532. Sileutia lunae. Milton, MA: Chowder, 1982

STEWART, Susan
   4533. Yellow stars and ice. Princeton, NJ: Princeton Uni-
         versity Press, 1981

STOCK, Susan
   4534. Early morning through the door. Whitehorn, CA:
         Holmgangers, 1983

STOKES, Terry
   4535. Punching in, punching out. Providence: Burning Deck,
         1973
   4536. House wrecking. Hartford, CT: Bartholomew's Cobble,
         1975
   4537. High school confidential. Providence: Diana's, 1976
   4538. The lady poems. Woodenhaven, NY: Cross Country,
         1977
   4539. Life in these United States. Memphis: St. Luke's,
         1978

STOKESBURY, Leon
   4540. Often in different landscapes. Austin: University of
         Texas Press, 1976

STOLOFF, Carolyn
    4541. Dying to survive. Garden City, NY: Doubleday, 1973
    4542. In the red meadow. New York: New Rivers, 1974
    4543. Lighter-than-night verse. San Francisco: Red Hill,
          1977
    4544. Swiftly now. Athens: Ohio University Press, 1982
    4545. A spool of blue. Metuchen, NJ: Scarecrow, 1983

STONE, Arlene
    4546. The image maker. Boston: Plowshare, 1976
    4547. Through a coal cellar darkly. La Crosse, WI: Juni-
          per, 1976
    4548. [No entry]
    4549. The women's house. Olean, NY: Allegany Mountain,
          1979
    4550. The double pipes of Pan. Berkeley: North Atlantic,
          1983

STONE, Carole
    4551. Legacy. Oneonta, NY: Swamp, 1979
    4552. A sentimental education. Amherst, MA: Swamp, 1981

STONE, John
    4553. In all this rain. Baton Rouge: Louisiana State Univer-
          sity Press, 1980

STONE, Naomi Burton
    4554. To be a pilgrim. Winona, MN: St. Mary's College
          Press, 1973

STONE, Ruth
    4555. Cheap. New York: Harcourt Brace Jovanovich, 1975

STOREY, Edward
    4556. A man in winter. Middletown, CT: Wesleyan Univer-
          sity Press, 1973

STOSS, John
    4557. Finding the broom. Fayetteville, AR: Lost Roads,
          1977

STOUT, Robert Joe
    4558. Trained bears on hoops. Berkeley: Thorp Springs,
          1973
    4559. Camping out. Richford, VT: Samisdat, 1976
    4560. Swallowing dust. Fairfax, CA: Red Hill, 1976
    4561. The trick. La Crosse, WI: Juniper, 1976

STOUTENBURG, Adrien
    4562. Greenwich mean time. Salt Lake City: University of
          Utah Press, 1979

STOWELL, Hal
    4563. Country crossings. Amherst, MA: Lynx House, 1976

STRAND, Mark
    4564. Elegy for my father. Iowa City: Windhover, 1973
    4565. The Sargentville notebook. Providence: Burning Deck,
           1973
    4566. The story of our lives. New York: Atheneum, 1973
    4567. The late hour. New York: Atheneum, 1978
    4568. The monument. New York: Ecco, 1978
    4569. Selected poems. New York: Atheneum, 1980

STRAND, Thomas
    4570. Questions to Brecht. Berkeley: Thorp Springs, 1975

STRONE, Celia
    4571. The drum and the melody. New York: The Smith,
           1983

STRONGIN, Lynn
    4572. Shrift, a winter sequence. Berkeley: Thorp Springs,
           1975
    4573. A hacksaw brightness. Tucson, AZ: Ironwood, 1977
    4574. Nightmare of mouse. Fort Collins, CO: L'Epervier,
           1977
    4575. Toccata of the disturbed child. Highland Park, MI:
           Fallen Angel, 1977
    4576. Dwarf cycle. Berkeley: Thorp Springs, 1978
    4577. Countrywoman/surgeon. Seattle: L'Epervier, 1980

STROUD, Joseph
    4578. In the sleep of rivers. Santa Barbara: Capra, 1974
    4579. Signatures. Brockport, NY: BOA, 1983

STRYK, Lucien
    4580. Awakening. Chicago: Swallow, 1973
    4581. Selected poems. Chicago: Swallow, 1976
    4582. Three Zen poems, after Shinkichi Takahashi. Knotting,
           Eng.: Sceptre, 1976
    4583. The duck pond. London: J. Joy, 1978
    4584. Cherries. Bristol, RI: Ampersand, 1983

STUART, Dabney
    4585. The other hand. Baton Rouge: Louisiana State Univer-
           sity Press, 1974
    4586. Friends of yours, friends of mine. Richmond, VA:
           Rainmaker, 1975
    4587. Round and round. Baton Rouge: Louisiana State Univer-
           sity Press, 1977
    4588. Common ground. Baton Rouge: Louisiana State Univer-
           sity Press, 1982

STUDEBAKER, William
  4589. Trailing the raven. Pocatello, ID: Limberlost Review,
         1982

STYRON, Rose
  4590. Thieves' afternoon. New York: Viking, 1973

SUBLETTE, Walter
  4591. The resurrection on Friday night. Chicago: Swallow,
         1977

SUK, Julie
  4592. The medicine woman. Laurinburg, NC: St. Andrews,
         1980

SUKENICK, Lynn
  4593. Houdini. Santa Barbara: Capra, 1973
  4594. Water astonishing. Holly Springs, MS: Ragnarok,
         1974
  4595. Problems & characteristics. Berkeley: Avocet Press,
         1975

SULLIVAN, Chuck
  4596. Vanishing species. Charlotte, NC: Red Clay, 1975
  4597. Catechism of hearts. Sullivan's Island, SC: Red Clay,
         1980

SULLIVAN, Francis
  4598. Spy Wednesday's kind. New York: The Smith, 1979

SULLIVAN, Nancy
  4599. Telling it. Boston: Godine, 1975

SULLIVAN, Rob
  4600. Hands in the stone. Diablo, CA: Holmgangers, 1974

SUMMERS, Hollis
  4601. Occupant, please forward. New Brunswick, NJ: Rut-
         gers University Press, 1976
  4602. Dinosaurs. Athens, OH: Rosetta, 1978

SUTHERLAND, Elizabeth
  4603. Mouth of the whale. Santa Barbara: Mudborn, 1979

SUTTER, Barton
  4604. Cedarhome. Brockport, NY: BOA Editions, 1977

SUTTON, Lorraine
  4605. Saycred Laydy. Bronx, NY: Sunbury, 1975

SWAN, Jim
  4606. A door to the forest. New York: Random House, 1979

SWANDER, Mary
    4607.   Needlepoint. Missoula, MT: SmokeRoot, 1977
    4608.   Succession. Athens: University of Georgia Press, 1979

SWANGER, David
    4609.   The shape of waters. Ithaca, NY: Ithaca House, 1978
    4610.   Inside the horse. Ithaca, NY: Ithaca House, 1981

SWANN, Brian
    4611.   The whale's scars. New York: New Rivers, 1974
    4612.   Roots. New York: New Rivers, 1976
    4613.   The middle of the journey. University: University of
          Alabama Press, 1982

SWARD, Robert
    4614.   Poems; new and selected (1957-1973). Chicago: Swal-
          low, 1973
    4615.   Letter to a straw hat. Victoria, BC: Soft, 1974
    4616.   Five Iowa poems. Iowa City: Stone Wall, 1975
    4617.   Honey bear on Lasqueti Island, B.C. Victoria, BC:
          Soft, 1978
    4618.   Half a life's history. Toronto: Aya, 1983

SWARTHOUT, Kathryn
    4619.   Lifesavors. Garden City, NY: Doubleday, 1982

SWENSON, Brigit
    4620.   The eagle and the flower. New York: Astra, 1976

SWENSON, Karen
    4621.   An attic of ideals. Garden City, NY: Doubleday, 1974

SWENSON, May
    4622.   New & selected things taking place. Boston: Little,
          Brown, 1978

SWISHER, Robert K., Jr.
    4623.   Touch me if you love me. Santa Fe, NM: Sunstone,
          1976

SYLVESTER, William
    4624.   Curses omens prayers. Ashland, OH: Ashland Poetry,
          1974

SZERLIP, Barbara
    4625.   The ugliest woman in the world and other histories.
          Arlington, VA: Gallimaufry, 1978

TAGGART, John
    4626.   Pyramid canon. Providence: Burning Deck, 1973
    4627.   The pyramid is a pure crystal. New Rochelle, NY:
          Elizabeth, 1974

4628.   Prism and the pine twig. New Rochelle, NY: Elizabeth, 1977

4629.   Dodeka. Milwaukee: Membrane, 1979

TAGLIABUE, John
4630.   Every minute a ritual.   Lewiston, ME: Grace Taglia-
        bue, 1973
4631.   Poems on the Winter's Tale.   Houghton, NY: Ktaadn, 1973

TALARICO, Ross
4632.   Simple truths. Raleigh, NC: Review, 1975
4633.   Trying to leave. La Mesa, CA: Helix House, 1978
4634.   Almost happy. Brooklyn: Release, 1981

TALL, Deborah
4635.   Ninth life. Ithaca, NY: Ithaca House, 1982

TALNEY, Ron
4636.   The anxious ground. Portland: Press-22, 1974

TANAKA, Ronald
4637.   Shinto suite. Greenfield, NY: Greenfield Review, 1981

TANKSLEY, Perry
4638.   For the good times. Jackson, MS: Allgood, 1975

TAPSCOTT, Stephen
4639.   Mesopotamia. Middletown, CT: Wesleyan University
        Press, 1975
4640.   Penobscot. Roslindale, MA: Pym-Randall, 1983

TARACHOW, Michael
4641.   From a cup of old coins. Milwaukee: Shelters, 1974
4642.   Sunrise. Milwaukee: Pentagram, 1975
4643.   Into it. Milwaukee: Pentagram, 1976
4644.   Waves. Dennis, MA: Salt-Works, 1977
4645.   Interlude. Markesan, WI: Pentagram, 1979
4646.   The turning point. Markesan, WI: Pentagram, 1981

TARGAN, Barry
4647.   Thoreau stalks the land disguised as a father.   Green-
        field Center, NY: Greenfield Review, 1975

TARN, Nathaniel
4648.   Lyrics for the bride of God: section: the artemission.
        Santa Barbara: Tree, 1973
4649.   The Persephones. Santa Barbara: Tree, 1974
4650.   Section: the artemission. Santa Barbara: Tree, 1974
4651.   Lyrics for the Bride of God. New York: New Direct-
        ions, 1975
4652.   Narrative of this fall. Los Angeles: Black Sparrow,
        1975

4653. The house of leaves. Santa Barbara: Black Sparrow, 1976
4654. The microcosm. Milwaukee: Membrane, 1977
4655. Birdscapes, with seaside. Santa Barbara: Black Sparrow, 1978

TASHJIAN, Georgian
4656. The quiet noise of remembering. Palo Alto, CA: Altoan, 1976

TATE, James
4657. Viper jazz. Middletown, CT: Wesleyan University Press, 1976
4658. The torches. Greensboro, NC: Unicorn, 1977
4659. Riven doggeries. New York: Ecco, 1979
4660. Land of little sticks. Worcester, MA: Metacom, 1981
4661. Hints to pilgrims. Amherst: University of Massachusetts Press, 1982
4662. Constant defender. New York: Ecco, 1983

TAYLOR, Diane
4663. A scoundrel breeze. Little Rock, AR: August House, 1983

TAYLOR, Henry
4664. An afternoon of pocket billiards. Salt Lake City: University of Utah Press, 1975

TAYLOR, Kent
4665. Driving like the sun. Ellensburg, WA: Vagabond, 1976

TAYLOR, Laurie
4666. Changing the past. St. Paul: New Rivers, 1981

TEDLOCK, Ernest
4667. Told by the weather. Whitehorn, CA: Holmgangers, 1983

TERR, Leonard
4668. Sitting in our tree house waiting for the apocalypse. Ithaca, NY: Ithaca House, 1975

TERRIS, Virginia R.
4669. Tracking. Urbana: University of Illinois Press, 1976

TESSLER, Clare
4670. Dreams & memories. Santa Fe, NM: Sunstone, 1976

THARAUD, Ross
4671. Openings. Ithaca, NY: Ithaca House, 1976

THOMAS, Daniel B.
4672. Momma, I know why. New York: Barlenmir, 1974

THOMAS, John
    4673. Epopoeia and the decay of satire. Fairfax, CA: Red
        Hill, 1976

THOMAS, Joyce Carol
    4674. Bittersweet. San Jose, CA: Firesign, 1973
    4675. Blessing. Berkeley: Jocato, 1975

THOMAS, Lorenzo
    4676. Dracula. New York: Angel Hair, 1973
    4677. Chances are few. Berkeley: Blue Wind, 1979
    4678. The bathers. Berkeley: I. Reed, 1981

THOMAS, Richard
    4679. Poems. New York: Avon, 1974
    4680. In the moment. New York: Avon, 1979

THOMAS, Ryan
    4681. Getting real. Berkeley: Images, 1977

THOMASEN, Suzi
    4682. A faraway whistle. San Luis Obispo, CA: Solo, 1978

THOMPSON, Marilyn
    4683. Saying things. Omaha: Abattoir, 1975

THOMPSON, Phyllis
    4684. The creation frame. Urbana: University of Illinois
        Press, 1973
    4685. The serpent of the white rose. Honolulu: Petronium,
        1976

THORNBURG, Thomas
    4686. Saturday town. Georgetown, CA: Dragon's Teeth, 1976

TIBBS, Ben
    4687. Bombs. Grand Rapids, MI: Pilot, 1975

TICHY, Susan
    4688. The hands in exile. New York: Random House, 1983

TICKLE, Phyllis A.
    4689. American genesis. Memphis, TN: St. Luke's, 1976

TILLINGHAST, Richard
    4690. The knife, and other poems. Middletown, CT: Wesle-
        yan University Press, 1980

TINKER, Carol
    4691. The pillow book of Carol Tinker. Santa Barbara: Cad-
        mus, 1980

TIPTON, David
    4692.   Departure in yellow. Santa Cruz, CA: Green Horse, 1976
    4693.   A graph of love. Newcastle-on-Tyne, Eng.: Galloping Dog, 1976

TIPTON, James
    4694.   Bittersweet. Austin, TX: Cold Mountain, 1975

TODD, Gail
    4695.   Family way. San Lorenzo, CA: Shameless Hussy, 1975

TOLSON, Melvin B.
    4696.   A gallery of Harlem portraits. Columbia: University of Missouri Press, 1979

TOMLINSON, Kerry
    4697.   Time payment. Santa Barbara: Mudborn, 1978

TORREGIAN, Sotere
    4698.   The age of gold. New York: Kulchur Foundation, 1976
    4699.   Amtrak trek. New York: Telephone, 1979

TOTH, Steve
    4700.   Traveling light. Berkeley: Blue Wind, 1977

TOUSTER, Alison
    4701.   The first movement. Georgetown, CA: Dragon's Teeth, 1976

TOWLE, Tony
    4702.   Autobiography, and other poems. New York: Sun, 1977

TOWNER, Daniel. Six poems. Cleveland: Bits, 1980

TOWNLEY, Rod
    4704.   Three musicians. New York: The Smith, 1978

TRAXLER, Patricia
    4705.   Blood calendar. New York: Morrow, 1975
    4706.   The glass woman. Brooklyn: Hanging Loose, 1983

TREMBLAY, Bill
    4707.   The anarchist heart. New York: New Rivers, 1977
    4708.   Home front. Amherst, MA: Lynx House, 1978

TREMBLAY, Cynthia
    4709.   Morning news. Amherst, MA: Lynx House, 1976

TRIAS, Peter
    4710.   That house in Venice. Laurinburg, NC: Saint Andrews, 1976

TRIMPI, Wesley
    4711. The desert house. Florence, KY: Barth, 1982

TRUDELL, Dennis
    4712. Eight pages. Madison, WI: Abraxas, 1975
    4713. Here a home, there a home. La Crosse, WI: Juniper,
        1976

TRUEBLOOD, Cynthia
    4714. A rare bird flies past. San Francisco: Lone Mountain,
        1976

TRUESDALE, C. W.
    4715. Doctor Vertigo. New York: New Rivers, 1976

TSONGAS, George
    4716. Addenda. San Francisco: Smoking Mirror, 1974
    4717. Love letters. San Francisco: Second Coming, 1975

TURCO, Lewis
    4718. The weed garden. Orangeburg, SC: Peaceweed, 1973
    4719. Courses in lambents. Oswego, NY: Mathom, 1977
    4720. A cage of creatures. Potsdam, NY: Banjo, 1978
    4721. The compleat melancholick. Madison, WI: Bieler, 1979
    4722. American still lifes. Oswego, NY: Mathom, 1981

·TURNER, Alberta T.
    4723. Learning to count. Pittsburgh: University of Pittsburgh
        Press, 1974
    4724. Lid and spoon. Pittsburgh: University of Pittsburgh
        Press, 1977
    4725. A belfry of knees. University: University of Alabama
        Press, 1983

TWICHELL, Chase
    4726. Northern spy. Pittsburgh: University of Pittsburgh
        Press, 1981

TYSH, George
    4727. Mecanorgane. Providence: Burning Deck, 1973
    4728. Shop posh. Providence: Burning Deck, 1973
    4729. Tea. Providence: Burning Deck, 1979

TYSON, William
    4730. We are love. Goldsboro, NC: Tybr, 1975

ULLMAN, Leslie
    4731. Natural histories. New Haven, CT: Yale University
        Press, 1979

UNGER, Barbara
    4732. Basement. San Francisco: Isthmus, 1975

UNTERECKER, John
    4733. Irish poems. Dublin: Dolmen, 1973
    4734. Dance sequence. Santa Cruz, CA: Kayak, 1975
    4735. Stone. Honolulu: University Press of Hawaii, 1977

UPDIKE, John
    4746. Cunts. New York: Hallman, 1974
    4747. Query. New York: Albondocani, 1974
    4748. From the journal of a leper. Northridge, CA: Lord
        John, 1976
    4749. Tossing and turning. New York: Knopf, 1977
    4750. Five poems. Cleveland: Bits, 1980

URDANG, Constance
    4751. The picnic in the cemetery. New York: Braziller,
        1975
    4752. The lone woman and others. Pittsburgh: University
        of Pittsburgh Press, 1980
    4753. Only the world. Pittsburgh: University of Pittsburgh
        Press, 1983

VAL, Stephen
    4754. Final leaves. Washington: Stephen Val Memorial Fund,
        1976

VALENTINE, Jean
    4755. Ordinary things. New York: Farrar, Straus, Giroux,
        1974
    4756. Turn. Oberlin, OH: Pocket Pal, 1977
    4757. The messenger. New York: Farrar, Straus, Giroux,
        1979

VAN ARSDALE, Philip
    4758. How to attain lasting peace. St. Petersburg, FL: Val-
        kyrie, 1974

VAN BRUNT, H. L.
    4759. Indian territory and other poems. New York: The
        Smith, 1974
    4760. For luck; poems, 1962-1977. Pittsburgh: Carnegie-
        Mellon University Press, 1977

VANDER MOLEN, Robert
    4761. Along the river, and other poems. New York: New
        Rivers, 1978
    4762. Circumstances. Fremont, MI: Sumac, 1978

VAN DUYN, Mona
    4763. Merciful disguises. New York: Atheneum, 1973
    4764. Letters from a father, and other poems. New York:
        Atheneum, 1982

VAN DYKE, Cheryl
    4765. Cheat grass. Port Townsend, WA: Copper Canyon, 1975

VANGELISTI, Paul
    4766. Air. Fairfax, CA: Red Hill, 1973
    4767. Pearl Harbor. San Francisco: Isthmus, 1975
    4768. The extravagant room. Fairfax, CA: Red Hill, 1976
    4769. Remembering the movies. San Francisco: Red Hill, 1977
    4770. 2x2. San Francisco: Red Hill, 1977

VAN WALLEGHEN, Michael
    4771. The Wichita poems. Iowa City: Stone Wall, 1973
    4772. The Wichita poems. Urbana: University of Illinois Press, 1975
    4773. More trouble with the obvious. Urbana: University of Illinois Press, 1981

VAS DIAS, Robert
    4774. Making faces. London: Joe Di Maggio, 1975
    4775. Ode. Omaha: Abattoir, 1977
    4776. Poems beginning "The world." London: Oasis, 1979

VEDDAR, Irene McCaleb
    4777. Sunlight and shadows. Escondido, CA: Omni, 1976

VEENENDAAL, Cornelia
    4778. The Trans-Siberian railway. Cambridge, MA: Alice James, 1973
    4779. Green shaded lamps. Cambridge, MA: Alice James, 1977

VEGA, J. see POMMY-VEGA, Janine
    4780. [No entry]

VERNON, John
    4781. Ann. Binghamton, NY: Iris, 1976

VIERECK, Peter
    4782. The tree witch. Westport, CT: Greenwood, 1973

VIERLING, Ronald
    4783. The prairie rider cantos. Vermillion, SD: Dakota, 1974

VILLANUEVA, Alma
    4784. Mother, may I. Pittsburgh: Motheroot, 1979

VINOGRAD, Julia
    4785. The Circus. Berkeley: Thorp Springs, 1974
    4786. Street feet. Berkeley: Thorp Springs, 1974

4787. Street pieces. Berkeley: Thorp Springs, 1975
4788. Berkeley Street cannibals. Berkeley: Oyez, 1976
4789. Time and trouble. Berkeley: Thorp Springs, 1976
4790. As if the street could die. Berkeley: Thorp Springs, 1977
4791. Leftovers. Berkeley: Ground Under, 1978

VINZ, Mark
4792. Letters to the poetry editor. Santa Barbara: Capra, 1975
4793. Red River blues. Texas City, TX: Poetry Texas, 1977
4794. Deep water Dakota. La Crosse, WI: Juniper. 1980
4795. Climbing the stairs. Peoria, IL: Spoon River, 1983
4796. The weird kid. St. Paul: New Rivers, 1983

VIOLI, Paul
4797. Automatic transmission. New York: Kulchur Foundation, 1973
4798. In Baltic circles. New York: Kulchur Foundation, 1973
4799. Waterworks. West Branch, IA: Toothpaste, 1973
4800. Harmatum. New York: Sun, 1977
4801. Splurge. New York: Sun, 1981

VIORST, Judith
4802. A visit from St. Nicholas (to a liberated household). New York: Simon and Schuster, 1976

VLIET, R. G.
4803. Water and stone. New York: Random House, 1980

VOELCKER, Hunce
4804. Within the rose. San Francisco: Panjandrum, 1976

VOIGT, Ellen Bryant
4805. Claiming kin. Middletown, CT: Wesleyan University Press, 1976
4806. The forces of plenty. New York: Norton, 1983

WADE, John Stevens
4807. Well water and daisies. La Crosse, WI: Northeast/ Jupiter, 1974
4808. Each to his own ground. La Crosse, WI: Juniper, 1976
4809. Some of my best friends are trees. West Lafayette, IN: Sparrow, 1977
4810. Up north. La Crosse, WI: Juniper, 1980

WAGONER, David
4811. Sleeping in the woods. Bloomington: Indiana University Press, 1974
4812. A guide to Dungeness Spit. Port Townsend, WA: Gray-wolf, 1975

4813.   Collected poems, 1956-1976. Bloomington: Indiana
        University Press, 1976
4814.   Travelling light. Port Townsend, WA: Graywolf, 1976
4815.   Whole hog. Boston: Little, Brown, 1976
4816.   Who shall be the sun? Bloomington: Indiana University
        Press, 1978
4817.   In broken country. Boston: Little, Brown, 1979
4818.   Landfall. Boston: Little, Brown, 1981
4819.   First light. Boston: Little, Brown, 1983

WAKOSKI, Diane
4820.   Dancing on the grave of a son of a bitch. Los Angeles:
        Black Sparrow, 1973
4821.   The owl and the snake. Mt. Horeb, WI: Perishable,
        1973
4822.   Sometimes a poet will hijack the moon. Providence:
        Burning Deck, 1973
4823.   Winter sequences. Los Angeles: Black Sparrow, 1973
4824.   Abalone. Los Angeles: Black Sparrow, 1974
4825.   Looking for the King of Spain. Los Angeles: Black
        Sparrow, 1974
4826.   Trilogy: Coins & coffins; Discrepancies and apparitions;
        The George Washington poems. Garden City, NY:
        Doubleday, 1974
4827.   The wandering tattler. Mt. Horeb, WI: Perishable,
        1974
4828.   The fable of the lion and the scorpion. Milwaukee:
        Pentagram, 1975
4829.   A portfolio. Providence: Burning Deck, 1975
4830.   Virtuoso literature for two and four hands. Garden
        City, NY: Doubleday, 1975
4831.   G. Washington's camp cups. Madison, WI: Red Ozier,
        1976
4832.   The last poem. Santa Barbara: Black Sparrow, 1976
4833.   Waiting for the King of Spain. Santa Barbara: Black
        Sparrow, 1976
4834.   Spending Christmas with the man from receiving at
        Sears. Santa Barbara: Black Sparrow, 1977
4835.   The man who shook hands. Garden City, NY: Double-
        day, 1978
4836.   Trophies. Santa Barbara: Black Sparrow, 1979
4837.   Making a sacher torte. Mount Horeb, WI: Perishable,
        1981
4838.   The lady who drove me to the airport. Worcester, MA:
        Metacom, 1982
4839.   The magician's feastletters. Santa Barbara: Sparrow,
        1982
4840.   Greed, parts 1-9, 11-13. Santa Barbara: Black Spar-
        row, 1983

WALDIE, D. J.
4841.   The fugitive vowels. Santa Cruz, CA: Greenhouse Re-
        view, 1976

WALDMAN, Anne
4842. Life notes. Indianapolis: Bobbs-Merrill, 1973
4843. Fast speaking woman. Detroit: Red Hanrahan, 1974
4844. Fast speaking woman and other chants. San Francisco:
    City Lights, 1975
4845. Sun the blond out. Berkeley: Arif, 1975
4846. Journals & dreams. New York: Stonehill, 1976
4847. Shaman. Boston: Munich, 1977
4848. To a young poet. Boston: White Raven, 1979
4849. Countries. West Branch, IA: Toothpaste, 1980
4850. First baby poems. New York: Hyacinth Girls, 1983
4851. Makeup on empty space. West Branch, IA: Toothpaste,
    1983

WALDRIDGE, Robert
4852. From a place which is no longer named. Moorhead, MN:
    Territorial, 1973

WALDROP, Keith
4853. Indifference point. Providence: Limestone, 1974
4854. A garden of effort. Providence: Burning Deck, 1975
4855. Human nature can be changed. Providence: Diana's
    Bimonthly, 1975
4856. Poem from memory. Philadelphia: Treacle, 1975
4857. Neither late nor sensitive. Paris: Orange Export, 1976
4858. Windfall losses. Woods Hole, MA: Pourboire, 1976
4859. The ruins of Providence. Providence: Copper Beech,
    1983
4860. The space of half an hour. Providence: Burning Deck,
    1983

WALDROP, Rosmarie
4861. Kind regards. Providence: Diana's Bimonthly, 1975
4862. Acquired pores. Paris: Orange Export, 1976
4863. The road is everywhere or stop this body. Columbia,
    MO: Open Places, 1978
4864. The ambition of ghosts. New York: Seven Woods, 1979
4865. Psyche and Eros. Peterborough, Eng.: Spectacular
    Diseases, 1980
4866. When they have senses. Providence: Burning Deck,
    1980

WALEY, Arthur
4867. The nine songs. San Francisco: City Lights, 1973

WALKER, Alice
4868. Revolutionary petunias. New York: Harcourt Brace
    Jovanovich, 1973
4869. Once. New York: Harcourt Brace Jovanovich, 1976
4870. Good night, Willie Lee, I'll see you in the morning.
    New York: Dial, 1979

WALKER, David
    4871. Moving out. Charlottesville: University Press of Virginia, 1976

WALKER, Jeanne Murray
    4872. Nailing up the home sweet home. Cleveland: Cleveland State University Poetry Center, 1980

WALKER, Jeff
    4873. Young dogs in the moonlight. Amherst, MA: Lynx House, 1976

WALKER, Margaret
    4874. October journey. Detroit: Broadside, 1973

WALLACE, Laura
    4875. The hour between dog and wolfe. Baltimore: New Poets Series, 1976

WALLACE, Ronald
    4876. Installing the bees. Madison, WI: Chowder, 1978
    4877. Plums, stones, kisses & hooks. Columbia: University of Missouri Press, 1981
    4878. Tunes for bears to dance to. Pittsburgh: University of Pittsburgh Press, 1983

WALMSLEY, Gordon
    4879. Kinesis. New Orleans: Bridgehead, 1983

WALSH, Chad
    4880. Hang me up my begging bowl. Chicago: Swallow, 1979

WALSH, Charlie
    4881. My summer vacation. Berkeley: As Is/ So & So, 1979

WALSH, Marnie
    4882. A taste of the knife. Boise, ID: Ahsahta, 1976

WALTHALL, Hugh
    4883. Ladidah. Ithaca, NY: Ithaca House, 1978

WANG, David Rafael
    4884. The intercourse. Greenfield Center, NY: Greenfield Review, 1975

WANIEK, Marilyn Nelson
    4885. For the body. Baton Rouge: Louisiana State University Press, 1978

WANN, David
    4886. Log rhythms. Berkeley: North Atlantic, 1983

WANTLING, William
   4887. San Quentin's strangers. Dunedin: Caveman, 1973
   4888. 10,000 rpm and diggin it, yeah! Cardiff: Second Aeon, 1973
   4889. 7 on style. San Francisco: Second Coming, 1975

WARD, Philip
   4890. The keymakers. New York: Oleander, 1978

WARING, Karen
   4891. Exposed to the elements. Salt Lake City: Litmus, 1976

WARN, Emily
   4892. The leaf path. Port Townsend, WA: Copper Canyon, 1982

WARREN, Peter Whitson
   4893. Al's ham-'n'-egger & body shop again. Fredonia, NY: Basilisk, 1974

WARREN, Robert Penn
   4894. Selected poems 1923-1975. New York: Random House, 1976
   4895. Now and then; poems 1976-1978. New York: Random House, 1978
   4896. Being here. New York: Random House, 1980
   4897. Rumor verified. New York: Random House, 1981
   4898. Chief Joseph of the Nez Percé: a poem. New York: Random House, 1983

WARSH, Lewis
   4899. Blue heaven. New York: Kulchur Foundation, 1978
   4900. Hives. New York: United Artists, 1979
   4901. Methods of birth control. College Park, MD: Sun & Moon, 1983

WATERMAN, Cary
   4902. The salamander migration and other poems. Pittsburgh: University of Pittsburgh Press, 1980

WATERS, Chocolate
   4903. To the man reporter from the Denver Post. New York: Eggplant, 1975
   4904. Take me like a photograph. New York: Eggplant, 1977

WATERS, Michael
   4905. Fish light. Ithaca, NY: Ithaca House, 1975
   4906. The scent of apples. Athens, OH: Croissant, 1977
   4907. Not just any death. Brockport, NY: BOA, 1979
   4908. The stories in the light. Birmingham, AL: Thunder City, 1983

WATSON, Robert
    4909. Selected poems. New York: Atheneum, 1974
    4910. Island of bones. Greensboro, NC: Unicorn, 1977
    4911. Night blooming cactus. New York: Atheneum, 1980

WATTEN, Barrett
    4912. Opera-works. Bolinas, CA: Big Sky, 1975
    4913. 1-10. Berkeley: This, 1980
    4914. Decay. Berkeley: This, 1981

WATTERLOND, Michael
    4915. Tropicana. Los Angeles: Black Sparrow, 1975

WEATHERLY, Tom
    4916. Thumbprint. Norwood, PA: Telegraph, 1973

WEAVER, Marvin
    4917. Hearts & gizzards. Laurinburg, NC: Curveship, 1976

WEBER, Elizabeth
    4918. Small mercies. Missoula, MT: Owl Creek, 1983

WEBER, Marc
    4919. 48 small poems. Pittsburgh: University of Pittsburgh
          Press, 1973

WECHTER, Vivienne Thaul
    4920. A view from the ark. New York: Barlenmir, 1976

WEIDEMANN, Anton
    4921. Seasons and seasoning. Milwaukee: Peacock, 1975

WEIGL, Bruce
    4922. Executioner. Tucson, AZ: Ironwood, 1976
    4923. Executioner on holiday. Tucson, AZ: Orchard, 1976
    4924. A sack full of old quarrels. Cleveland: Cleveland
          State University Poetry Center, 1976
    4925. A romance. Pittsburgh: University of Pittsburgh Press,
          1979

WEIGNER, Kathleen see WIEGNER, Kathleen
    4926. [No entry]

WEIL, James L.
    4927. To her hand. New Rochelle, NY: Elizabeth, 1973
    4928. Your father. New Rochelle, NY: Elizabeth, 1973
    4929. Perfectly yours. New Rochelle, NY: Elizabeth, 1974
    4930. Uses. New Rochelle, NY: Elizabeth, 1974
    4931. Portrait of the artist painting her son. West Lafayette,
          IN: Sparrow, 1976
    4932. Three. Knotting, Eng.: Sceptre, 1976
    4933. Aleksis. New Rochelle, NY: Elizabeth, 1977
    4934. [No entry]

4935. Quarrel with the rose. New Rochelle, NY: Elizabeth,
       1978
4936. Uses and other selected poems. West Lafayette, IN:
       Sparrow, 1981

WEINER, Bernard
4937. The Bellingham poems: Bellingham, WA: Goliards,
       1973

WEINER, Hannah
4938. The selected code poems. Providence: Diana's, 1978
4939. Little books/Indians. New York: Segue Foundation,
       1980
4940. Nijole's house. Elmwood, CT: Potes & Poets, 1981
4941. Code poems. Barrytown, NY: Station Hill, 1983

WEINGARTEN, Roger
4942. What are birds worth. Omaha: Abattoir, 1975
4943. The Vermont suicides. New York: Knopf, 1978
4944. Tables of the meridian. Des Moines, IA: Blue Build-
       ings, 1982

WEINSTEIN, Norman
4945. Nigredo. Barrytown, NY: Station Hill, 1982

WEISS, Dale
4946. After the war. Santa Fe, NM: Sunstone, 1975

WEISS, Mark
4947. Letter to Maxine. Deerfield, MA: Heron, 1974
4948. Intimate wilderness. New York: New Rivers, 1976

WEISS, Ruth
4949. Light. San Francisco: Peace & Pieces, 1976
4950. Desert journal. Boston: Good Gay Poets, 1977

WEISS, Theodore
4951. Fireweeds. New York: Macmillan, 1976
4952. Views & spectacles. New York: Macmillan, 1979
4953. Recoveries: a poem. New York: Macmillan, 1982

WELBURN, Ron
4954. Peripheries. Greenfield Center, NY: Greenfield Re-
       view, 1973
4955. Brownup, and other poems. Greenfield Center, NY:
       Greenfield Review, 1977
4956. Heartland. Detroit: Lotus, 1982

WELCH, Don
4957. Dead horse table. Lincoln, NE: Windflower, 1975
4958. The rarer game. Kearney, NE: Kearney State College
       Press, 1980

WELCH, James
4959.   Riding the Earthboy 40.   New York: Harper & Row,
        1975

WELCH, Lew
4960.   Ring of bone; collected poems 1950-1971.   Bolinas, CA:
        Grey Fox, 1973
4961.   Selected poems.   Bolinas, CA: Grey Fox, 1976

WELT, Bernard
4962.   Serenade.   Calais, VT: Z Press, 1979

WENDT, Viola
4963.   You keep waiting for geese.   Waukesha, WI: Carroll
        College, 1975
4964.   The wind is rising.   Waukesha, WI: Carroll College,
        1979

WEST, Don
4965.   O mountaineers!   A collection of poems.   Huntington,
        WV: Appalachian, 1974

WEST, John Foster
4966.   Wry wine.   Winston-Salem, NC: Blair, 1977

WEST, Kathleene
4967.   Landbound.   Port Townsend, WA: Copper Canyon, 1978
4968.   No warning.   Waldron Island, WA: Jawbone, 1978

WESTCOTT, Joan
4969.   Taffeta and lace.   St. Paul: Trunk, 1976

WESTERBACK, Arnold J.
4970.   In the oriental forms.   Detroit: Harlo, 1976

WESTLAKE, Diane
4971.   Gentle freedom, gentle courage.   Boulder, CO: Blue
        Mountain, 1980

WHALEN, Philip
4972.   The kindness of strangers, poems 1969-1974.   Bolinas,
        CA: Four Seasons, 1975
4973.   Decompressions.   Bolinas, CA: Grey Fox, 1977
4974.   Enough said.   San Francisco: Grey Fox, 1980
4975.   Heavy breathing.   San Francisco: Four Seasons, 1983

WHEELER, Billy Edd
4976.   Travis and other poems of the Swannanoa Valley.   Swan-
        nanoa, NC: Wild Goose, 1977

WHEELER, Sylvia
4977.   City limits.   Shawnee Mission, KS: BkMk, 1974

WHIMPLE, Myrtle
4978.   Myrtle Whimpler's sampler.   St. Paul: Trunk, 1976

WHITE, James L.
4979.   A crow's story of deer.   Santa Barbara: Capra, 1974
4980.   The Del Rio Hotel; new and selected poems.   Moorhead,
        MN: Territorial, 1975
4981.   The salt ecstasies.   Port Townsend, WA: Graywolf,
        1982

WHITE, Mimi
4982.   Into the darkness we go.   Sacramento, CA: Cougar,
        1982

WHITE, Paulette C.
4983.   Love poems to a Black junkie.   Detroit: Lotus, 1975

WHITEBIRD, Joanie
4984.   Naked.   Berkeley: Thorp Springs, 1976
4985.   Spare poems.   Texas City: Texas Portfolio, 1976
4986.   Birthmark.   San Francisco: Second Coming, 1977
4987.   24.   San Francisco: Second Coming, 1978

WHITED, David
4988.   Poemoptrics.   Bowling Green, OH: Newedi, 1975
4989.   Hollow fix.   Portland: Skydog, 1979

WHITEHEAD, James
4990.   Local men.   Urbana: University of Illinois Press, 1979

WHITENER, Barbara
4991.   Dreams are not enough.   Louisville, KY: Love Street,
        1977

WHITESIDE, Tom
4992.   An inland journey.   Little Rock, AR: August House,
        1983

WHITING, Nathan
4993.   Distancing.   Berkeley: New Rivers, 1974
4994.   Running.   New York: New Rivers, 1975
4995.   This slave dreads her work as if she were a lamb
        commanded to be a musician.   Brooklyn: Hanging
        Loose, 1980

WHITMAN, Ruth
4996.   Tamsen Donner.   Cambridge, MA: Alice James, 1977
4997.   Permanent address; new poems 1973-1980.   Cambridge,
        MA: Alice James, 1980

WHITMAN, William
4998.   The dancing galactic bear.   Trumansburg, NY: Crossing,
        1974

WHITNEY, John Denison
    4999. Tongues. New Rochelle, NY: Elizabeth, 1976

WHITTEMORE, Reed
    5000. The mother's breast and the father's house. Boston:
          Houghton Mifflin, 1974
    5001. The feel of rock: poems of three decades. Washington:
          Dryad, 1982

WICKLUND, Millie May
    5002. The Marisol poems. New York: New Rivers, 1975
    5003. Outlaw. Santa Barbara: Mudborn, 1979
    5004. The Marisol poems, II. East Lansing, MI: Ghost
          Dance, 1981
    5005. The parachute poems. East Lansing, MI: Ghost Dance,
          1983

WIEDER, Laurance
    5006. No harm done. Ann Arbor, MI: Ardis, 1975

WIEGNER, Kathleen
    5007. Country Western breakdown. Trumansburg, NY: Cross-
          ing, 1974
    5008. Freeway driving. Brooklyn: Hanging Loose, 1981

WIENERS, John
    5009. Hotels. New York: Angel Hair, 1974
    5010. Behind the state capitol; or Cincinnati Pike. Boston:
          Good Gay Poets, 1975

WIENERT, Christopher
    5011. The everywhere province. Baltimore: White Dot, 1975
    5012. The love unit. Baltimore: White Dot, 1976

WIER, Dara
    5013. Blood, hook & eye. Austin: University of Texas Press,
          1977
    5014. The 8-step grapevine. Pittsburgh: Carnegie-Mellon
          University Press, 1980

WILBUR, Richard
    5015. Seed leaves: homage to R. F. Boston: Godine, 1974
    5016. The mind-reader. New York: Harcourt Brace Jovano-
          vich, 1976

WILCOX, Patricia
    5017. A public and private hearth. Binghamton, NY: Belle-
          vue, 1978

WILD, Peter
    5018. Cochise. Garden City, NY: Doubleday, 1973
    5019. New and selected poems. New York: New Rivers, 1973
    5020. The cloning. Garden City, NY: Doubleday, 1974

5021.   Tumacacori. Berkeley: Two Windows, 1974
5022.   Chihuahua. Garden City, NY: Doubleday, 1976
5023.   Health. Berkeley: Two Windows, 1976
5024.   The island hunter. Tannersville, NY: Tideline, 1976
5025.   House fires. Santa Cruz, CA: Greenhouse Review,
        1977
5026.   Barn fires. Point Reyes, CA: Floating Island, 1978
5027.   Gold mines. Iola, WI: Wolfsong, 1978
5028.   Zuni Butte. Bisbee, AZ: San Pedro, 1978
5029.   The lost tribe. Iola, WI: Wolfsong, 1979
5030.   Jeanne D'Arc. Memphis, TN: St. Luke's, 1980
5031.   Rainbow. Des Moines, IA: Blue Buildings, 1980
5032.   Wilderness. St. Paul: New Rivers, 1980
5033.   Heretics. Madison, WI: Ghost Pony, 1981

WILK, David
5034.   For you/for sure. Berkeley: Tuumba, 1977
5035.   Tree taking root. St. Paul: Truck, 1977

WILL, Frederic
5036.   Guatemala. Binghamton, NY: Bellevue, 1973
5037.   Epics of America. Sunderland, MA: Panache, 1977
5038.   Our thousand-year-old bodies. Amherst: University of
        Massachusetts Press, 1980

WILLARD, Nancy
5039.   The carpenter of the sun. New York: Liveright, 1974
5040.   Household tales of moon and water. New York: Har-
        court Brace Jovanovich, 1983

WILLEMS, J. Rutherford
5041.   And she finishes. San Francisco: Isthmus, 1973
5042.   Opening the cube. Berkeley: Tree, 1975

WILLIAMS, C. K.
5043.   With ignorance. Boston: Houghton Mifflin, 1977
5044.   The lark, the thrush, the starling. Providence: Burn-
        ing Deck, 1983
5045.   Tar. New York: Random House, 1983

WILLIAMS, Emmett
5046.   Selected shorter poems. Barton, VT: Something Else,
        1973
5047.   A valentine for Noel. Barton, VT: Something Else,
        1973
5048.   Selected shorter poems, 1950-1970. New York: New
        Directions, 1975
5049.   The voyage. Stuttgart: H. Mayer, 1975

WILLIAMS, Eugene
5050.   Cream dreams for Eugene in Germany. West Glover,
        VT: Unpublished Editions, 1973

WILLIAMS, Jonathan
  5051. Imaginary postcards. London: Trigram, 1973
  5052. Five from up t' date. Kendal, Cumbria: Finial, 1974
  5053. Who is Little Enis? Highlands, NC: Jargon, 1974
  5054. Gists from a Presidential report on hardcornponeography. Highlands, NC: Jargon, 1975
  5055. Hassidic exclamation on Stevie Smith's poem, "Not Waving But Drowning." Storrs: University of Connecticut Library, 1975
  5056. How what? Laurinburg, NC: Mole, 1975
  5057. My Quaker-atheist friend. London: Bryden, 1975
  5058. gAyBC's. Champaign, IL: Finial, 1976
  5059. In the field at the solstice. Champaign, IL: Finial, 1976
  5060. A Blue Ridge weather report. Lexington, KY: Gnomon, 1977
  5061. An omen for Stevie Smith. New Haven, CT: Yale University Sterling Library, 1977
  5062. Untinears & antennae for Maurice Ravel. St. Paul: Truck, 1977
  5063. A hairy coat near Yanwath Yat. Rocky Mount: North Carolina Wesleyan College, 1978
  5064. Elite/elate poems. Highlands, NC: Jargon, 1979
  5065. Shankum Naggum. Rocky Mount: North Carolina Wesleyan College Friends of the Library, 1979
  5066. Get hot or get out: a selection of poems, 1957-1981. Metuchen, NJ: Scarecrow, 1982

WILLIAMS, Miller
  5067. Halfway from Hoxie. New York: Dutton, 1973
  5068. Why God permits evil. Baton Rouge: Louisiana State University Press, 1977
  5069. Distractions. Baton Rouge: Louisiana State University Press, 1981
  5070. The boys on their bony mules. Baton Rouge: Louisiana State University Press, 1983

WILLIAMS, Paul
  5071. Des energi. New York: Elektra, 1973
  5072. You and me against the world. Boulder, CO: Blue Mountain, 1979

WILLIAMS, Sherley
  5073. The peacock poems. Middletown, CT: Wesleyan University Press, 1975
  5074. Some one sweet angel chile. New York: Morrow, 1982

WILLIAMS, Tennessee
  5075. Androgyne, mon amour. New York: New Directions, 1977

WILLIAMS, Willie J.
5076. A flower blooming in concrete. Detroit: Lotus, 1977

WILLIAMSON, Alan
5077. Presence. New York: Knopf, 1983

WILLIS, Leydel Johnson
5078. A black snowball. Detroit: Harlo, 1977

WILLS, Jesse
5079. Selected poems. Nashville: Vanderbilt University
       Press, 1975

WILNER, Eleanor
5080. Maya. Amherst: University of Massachusetts Press,
       1979

WILSON, Emily Herring
5081. Balancing on stones. Winston-Salem, NC: Jackpine,
       1975
5082. Arise up and call her blessed. Emory, VA: Iron
       Mountain, 1982

WILSON, Keith
5083. Thantog. Dennis, MA: Salt-Works, 1977
5084. Desert cenote. Fort Kent, ME: Great Raven, 1978
5085. Shaman deer. Dennis, MA: Salt-Works, 1978
5086. Streets of San Miguel. Tucson, AZ: Maguey, 1978
5087. While dancing feet shatter the earth. Logan: Utah
       State University Press, 1978
5088. Stone roses. Logan: Utah State University Press, 1983

WILSON, Kirk
5089. The early word. Providence: Burning Deck, 1973

WILSON, Robley Jr.
5090. Returning to the body. La Crosse, WI: Juniper, 1977

WILSON, Sandra
5091. Inventing the cats. Shawnee Mission, KS: BkMk, 1973

WINANS, A. D.
5092. Straws of sanity. Berkeley: Thorp Springs, 1975
5093. Tales of crazy John: or, beating Brautigan at his own
       game. San Francisco: Second Coming, 1975
5094. All the graffiti on all the bathroom walls of the world
       can't hide these scars. San Francisco: Fallen Angel,
       1977
5095. North Beach poems. San Francisco: Second Coming,
       1977
5096. Org 1. Millbrae, CA: Poor Souls/Scaramouche, 1977
5097. The further adventures of Crazy John. San Francisco:
       Second Coming, 1979

WINANT, Fran
    5098. Dyke jacket. New York: Violet, 1976

WINCH, Terence
    5099. Luncheonette jealousy. Washington: Washington Writers', 1975

WINES, Vietta B.
    5100. Wines & roses. Bigfork, MN: Northwoods, 1974

WINNER, Robert
    5101. Green in the body. Pittsburgh: Slow Loris, 1979
    5102. Origins. Pittsburgh: Slow Loris, 1982
    5103. Flogging the Czar. New York: Sheep Meadow, 1983

WINSLOW, Pete
    5104. A daisy in the memory of a shark. San Francisco: City Lights, 1973

WISENFARTH, Joseph
    5105. Plane words. Madison, WI: Halfpenny, 1975

WITHERUP, William
    5106. Bixby Creek poems and Four from Kentucky. Mount Carroll, IL: Uzzano, 1977

WITT, Harold
    5107. Now, swim. Ashland, OH: Ashland Poetry, 1974
    5108. Surprised by others at Fort Cronkhite. West Lafayette, IN: Stefanile, 1975
    5109. Winesburg by the sea. Berkeley: Thorp Springs, 1979
    5110. The snow prince. Kensington, CA: Blue Unicorn, 1982
    5111. The light at Newport. Norristown, PA: Black Willow, 1983

WITTE, John
    5112. Loving the days. Middletown, CT: Wesleyan University Press, 1978

WITTENBERG, Rudolph M.
    5113. A threat to Genesis, and other poems. Georgetown, CA: Dragon's Teeth, 1976

WITTLINGER, Ellen
    5114. Breakers. New York: Sheep Meadow, 1979

WOESSNER, Warren
    5115. Landing. Ithaca, NY: Ithaca House, 1974
    5116. Lost highway. Texas City, TX: Poetry Texas, 1977
    5117. No hiding place. Peoria, IL: Spoon River, 1979

WOIWODE, Larry
    5118. Even tide. New York: Farrar, Straus & Giroux, 1977

WOJAHN, David
5119. Icehouse lights. New Haven, CT: Yale University
       Press, 1982

WOLFE, Marianne
5120. The berrypicker. Denver: Copper Canyon, 1973
5121. The poem you asked for. Iowa City: Spirit That
       Moves Us, 1977

WOOD, Nancy
5122. Many winters. Garden City, NY: Doubleday, 1975
5123. War cry on a prayer feather. Garden City, NY:
       Doubleday, 1979

WOOD, Renate
5124. Points of entry. Golden, CO: Riverstone, 1981

WOODS, John
5125. Alcohol. Grand Rapids, MI: Pilot, 1973
5126. A bone flicker. La Crosse, WI: Juniper, 1973
5127. Striking the earth. Bloomington: Indiana University
       Press, 1976
5128. Thirty years on the force. La Crosse, WI: Juniper,
       1977
5129. The valley of minor animals. Port Townsend, WA:
       Dragon Gate, 1982

WORLEY, Stella
5130. In dressing for the part. Broderick, CA: Hearthstone,
       1976

WORMSER, Baron
5131. The white words. Boston: Houghton Mifflin, 1983

WORSHAM, Fabian
5132. The green kangaroo. Tallahassee, FL: Anhinga, 1978

WORTHAM, Jim
5133. Love touching love. Louisville, KY: Love Street, 1974
5134. Loving you. Louisville, KY: Love Street Books, 1975
5135. Searching for someone. Louisville, KY: Love Street,
       1976
5136. Thinking of you. Louisville, KY: Love Street, 1977
5137. Be gentle with your goodbye. Louisville, KY: Love
       Street, 1978

WRIGHT, C. D.
5138. Alla breve loving. Seattle: Mill Mountain, 1976
5139. Room rented by a single woman. Fayetteville, AR:
       Lost Roads, 1977
5140. Terrorism. Fayetteville, AR: Lost Roads, 1979
5141. Translations of the Gospel back into tongues. Albany:
       State University of New York Press, 1982

WRIGHT, Carolyne
  5142. Stealing the children. Boise, ID: Ahsahta, 1978
  5143. Returning what we owed. Missoula, MT: Owl Creek, 1980
  5144. Premonitions of an uneasy guest. Abilene, TX: Hardin-Simmons University Press, 1983

WRIGHT, Charles
  5145. Hard freight. Middletown, CT: Wesleyan University Press, 1973
  5146. Bloodlines. Middletown, CT: Wesleyan University Press, 1975
  5147. China trace. Middletown, CT: Wesleyan University Press, 1977
  5148. Colophons. Iowa City: Windhover, 1977
  5149. Wright: a profile. Iowa City: Grilled Flowers, 1979
  5150. Dead color. Salem, OR: Charles Seluzicki, 1980
  5151. The Southern Cross. New York: Random House, 1981
  5152. Country music: selected early poems. Middletown, CT: Wesleyan University Press, 1982

WRIGHT, Franz
  5153. The earth without you. Cleveland: Cleveland State University Poetry Center, 1980
  5154. The one whose eyes open when you close your eyes. Roslindale, MA: Pym-Randall, 1982

WRIGHT, James
  5155. Two citizens. New York: Farrar, Straus & Giroux, 1973
  5156. Fresh wind in Venice. Pittsburgh: Slow Loris, 1976
  5157. Moments of the Italian summer. Washington: Dryad, 1976
  5158. Old booksellers and other poems. Melbourne: Cotswold, 1976
  5159. To a blossoming pear tree. New York: Farrar, Straus & Giroux, 1977
  5160. The temple in Nimes. Worcester, MA: Metacom, 1982
  5161. This journey. New York: Random House, 1982

WRIGHT, Jay
  5162. Dimensions of history. Santa Cruz, CA: Kayak, 1976
  5163. Soothsayers and omens. New York: Seven Woods, 1976
  5164. The double inventions of Komo. Austin: University of Texas Press, 1980

WRIGHT, John W.
  5165. Poems and woodcuts. Omaha: Abattoir, 1976

WRIGHT, Rebecca
  5166. Ciao Manhattan. New York: Telephone, 1977

WYLIE, Andrew
5167. Gold. Norwood, PA: Telegraph, 1973
5168. Yellow flowers. New York: Unmuzzled Ox, 1975

YAMADA, Mitsuye
5169. Camp notes and other poems. San Lorenzo, CA:
       Shameless Hussy, 1976

YATES, Peter
5170. The garden prospect: selected poems. Highlands, NC:
       Jargon Society, 1980

YAU, John
5171. Crossing Canal Street. Binghamton, NY: Bellevue,
       1976
5172. The reading of an ever changing tale. Lansing, NY:
       Nobodaddy, 1977
5173. Sometimes. New York: Sheep Meadow, 1979
5174. Broken off by the music. Providence: Burning Deck,
       1982
5175. Corpse and mirror. New York: Holt, Rinehart, and
       Winston, 1983

YOUNG, Al
5176. Some recent fiction. San Francisco: San Francisco
       Book Co., 1974
5177. Geography of the near past. New York: Holt, Rinehart,
       and Winston, 1976
5178. The blues don't change: new and selected poems. Baton
       Rouge: Louisiana State University Press, 1982

YOUNG, David
5179. Boxcars. New York: Ecco, 1973
5180. Work lights. Cleveland: Cleveland State University
       Poetry Center, 1978
5181. The names of a hare in English. Pittsburgh: University
       of Pittsburgh Press, 1979

YOUNG, Gary
5182. Hands. Los Angeles: Jazz, 1982

YOUNG, Ian
5183. Double exposure. Trumansburg, NY: Crossing, 1974

YOUNG, Jim
5184. Take it with you. Crete, NE: Best Cellar, 1973

YOUNG, Jordan R.
5185. A night in the Hard Rock Cafe. Anaheim, CA: Moon-
       stone, 1980
5186. Soft light falling quickly. Anaheim, CA: Moonstone,
       1983

YOUNG, Karl
  5187. Cried and measured. Berkeley: Tree, 1977

YOUNG, Tommy Scott
  5188. Black blues and shiny songs. Charlotte, NC: Red
        Clay, 1977

YOUNG, Virginia Brady
  5189. Circle of thaw. New York: Barlenmir, 1976

YOUNG BEAR, Ray A.
  5190. Waiting to be fed. Port Townsend, WA: Graywolf,
        1975
  5191. Winter of the salamander: the keeper of importance.
        New York: Harper & Row, 1980

ZAHNISER, Ed
  5192. The ultimate double play: Washington: Some of Us,
        1974

ZALLER, Robert
  5193. Wind songs. Birmingham, AL: Ragnarok, n.d.
  5194. Lives of the poet. New York: Barlenmir, 1974

ZAMORA, Sheila
  5195. Leaf's boundary. Fort Collins, CO: L'Epervier, 1980

ZANDER, William
  5196. Distances. San Luis Obispo, CA: Solo, 1979

ZATURENSKA, Marya
  5197. The hidden waterfall. New York: Vanguard, 1974

ZAVATSKY, Bill
  5198. Theories of rain and other poems. Albuquerque, NM:
        Sun, 1975

ZAVRIAN, Suzanne Ostro
  5199. Demolition zone. New York: New Rivers, 1975
  5200. The dream of the whale. West Branch, IA: Toothpaste,
        1982

ZAWADIWSKY, Christine
  5201. Kissing the murderer. Chicago: Ommation, 1979

ZEIDNER, Lisa
  5202. Talking cure: poems. Lubbock, TX: Texas Tech,
        1982

ZELEVANSKY, Paul
  5203. The book of takes. New York: Zartscarp, 1976

ZIEGLER, Alan
  5204. Planning escape: Brooklyn: Release, 1973

ZIMMER, Paul
  5205. The Zimmer poems. Washington: Dryad, 1976
  5206. With Wanda; town and country poems. Washington:
       Dryad, 1979
  5207. The ancient wars. Pittsburgh: Slow Loris, 1981
  5208. Earthbound Zimmer. Milton, MA: Chowder, 1983
  5209. Family reunion: selected and new poems. Pittsburgh:
       University of Pittsburgh Press, 1983
  5210. With Wanda: town and country poems. Milton, MA:
       Chowder, 1983

ZIMMERMAN, Toni Ortner
  5211. Woman in search of herself: Pittsburgh: Know, Inc.,
       1973
  5212. Entering another country. Fredonia, NY: Basilisk,
       1976
  5213. Never stop dancing. Greenfield Center, NY: Greenfield
       Review, 1976
  5214. Stones. Alexandria, VA: Huffman, 1976

ZIMROTH, Evan
  5215. Giselle considers her future. Columbus: Ohio State
       University Press, 1978

ZINNES, Harriet
  5216. I wanted to see something flying. New York: Folder,
       1976
  5217. Entropisms. Arlington, VA: Gallimaufry, 1978
  5218. Book of ten. Binghamton, NY: Bellevue, 1979

ZMEZQUITA, Ricardo M. see AMEZQUITA, Richard M.
  5219. [No entry]

ZOLYNAS, Al
  5220. The new physics. Middletown, CT: Wesleyan Univer-
       sity Press, 1979

ZU-BOLTON, Ahmos
  5221. A niggered amen. San Luis Obispo, CA: Solo, 1975

ZUCKROW, Edward
  5222. Slowly, out of stones. New York: Smith, 1980

ZUKOFSKY, Louis
  5223. "A" 22 & 23. New York: Grossman, 1975

ZWEIG, Martha
  5224. Powers. Montpelier, VT: Vermont Council on the
       Arts, 1976

"A" 22 & 23   5223
ABC   4300
A cappella   148
a. k. a.   3649
Aba   986
Abalone   4824
The abandoned music room
  3720
Able was I ere I saw Elba;
  selected poems 1954-1974
  2127
Above the treeline   1590
Abracadabra   49
Absence of unicorns, presence
  of lions   3336
Abulafia's circles   4021
Abyss   258
The academy of goodbye   3683
Accidental postures   2118
Accidental weather   4114
Accompanied   4149
Acquired pores   4862
Across the loud stream   4254
Across water   4328
The act proves untenable   3805
Acts   3522
Adam's dream   591
Adapt the living   879
Addenda   4716
Adirondacks   2595
Adlai Stevenson   2624
Admit impediment   3759
Admonitions   4441
Adorning the buckhorn helmet
  641
Adult bookstore   4248
Adulterers anonymous   2875
Advice to a vampire at puberty
  3024
Aegis   40
Aegis; selected poems 1970-1980
  920

The aerial tide coming in   2806
Aerial view of Louisiana   3118
The aerialist's fall   1858
Aesthetics   3512
The affinities of Orpheus   2166
Afghanistan   3316
Africa, Paris, Greece   633
Africa to me   1901
African in America   344
African journals   3752
African violet: poems for a
  black woman   2473
Afrikan revolution   252
After a cremation   2951
After drought   4138
After h(ours)   2174
After Lucretius   3940
After one   4352
After our war   232
After the drought   236
After the hunt   4105
After the ifaluk   4032
After the killing   3817
After the rain   2887
After the rhymer's guild   2488
After the war   4946
After the war (a long novel with
  few words)   167
After touch   807
The afterlife   2754
Afterlight   2201
An afternoon of pocket billiards
  4664
Afterwards   1002
Against a garden wall   2866
Against nature: wildness poems
  2943
Against that time   4171
Against the silences   435
The Agamenticus poems   2365
The age of gold   4698
Agua Negra   3959

Ain't no melody like the tune 1004
Air 4766
The airplane burial ground 976
Akiba's children 1946
Al la poems 326
Alba genesis 355
Alba nemesis: the China poems 356
The alchemist to Mercury 2433
Alcohol 5125
Aleksis 4933
Alice ordered me to be made 3450
Alive and taking names, and other poems 2237
All beautiful things 1433
All beautyfull & foolish souls 1312
All my mirrors lie 4030
All pieces of a legacy 1366
All roads at once 922
All that autumn 4301
All that is left 3443
All that, so simple 3360
All the bar room poetry in this world can't mend this heart of mine, dear 3935
All the days are 217
All the graffiti on all the bathroom walls of the world can't hide these scars 5094
All the night wings 1304
All this every day 2600
All wet 1076
Alla breve loving 5138
The alleys of Eden 669
Alliance, Illinois 1400
Almazora 42 1529
Almost a rainbow 163
Almost happy 4634
Alone 1648
Along the river, and other poems 4761
Along this water 2066
An alphabet 3995
Alphabet for the lost years 4141
Alphabet poems 3656
The alphabet work 1325
Alphabetical order 3032
Al's ham-'n'-egger & body shop again 4893

Alsace-Lorraine 2188
Altamira 1715
Altar pieces 4025
Alvin Turner as farmer 2494
Amaranth 4256
The ambition of ghosts (Feldman) 1441
The ambition of ghosts (Waldrop) 4864
The American book of the dead 269
American dusk 771
The American fantasies: collected poems, 1945-1981 4156
An American gallery 3885
American gasoline dreams 3348
American genesis 4689
American handbook 4510
American journal 1971
American light 3691
American primitive 3494
American still lifes 4722
American tantrums 606
Americruiser 3395
Ameriki 1267
The Amerindian coastline poem 2186
Among the stones 4258
AM/TRAK 254
Amtrak trek 4699
The anarchist heart 4707
Anarchistic murmurs from a high mountain valley 327
Ancestors to come 1275
Anchors of light 1569
The ancient rain 2396
The ancient wars 5207
& collected conjunctions 549
& everybody is a children 4321
And finding no mouse there 4353
And live apart 3626
And morning 1501
And she finishes 5041
And the dew lay all night upon my branch 1795
And the master said 778
Andean town circa 1980 528
Androgyne, mon amour 5075
Andy 1687
Angel 2801
Angel at the gate 2803
Angel fire 3465
The angelic orders 2220

Angle of ascent; new and select-
ed poems 1969
Angle of geese and other poems
    3274
The angled road 708
Angry candy 3616
Anima 2862
Animae 1882
Animal 4315
The animal in the bush 2231
The animal kingdom 1421
Animal snackers 2762
Animals 3132
The animals 1800
Animals that stand in dreams
    1314
Ann 4781
Anna's song 3471
The anonymous lover 2837
Another kind of autumn 1303
Another light 686
Another place 32
Another poet in New York 870
A'nque 108
Anse on Island Creek and other
    poems 4496
Antarctic traveller 3753
Antares 3928
Antechamber & other poems
    2939
Antedeluvian dream songs 704
Antelope are running 1751
Anthem for rusty saw and blue
    sky 3486
Anthracite country 3588
Anti-history 663
The Antioch suite-jazz 1310
Ants 359
Any body's song 2626
Any day of your life 2465
Any minute 453
Anxiety and ashes 2292
The anxious ground 4636
Anything, anything 2962
Anything on its side 1283
Apollo helmet 4210
An apology for loving the old
    hymns 4373
Appalachia 1206
Appalachian winter 4281
Apparitions of a black pauper's
    suit: 13 eulogies 3076
The appassionata poems 782

Approached by fur 2997
The April wars 2347
The arable mind 1798
Arachnids and other friends
    1045
The Ararat papers 248
The arc from now 1815
The arcanes of Le Comte de St.
    Germain 2109
Archipelago 2248
Arctic summer 4124
Are you a kid? 3747
Are you tough enough for the
    eighties? 413
Areas 3220
The argot merchant disaster:
    poems new and selected 4492
Ariana Olisvos: her last works
    and days 1243
Arioso 37
Arise up and call her blessed
    5082
Arkansas bench stone 4480
Armed love 2721
Arnulfsaga 1307
Around you, your house and A
    catechism 4471
Arriving at the nadir 2320
Arriving on Paumanok 2564
Arriving on the playing fields
    of paradise 3087
The art of love 2516
The art/the veil 3164
Articulation in blue 3219
Artist, come home 4464
As I go 4257
As I magic 3997
As if anything could grow back
    perfect 3546
As if it will matter 75
As if the street could die 4790
As is (Albert) 58
As is (Benson) 339
As one 2264
As we know 197
Ascending red cedar moon 3409
The ash 2054
Ash in the candle's wick 2552
Ashes; poems new and old 2748
Asian figures 3183
Asleep in another country 3344
Asparagus, asparagus 2470
Aspects of a Southern story 4117

Aspects of Eve   3603
Aspects of the vertical   2729
Assuming the position   1190
Astralphonic voices   1049
Asylums   371a
Asymmetries 1-260   3008
At a loss   3099
At a time; a dance for voices
    2413
At fifty   3527
At Malibu   794
At night the salmon move   725
At Park and East Division
    2775
At rest in the Midwest   2998
At sixes   2164
At the barre   810
At the edge of the body   2340
At the house of the tin man
    2965
Atlantic flyway   1594
Atlantic wall   858
An attic of ideals   4621
Attitude: uncollected poems of
    the seventies   2614
The attraction of heavenly bod-
    ies   2100
Auctions   4253
Auden (1907-1973)   4247
Audible dawn   2857
August fires and other poems
    1054
Aur sea   2102
Aura   717
Aurora; 10 poems   1488
Auspices   917
Austerities   4310
The Austin tower   4098
Autobiography, and other poems
    4702
Autograph   304
Automatic transmission   4797
Aux morts   1375
Available light   486
The avenue bearing the initial
    of Christ into the new world
    2477
Average nights   3382
Avis   1671
Awakening   4580
Away   963
Away from home   366
The awful rowing toward God
    4227

An awkward silence   1277
Awkward song   2546
Axe handles   4404
Axes 52   1362
Axis: parataxis   550

Bacchae sonnets   4193
The Bacchae sonnets 1-7   4197
Back into my body   2877
Back to black basics   1264
Backroads   1866
Backtalk   309
Backwards   962
Bad boats   2293
Badlands   934
The badminton at Great Barring-
    ton   321
Balancing on stones   5081
Ballads of a bench warmer   3709
Ballet of oscillations   2155
The Balthus poems   1153
Bandwagon   2547
Barbed wire   1925
The bard owl   3758
The bare wires   682
The bared and bended arm   240
Bark, a polemic   3156
Barn fires   5026
BART   4299
Baseball   795
Basement   4732
Bastard moons   1559
The bathers   4678
The battlefield where the moon
    says I love you   4481
Bay is the land   1082
Be gentle with your goodbye
    5137
Beach glass   1575
Bean Street   3322
The beared mother   1865
The beasts & the elders   4290
Beasts did leap   4382
Beautiful cages   4251
A beautiful woman moves with
    grace   3977
Beauty shop monologues   4528
Because the death of a rose   147
Beckonings   582
Becoming   4250
Becoming visible   2616
Becos   2512
The bees   2061

Before I go out on the road 667
Before sleep 487
Before the trees turn gray 165
Begin, distance 4113
Beginning with O 594
Beheading the children 845
Behind the state capitol; or Cin-
    cinnati Pike 5010
Being here 4896
A belfry of knees 4725
The bell clerk's tears keep
    flowing 3943
A bell or a hook 1514
The Bellingham poems 4937
Bells & clappers 95
Belly song 2503
The bend, the lip, the kid 1726
Beneath the smoke rings 1445
Beneath this calm exterior 4508
Beowulf to Beatles & beyond
    3706
Berkeley Street cannibals 4788
The berrypicker 5120
Beside herself; Pocahontas to
    Patty Hearst 1827
The best hour of the night 4326
A bestiary 3169
The bestowal 1962
Between high tides 62
Between lives 3384
Between Lunatic Ears 1158
Between our selves 2853
Between revolutions 1033
Between the morning and the
    evening star 2699
Between two rivers 1208
Beyond mars 483
Beyond the summerhouse 2225
Beyond the wall 3061
Bezerkley sun and rain dance
    poems 4130
The Bible of the beasts of the
    little field 4145
Bicycle consciousness 1005
The bicycle in the snowbank
    3789
Bidato: Ten Mile River poems
    419
Big nose 4351
The big parade 1884
Big winds, glass mornings,
    shadows cast by stars 3073
Biography 1807

Biography and a lament 4304
Bird as 1670
Birds of the West 568
Birdscapes, with seaside 4655
Birth sores/bands 1889
Birthcords 2301
Birthmark 4986
Biting Sun 2486
Bits of thirst 3088
Bits of thirst & other poems &
    translations 3089
Bittersweet (Thomas) 4764
Bittersweet (Tipton) 4694
Bixby Creek poems and Four
    from Kentucky 5106
Black blues and shiny songs 5188
Black cinema 2836
Black earth, blue sky 2687
The Black Hawk songs 491
Black hills 1406
Black leaves 3992
Black man abroad 1329
Black of the wind-vane hen 2314
A black snowball 5078
Black sun 866
The black unicorn 2855
Black woman sorrow 474
Blackbird sundown 1412
Blackdog in the headlights 4255
Blame it on the jet stream!
    1413
Blank like me 1482
Bleeding the radiator 3096
Blenheim Palace 3600
Blessed art thou 4341
Blessing 4675
The blessing of the fleet 584
The blessing of winter rain 3931
A blessing outside us 3313
The blind lion 82
Blood calendar 4705
Blood, hook & eye 5013
Blood Lord 4220
Blood mountain 1334
Bloodfire 749
Bloodlines 5146
Bloodwhispers/blacksongs 1188
The Bloomingdale papers 715
Blowing mouth: the jazz poems,
    1958-1970 546
Blue (Albert) 53
Blue (Clark) 791
The Blue and the Gray 3446

The blue belly of the world
  3253
A blue book 1598
Blue chicory 3417
Blue Dust, New Mexico 2794
Blue heaven 4899
Blue hooks in weather 627
The blue horse, and other night
  poems 1537
Blue is the hero: poems 1960-
  1975 364
The blue man 4143
Blue Monday 1508
Blue Mountain 233
The blue narrator 3514
Blue orchid numero uno 3745
Blue rags 3160
A Blue Ridge weather report
  5060
A blue shovel 2024
Blue springs 3472
Blue sunrise 93
A blue tongue 2751
Blue wine and other poems
  2151
A blue wing tilts at the edge of
  the sea; selected poems
  1964-1974 1849
Blue woman dancing in the nerve
  846
Blues & ballads 86
A blues book for blue black
  magical women 4088
The blues don't change: new
  and selected poems 5178
Blues of the Egyptian kings 563
Blues of the sky 3994
The board of directors 3325
Boardwalk 4447
The body & the body's guest
  2896
Body bee calling from the 21st
  century 72
Body India 2992
Body of work 3896
The body's symmetry 3761
Bohemian airs & other kefs
  126
Bolero 3162
The Bolinas book 4119
Bombs 4687
Bone china beliefs 3218
A bone flicker 5126

Bone love 1673
The bones of the Earth 250
Bonfire 1631
The book of death 3373
The book of folly 4225
The book of Joanna 2927
Book of life 3028
The book of madness 1478
Book of palaces: the gatekeepers
  4014
The book of Persephone 2428
The book of Rimbaud 6
The book of rose 2879
Book of stones, or, stone songs
  4234
The book of takes 5203
Book of ten 5218
The book of the body 417
Booking passage 1998
The Booth interstate 3801
Border crossings 3586
Born 3748
Born of a woman 2504
Both hands screaming 3644
Bottom falling out of the dream
  68
The bottom land 3119
A bowl of sorrow 324
The boy under the bed 1025
The boys on their bony mules
  5070
A box of sandalwood 2506
Boxcars 5179
BPQD 1095
Braided apart 4458
Braille 3648
The braless express 558
A branch of California redwood
  3464
Brant Point 2607
Brass furnace going out 1140
Brass furnace going out 1143
Brass knuckles 1248
Breakers 5114
Breaking open 4044
The breathers 3865
Breathing space 3131
Brevities 485
The bridge of change 2839
Brief but warm the rain 989
Brief lives 1613
Bright eyes talks crazy to Rem-
  brandt 1814

Bright Mississippi 1394
Bright orbits 2890
The brindle mule 2701
Bring in the plants 1129
Bringing back slavery 1899
Bringing home breakfast 1077
The bristle cone pine & other
poems 995
B*R*M*Tz*V*H 4022
Brockport's poems 2050
The broken blockhouse wall
3630
The broken boat 142
The broken bowl 1331
The broken face of summer:
poems 2139
The broken juke 3874
The broken lock 1778
Broken off by the music 5174
The broken pot 414
Broken treaties 876
Bronchial tangle, heart system
3670
Bronze age 3304
Brooming to paradise 928
Brooms; selected poems 4306
Brotherly love 2128
Brothers, I loved you all 718
Brown bag 3248
Brownup, and other poems 4955
Bucks County blues 3807
Buddha's kisses and other poems
3961
The buddhist car and other
characters 4152
Buddhist poems 3263
The buffalo in the Syracuse zoo
613
Buffalo marrow on black 2018
The buffalo shoot 2591
Building poems 495
Buncha crocs in surch of snac
1588
Burglaries and celebrations
789
Buried city 3332
Burn down the icons 4173
Burning in water, drowning in
flame: selected poems 1955-
1973 632
The burning mystery of Anna in
1951 2518
The burning of Bilskirnir 3385

Burning the empty nests 3535
Burning village 2393
Burnsite 830
The bus to Veracruz 4261
The busses 340
Busy being born 1667
By breathing in and out 1192
By dawn's early light at 120
miles per hour 172
By lingual wholes 994
By the well of living and seeing:
Poems 1918-1973 3887
By the wreckmaster's cottage
3827

Cafe/Charivari, Charlatan/Chrom
2328
Cafe isotope 370
A cage of creatures 4720
A caged bird in spring 999
Calendar 973
Caliban in blue, and other poems
2961
California frescoes 2359
A call in the midst of the crowd
923
The calling across forever 1879
Calling collect 1223
Calling me from sleep; new and
selected poems 1961-1973
894
Calling myself home 2131
Calling the dead 1907
Cambodian spring 2674
Camouflage 3352
Camp notes and other poems
5169
Camping out 4559
Camptown spaces 4274
Canadian gothic and other poems
896
Cancer in my left ball 1658
Cancer quiz 1446
The candleflame 2094
Candles in Babylon 2738
A cannon between my knees 84
The canters of Thomas Parkin-
son 3593
Cantillations 2103
Canto the last 2384
Cantos V & VI, chicken mishigas
4409

Cape Canaveral cape of storms and wild cane fields 706
Capricorn 2468
Capsule Cranium 4355
The captains that dogs aren't 3953
Captive of the vision of paradise 183
Carapace 2387
Carbon 14 1069
The carbon gang 2767
Cardinals/The cardinal 2036
The cards 4011
Carlota 3823
Carmela Bianca 1669
Carmina 1351
Carnal refreshment 683
Carnivorous saint; gay poems, 1941-1976 3440
The carpenter at the asylum 3277
The carpenter of the sun 5039
Cartography 1769
Cascades 4531
Case history 1202
Cassandra speaking 2130
Casting for the cutthroat & other poems 1367
Casting stones 755
The cat approaches 2469
Cat eyes and dead wood 507
Catalpa; poems 1968-1973 2249
Catawba; omens, prayers and songs 3769
Catechism of hearts 4597
The cat's meow 3326
Caught in the revolving door 4264
Caviare at the funeral 4325
Cedar light 2124
Cedarhome 4604
The celebrated running horse messenger 3697
Celebrations 996
Celebrations after the death of John Brennan 2442
Centennial portraits 2633
The center of attention 2126
Centers; chiefly concerning John Wayne and his horse and many incredibilities 3594

The central motion; poems 1968-1979 1118
Ceremony Latin 3135
A certain distance 1542
A certain hunger 1618
Certain minutes 2986
Certain women 2969
The chain saw dance 628
Chances are few 4677
A change in the weather 2902
Change of territory 1147
Changes 1210
The changes 2180
Changing appearance 3504
Changing-ever changing 1921
Changing faces 4280
The changing light at Sandover 3176
Changing the past 4666
Charisma 2612
Charle Kiot 3765
Charms 940
Charon's cosmology 4305
Chattanooga 3860
Cheap 4555
Cheap thrills 1194
Cheapthrills 2522
Cheat grass 4765
The cheer 3168
Chekov on the West Heath 2733
Cherries 4584
Cheyenne River wild track 2394
Chicago (Clark) 792
Chicago (Nelson) 3380
Chicken 2419
Chicken & in love 1711
Chicken beacon 3013
Chief Joseph of the Nez Percé: a poem 4898
Chiemaxions 3065
Chihuahua 5022
A childhood in Reno 1723
Childhood, Namhood, manhood 3707
Childhood poems 1604
The children (Heyen) 2055
The children (Ott) 3556
Child's game, on a journey and other poems 600
China poems 272
China trace 5147
The Chinese insomniacs; new poems 2261

The Chinese poems 1611
The Chinese quartet: poems 3429
A chisel in the dark 1330
The choice 1187
Chokecherry hunters and other poems 863
Chords & tunings 4527
Chosen place 4259
Chosen poems: old and new 2856
Christmas tree 493
Christs and other poems 1044
Chrome grass 2810
Chronicle 3354
Chrysalis 1093
Chunder Hara 3732
Chunk off and float 767
Ciao Manhattan 5166
Cicada 1841
Ciderman 551
Cimarron 96
The circa poems 3596
Circle of fire 1497
Circle of hearts 3455
Circle of thaw 5189
The circle of the spirit 164
Circles on the water; selected poems 3715
The circular gates 3583
Circumstances 4762
The Circus 4785
Circus black, circus white 2685
A circus of needs 1238
City 3501
A city 1677
City air 1663
City joys 133
City limits 4977
The city of the Olesha fruit 1217
The city parables 2056
Cities and other disasters 3819
Claiming an identity they taught me to despise 812
Claiming kin 4805
The clam theater 1270
Clarifications 3611
Clash 43
Classic ballroom dances 4308
Classic plays 2080
Clean asshole poems & smiling vegetable songs 3534

Clear & present danger to society 2829
Cleared for landing 1047
Clearing 398
Clearwater 1578
Clenched horizon 4416
Climb to the high country 2176
The climbers 1940
Climbing and diving, flying and swimming 696
Climbing down 1091
Climbing into the roots 4107
Climbing the stairs 4795
Climbing up to light 4478
The clock of moss 985
The cloning 5020
Close quarters 648
A closed book 451
Closing the moviehouse 1220
Cloud, invisible air 1291
Cloud train 67
The clouds 899
Clouds and red earth 1566
The clouds of that country 135
Clovin's head 1148
Clown birth 3834
The club fits either hand 3645
Coal 2854
The coal miners 247
A coast of trees 119
The coat without a seam; sixty poems 1930-1972 2582
Cobblestones 4267
Cochise 5018
Cockroach 2105
Code poems 4941
Cogollo 1378
Coils 1372
Cold frames 2906
Collapsing spaces 226
The collected books of Jack Spicer 4444
Collected earlier poems, 1940-1960 2736
Collected poems (Barnard) 266
The collected poems (Brown) 602
Collected poems (Cannon) 688
Collected poems (Denby) 1089
Collected poems (Douglas) 1180
Collected poems (Feibleman) 1436
Collected poems (Golffing) 1716
Collected poems (Goodman) 1720
Collected poems (Mayo) 3140

Collected poems (Oppen) 3517
The collected poems (Plath)
3734
Collected poems (Roethke) 3955
The collected poems (Rukeyser)
4047, 4049
The collected poems, 1956-1974
(Dorn) 1168
Collected poems, 1956-1976
(Wagoner) 4813
Collected poems, 1953-1977
(Sandeen) 4091
Collected poems 1940-1978
(Shapiro) 4249
The collected poems, 1945-1975
(Creeley) 971
Collected poems, 1930-1983
(Miles) 3214
Collected poems, 1930-1976
(Eberhart) 1257
Collected poems, 1930-1973
(Sarton) 4121
Collected poems, 1936-1976
(Francis) 1543
Collected poems, 1924-1974
(Beecher) 310
The collected poems of George
Oppen; 1929-1975 3518
The collected poems of Howard
Nemerov 3391
The collected poems of Theo-
dore Roethke 3956
The collected poems of Thomas
Merton 3181
The collected poems of Weldon
Kees 2410
Collectibles 1833
Collecting the animals 1419
The collector of cold weather
3799
Colophon of the rover 1254
Colophons 5148
Color 1300
Color photos of the atrocities
3725
Color poems 1536
Columbus Square journal 902
Combing the waves 3842
Come 187
Come in and get lost 1601
Come the sweet by and by 2722
Cometh with clouds 2901
Comforting the wilderness 4252

Coming alive 1727
Coming to terms 3213
Comings back 1701
Commercial break 1448
Common ground 4588
The common life 2981
The common wages 4354
Communications equipment 1326
The company of strangers 881
The compass flower 3187
The compleat melancholick 4721
Complete poems (Jarrell) 2278
The complete poems (Sexton)
4229
The complete poems, 1927-1979
(Bishop) 425
The complete poems of Charles
Reznikoff; vol. I, poems 1918-
1936 3888
The complete poems of Charles
Reznikoff; vol. II, poems
1937-1975 3889
Concentrations 1355
Concise dictionary of Lead River,
MO 1119
Conclusions from memory 210
The condom poems 1023
Confederate jasmine 3419
The conquistador dog texts 819
The conservation of strangeness
4003
Constant defender 4662
Contending to be the dream 1012
Contending with the dark 4190
The contraband poems 3726
Contrasts in keening: Ireland
2817
Controlling interests 374
The convections 2429
Conversations 2234
Conversations in the gallery
3598
Conversions 4393
The cool boyetz cycle 2106
Cool zebras of light 3669
Coot and other characters 3966
Coprolites 1696
Cora Fry 599
Core meander 1380
Cornfields 1398
Cornflakes 3044
Cornucopia 3622
Corona 149

Corpse and mirror   5175
The Corrie White auction at
  Brockport, May, 1974   2037
Cotton candy on a rainy day
  1660
The countess from Minneapolis
  1805
Counting the days   137
Countries   4849
The country between us   1511
The country changes   4038
Country crossings   4563
Country music: selected early
  poems   5152
The country of marriage   391
Country of resemblances   343
Country of survivors   1135
Country pleasures   1644
Country Western breakdown
  5007
Countrywoman/surgeon   4577
Coup   3365
Courses in lambents   4719
The courtesy   4242
Cowboy   8
The coyot: Inca texts   820
Coyote space   132
Coyote's daylight trip   83
Crazy arms   2786
Crazy compositions   3573
Crazy Da must sing, inclined
  to his weaker side   2303
Crazy face   2527
Crazy girl on the bus   330
Cream dreams for Eugene in
  Germany   5050
The creation frame   4684
Creature comforts   733
Creatures   3379
The creek   1099
Crib death   4482
Cried and measured   5187
The crime of luck   2194
Crimes   1834
The criminal mentality   2825
Croquet lover at the dinner table
  63
Crossing   3130
The crossing   4477
Crossing America   871
Crossing by ferry: poems new
  and selected   2364
Crossing Canal Street   5171

Crossing Cocytus   3080
Crossing the Phantom River
  3269
Crossing the same river   1692
Crossings   2093
The crossings   655
A crow's story of deer   4979
Cruelty   46
The cruise of the Pnyx   2430
The cry of Oliver Hardy   2000
Crystal   2881
Crystals   3952
C's songs   3581
CTA   2952
Cuiva sails   1133
Cumberland Station   4359
Cunts   4746
Cup of cold water   1530
Currently   2269
Curse of the oval Room   2692
Curses and blessings   4278
Curses & songs & poems   4037
Curses omens prayers   4624
Curtains for you   1484
Curve   1702
Curve in the road   1713
Custer lives in Humboldt County
  & other poems   1847
Cute, and other poems   1405
Cutting our losses   2558
Cutting the firebreak   1414

Dabble: poems, 1966-1980   1689
The daffodil farmer   3515
The daily news   1717
Daily rites   380
The daily round   2847
A daisy in the memory of a
  shark   5104
Dakota incantations   2262
Damage within the community
  3355
Dame   200
Dance script with electric baller-
  ina   1570
Dance sequence   4734
A dancer's step   1972
Dancing back strong the nation
  2445
The dancing galactic bear   4998
Dancing on the edges of knives
  3475

Dancing on the grave of a son of a bitch 4820
Dancing the slack wire 545
Dandelions have their own gold standard 3288
Dangerous body 4064
Dangerous music 1830
Dangers 2978
Dangling in the tournefortia 638
Dante 1232
Dare 3614
The dark and bloody ground 3291
Dark lands 1747
Dark leverage 652
A dark light 3572
The dark playground 4446
Dark smoke 42
Dark world 714
Darkness 2046
Darkness at each elbow 1316
The darkness in my pockets 675
Darkness of snow 390
Darkwood 99
Das illustrite Mississippithal revisped 821
A daughter's geography 4237
Dawn chorus 3884
Day by day 2869
A day in the life 693
A day in the life of Sobi-Shi 3984
A day in the world 2593
Day to day 1007
The daybook of Western heroes 3597
Daylight saving 2099
The daynight lamp 3308
Days and nights 2519
Days off 3383
A day's work 3010
The dead and the living 3488
Dead color 5150
Dead horse table 4957
Dead letter 1880
Dead of winter 3011
Dead on arrival 1745
Dead reckoning (Ballard) 246
Dead reckoning (Overton) 3559
Dead's good company 4272
Dear anyone 2409
Dear blood 3370
Dear sky 1782

The death collection 106
Death mother and other poems 3299
The death notebooks 4226
The death of an elder Klallam 3410
Death perception: new poems and a masque 3307
Death's legacy 998
Debridement 1918
A decade of dreams 2800
Decay 4914
December 31, 1979 2063
Deck 4078
Decompressions 4973
Deep water Dakota 4794
The deer on the freeway 4385
The defense of the Sugar Islands 729
The defenestration of Prague 2193
Defying gravity 158
The Del Rio Hotel; new and selected poems 4980
Delayed, not postponed 1065
Delivery 314
Demolition zone 5199
Denizens 3666
Dented fenders 439
Departure 1610
Departure in yellow 4692
Departures 2366
Des energi 5071
Descending figure 1685
The descent 2057
Desemboque 1740
Desert cenote 5084
The desert house 4711
Desert journal 4950
The design on the oriole 4466
Designing women 1826
Desire 1545
Desperate affections 772
Desperate measures 4490
A desperate thing: marriage is a desperate thing 1427
Destroy all monsters 3393
Desultory days 968
Devils live so near 2376
Devils' wine 4135
Dial artemis 1516
Dialogue with a dead man 3224
The dialogues of Lewis and Clark 2700

Diapers on the snow 834
Diary from Baja 529
A diatribe to Dr. Steele 1809
Did you know they're beheading
  Bill Johnson today? 2414
Die Winterreise 98
Diet Pepsi & nacho cheese 3444
The difference between night and
  day 3811
Different arrangements 773
Different fleshes 1703
Different ways to pray 3458
The difficulty 4099
Digging in, burrowing out 1186
Digging out the roots 3411
The Dillinger poems 3290
Dimensions of history 5162
Dinner 650 Warburton Avenue
  Yonkers 3661
Dinner with Uncle Jozef 3719
Dinners and nightmares 1138
Dinosaurs 4602
Director of alienation 1450
The dirty old man's guide to
  young girls 2555
Disappearances 853
Disappearing work 1301
Dis/courses 87
The discovery of music 306
Disfrutes 375
Disguises 4201
Dispatch DP 163, and other
  poems 4092
Dispatches from the fields 2014
Dissolves 608
The distance 3000
Distances 5196
Distancing 4993
Distant thunder 3772
Distant topologies, poems, 1974-
  1976 351
Distractions 5069
Diversification 113
Diversion Road 2605
Divine comedies 3172
Diving into the wreck 3897
Djackson 2104
Do you fear no one 1242
Do you think we could have made
  it? and other love poems for
  the separated and divorced
  644
Doctor Miriam 3511

Doctor Vertigo 4715
The doctrine of selective depra-
  vity 1016
Document for an anonymous In-
  dian 2009
Dodeka 4629
The dodo bird 1556
Dog light 822
Dog moon 2798
The dog that was barking yester-
  day 1693
Dog's breakfast 3855
The dollmaker's ghost 2755
Domestic scenes 843
Don't dress your cat in an apron
  4436
A door to the forest 4606
Door to the sun 3243
Dot town 3312
Double derivation, association,
  and cliche from the Great
  Tournament Roll of Westmin-
  ster 3128
The double dream of spring 194
Double exposure 5183
The double inventions of Komo
  5164
The double pipes of Pan 4550
The double witness: poems
  1970-1976 313
Dowry 311
A dozen for Leah 1908
A dozen oranges 4418
Dozens 4350
Dracula 4676
The Dracula poems 2922
Dragons of mist and torrent
  4129
Drastic measures 3431
Dream 2226
Dream farmer 508
Dream flights 4363
Dream in Pienza and other
  poems: selected poems
  1963-1977 3547
The dream of a common lan-
  guage: poems 1974-1977
  3901
A dream of feet 213
A dream of springtime; poems
  1970-1978 3553
Dream of the traveler 2908
The dream of the whale 5200

Dream tree 847
Dreaming in color 2720
Dreamline express 3258
Dreams 4157
Dreams and memories (Bloom) 452
Dreams & memories (Tessler) 4670
Dreams are not enough 4991
Dream's navel 3637
Dreams of a native son 281
The dreams of exiles 3784
The dreams of Mercurius 1859
Dreams of state 2911
Dreams of straw 3773
A drift of swine 3477
Drinking beer at 22 below 3936
Driving and drinking 2697
Driving at night 2390
Driving like the sun 4665
Driving to New Mexico 2984
Droles de journal 3810
The drowned man to the fish 3675
Drowning from the inside out 2334
Drugs and all that 3737
The drum and the melody 4571
Drunk on a Greyhound 1120
Drunks 4357
Dry leaves 1988
Dry season 2312
The duck pond 4583
Dues 2609
Dumb show 1947
Duplicate keys 511
The duplications 2517
Durango 2438
Duration 809
During the growing season 3958
Dusk 2038
Dusk and ocean 3979
Dust of uncertain journey 3228
Duwamish head 2211
Dwarf cycle 4576
Dying 1247
Dying to survive 4541
Dyke jacket 5098

Each next 1551
Each soul is where it wishes to be 4239
Each to his own ground 4808
The eagle and the flower 4620
Early in '71 4184
Early morning through the door 4534
The early motion 1115
Early Plymouth women 2788
The early poems 4370
Early warning 722
The early word 5089
Earth birds: forty six poems written between May 1964 and June 1972 1297
Earth egg 930
The earth without you 5153
Earthbound Zimmer 5208
Earthsleep 750
East River nocturn 4498
An Eastward look 392
The eating of names 50
Eating stones 111
Echoes 972
Echoes from an ivory tower 1580
Echoes in the wind 2712
Echoes inside the labyrinth 2977
Eclipse (Johnson) 2307
Eclipse (Robins) 3939
Eco-catastrophe 1317
Edge 150
Edges of night 547
Edible fire 448
Egg tooth 3350
The eggplant and other absurdities 23
The eggplant skin pants, and poems 2608
Egyptian hieroglyphics 4093
Eight fairy tales 2834
Eight minutes from the sun 2238
Eight pages 4712
Eight poems 1579
The 8-step grapevine 5014
Eighteen poems 649
8th day, 13th moon 740
El clutch y los klinkies 993
El Canon and other poems 2382
Elderberry flood 3016
Election 1538
The electric banana 299
Electric holding company 3074
Elegy for my father 4564

Elegy in a country church yard
    4489
Elements of a coffee service
    1688
The elements of San Joaquin
    4422
Elite/elate poems   5064
The elm's home   2047
Embodiment   1774
Emergency exit   1178
The emerging detail   238
Emily Dickinson in Southern Cali-
    fornia   2441
Emperor of midnight   3948
Emplumada   738
EMPO   1096
The empress of the death house
    1103
Empty your body in mine   516
Encephalogeorgics   4059
Ency   3062
The end beginning   1425
The end of the ice age   3476
End of the picaro   4102
The end of the world   29
The end of this set   1467
An end to pinball   3106
Endless life   1455
Energumen   3832
The Englewood readings   805
Enigma Variations   363
Enlightenment   307
The ennead of Set-Heru   705
Enough cordwood for a hundred
    years   3460
Enough of flying   3848
Enough said   4974
Entering another country   5212
Entering Onondaga   619
Entries   3495
Entropisms   5217
Epics of America   5037
Epopoeia and the decay of satire
    4673
Erase words   7
Erat   3063
Erika: poems of the Holocaust
    2067
Erogenous zone   3892
Erogeny   587
Eros at the world kite pageant:
    poems 1979-1982   2773

Eros unbound   4126
Erosion   1733
Escape of the leopard   3273
Establishing a vineyard   3480
Esther K comes to America
    1931   4012
Etai-eken   3930
An ethnic connection and goals
    beyond   2228
Etruscan things   2726
Eurekas   1705
Eve, singing   3815
Even as we sleep   3607
Even dozen   2606
Even tide   5118
Evening comes slow to a field-
    hand   1000
Evening drowning   2058
Evening in the Antipodes   2121
Evening song; selected poems
    3372
Evenly distributed rubble   3804
The ever increasing dawn   4288
The everlastings   1218
Every bone a prayer   59
Every minute a ritual   4630
Everyday life   2598
Everyone has sher favorites (his
    or her)   2081
Everything all at once   2705
Everything dark is a doorway
    101
Everything else   2489
The everywhere province   5011
Evidence of light   679
The evolution of death   3621
The evolution of love   1609
Ex cranium, night   3808
Excavations   1725
Excommunicate   155
Executioner   4922
Executioner on holiday   4923
Exercises in memorizing myself
    447
Exhibition game   4387
Exile   3800
The exiled angel   3602
Exits and entrances   3027
Exits off a toll road   2768
The expectations of light   3957
Expecting Ginger Rogers   4273
An explanation of America   3723

Exploring another leg 1030
Explosion in the puzzle factory
  865
Exposed to the elements 4891
Exposure 611
Express 3866
The extravagant room 4768
Extreme unction 806
Extremes 268
Extremities 185
Eye la view 347
Eye level 4282
The eye of reason 336
Eyes 368
Eyes & objects 2316
The eyes don't always want to
  stay open 2848
Eyes on the land 1308
Eyes on the street 3999
The eyes, the blood 3157

F. P. 1364
The fable of the lion and the
  scorpion 4828
The fabulous beasts 3468
Face at the bottom of the world
  31
The face of Guy Lombardo 1527
Face value 4335
Faced with love 3071
Faces and spirits 3457
The faces of Americans in 1853
  3014
Facing the music 208
Facing the tree 2229
Factory 170
Factory dances 3796
Faith 1708
A fall from grace 4110
Falling 2207
Falling man 1469
Falling, May Day sermon, and
  other poems 1116
Falling off the roof 2808
Falling upwards 293
False clues 4170
False trees 3837
Familiar as a sparrow 3418
Family photographs 407
Family reunion: selected and
  new poems 5209
Family salt 2991

The family war 3358
Family way 4695
Fantoccini: a little book of
  memories 867
The far journey and final end of
  Dr. Faustwitz, spaceman
  2812
The far traveller 1166
A faraway whistle 4682
The farm in Calabria and other
  poems 3850
Fast asleep 3430
A fast life 1150
Fast speaking woman 4843
Fast speaking woman and other
  chants 4844
Father Fisheye 234
Father is a pillow tied to a
  broom 4424
Father of Waters 2181
The father poems 2521
Faustwitz Part I 2813
The fearful child 1563
Fears of the night 944
The feathered trees 1041
Feathers from the hill 3188
The feel of rock: poems of three
  decades 5001
The feel of the sun 3658
A feeling for leaving 382
Feeling through 204
Fellow feelings 2184
Felon's Journal 1520
Fergus falling 2479
A festering sweetness 857
Fever coast 3836
Fever poems 1343
A few pianos 859
Field guide 1951
Field poems 1203
Fields of vision 4042
Fierce meadows 3792
15 false propositions about God
  4442
The fifth direction 1360
The fifth season 4266
50 selected poems 1970-1976
  689
'53 Ford 988
Fighting death 907
The figure of fulfillment 2719
A figure of plain force 1999
Figures of speaking 2005

Film noir 152
Filming assassinations 2417
Final leaves 4754
Finding an old ant mansion 466
Finding losses 574
Finding my face 488
Finding the broom 4557
Finding the day 3687
Finding the islands 3189
Finding the lamb 3404
Finding the path 4384
Finding true north 3828
Finding words in winter 2351
Fire in the conservatory 1771
Fire in the dust 331
Fire in Whiting, Indiana 1979
Fire of eyes: a Guatemalan se-
    quence 4155
Fire under water 1246
Fireclock 3969
Firefly in my eyecup 3986
The fireproof floors of Witley
    Court 4178
Fires 2048
Fires; selected poems 1963-
    1976 1521
Firesign 1263
Fire-tested 2361
Fireweeds 4951
First baby poems 4850
First blues 1652
First book of gathas 3004
First edition 40 poems 4034
The first four books of poems:
    A mask for Janus; The danc-
    ing bear; Green with beasts;
    The drunk in the furnace
    3185
First light 4819
The first movement 4701
First poems 2630
First selected poems (Connellan)
    872
First selected poems (Packard)
    3571
The first thing in the field
    2912
First things 2576
First words 1744
First z poems 4073
Firstborn 1686
The fish hook 2954
Fish light 4905

The fisherman's whore 4358
Fishing 3500
Fishing the lower Jackson 1057
Fishing the morning lonely 3167
A fist full (1956-1957) 2930
Five 2406
Five faces 2809
Five from up t' date 5052
Five Iowa poems 4616
Five poems 4750
The five stages of grief 3605
Flagpole riding 1292
The flame behind the eye 2375
Flashbacks 3846
The flaw 2236
Fleas 189-195 2931
A flight of arrows 305
Flim Flam 123
Flogging the Czar 5103
Flood 3127
The Florence poems 3513
Florida poems 1261
Flow 616
A flower blooming in concrete
    5076
Flowering time 2325
Flute over Walden 3976
The flutes of Gama 4366
Fly free my love 290
Flying inland 4449
The follies 1370
Following gravity 178
Folly River 4074
Fool at the funeral 3489
A fool's bubble 2571
Footholds 2318
Foot-prints in the sands of time
    1075
For a living 3698
For Anna Akhmatova and other
    poems 3678
For colored girls who have con-
    sidered suicide, when the rain-
    bow is enuf 4235
For dear life 913
For earthly survival 287
For Eugene in Germany 2077
For instance 780
For luck; poems, 1962-1977 4760
For Max Jacob 833
For my brother 2596
For my mother 957
For rent or for sale 2944

For the birds 449
For the body 4885
For the four corners 1690
For the going 377
For the good times 4638
For the salamander 3557
For the sleepwalkers 2101
For you/for sure 5034
Foraging 1956
The force of desire 579
Forced-marching to the Styx:
  Vietnam-War poems 279
Forcehymn 2203
The forces of plenty 4806
Foreseeing the journey 179
A forest utilization family 271
Forget the sky 2290
Forgiving the beasts 1506
Formal application: selected
  poems, 1960-1980 228
Forms, coda 1344
Forms of praise 13
The forms of silence 3094
The forty days 2897
40 days, apple nights 2777
48 small poems 4919
45 Mercy Street 4228
Found in space 3919
Found poems 3763
The fount of dreams 2820
Four dozen songs 2715
Four for Roethke 3091
Four good things 3012
Four lectures 3945
Four poems 1781
Four ramages 469
Four seasons five senses 3589
Four trains, 4-5 December,
  1964 3001
The fourth 4079
Fox 603
Fractionally awake monad 438
Fracture 1390
Fragments 1615
Fragments of Perseus 2941
Fram 298
Framing 1463
Freddie poems 1139
The freeing of the dust 2732
Freely espousing 4182
Freestone: sections 25 and 26
  4103
Freeway driving 5008

French broom 3158
Fresh wind in Venice 5156
Friend 2945
Friends dreaming 2741
Friends of yours, friends of
  mine 4586
Frisco epic 2827
From a cup of old coins 4641
From a land where other people
  live 2851
From a place which is no longer
  named 4852
From a serpent's scroll 90
From a southern France notebook
  783
From a Swedish notebook 752
From an age of cars 817
From down to the village 629
From "Freestone" 4100
From Jordan's delight 437
From Mesoamerica 3239
From one life to another 2399
From one to another 191
From planet to planet 2698
From room to room 2450
From Sand Creek: rising in this
  heart which is our America
  3544
From Sheepshead, from Pauma-
  nok 1741
From snow and rock, from
  chaos 713
From the abandoned cities 3875
From the backyard of the Dias-
  pora 4340
From the book of shine 1509
From the boundary waters 3550
From the Chicago notebook
  3926
From the diary of Peter Doyle
  1645
From the fire 4457
From the first nine: poems
  1946-1976 3178
From the Golan Heights 816
From the high dive 4383
From the journal of a leper
  4748
The fugitive vowels 4841
Fugues in the plumbing 1812
The fuhrer bunker 4394
Full flower moon 2679
A full heart 1464

Full of lust and good usage 1237
Full summer 630
The funeral parlor 2068
Funny ducks 1680
The further adventures of Crazy
   John 5097
The further regions 1354
The furtive wall 1820
The future unscratched 2412
Futures 2117

G. Washington's camp cups
   4831
Gabriel 263
A gallery of Harlem portraits
   4696
The gallows lord 4033
The gambler 2716
Games and puzzles 159
Garage 1200
The garbage poems 245
The garden 1684
The garden in winter and other
   poems 3287
A garden of effort 4854
The garden prospect: selected
   poems 5170
The gardens of our going 2321
Gardens of the world 4455
Gas 898
Gasoline; the vestal lady on
   Brattle 932
The gates 4046
The gates of disappearance
   4343
Gathering fire 1646
Gathering firewood, new poems
   and selected 3847
Gathering the bones together
   3536
Gathering the light 598
Gathering the tribes 1510
Gathering time 237
The gaudy book 3634
Gaughin and food 292
Gauguin's chair, poems 1964-
   1974 3674
gAyBC's 5058
Gemini 3086
Genealogy 1230
The general mule poems 1157
A generation of peace 1276

A generous wall 122
Genetic memories 1020
Gentle freedom, gentle courage
   4971
Gentle subsidy 694
Geography of the near past 5177
Geography III 424
Geographies: William James,
   Gertrude Stein, General Booth
   & Ives 933
A geology 889
Georgia 1470
Gerard Manley Hopkins meets
   Walt Whitman in heaven 1026
The gestures 409
Get back insanity 3345
Get hot or get out: a selection
   of poems, 1957-1981 5066
Getting over it 259
Getting real 4681
Ghost call 823
Ghost hiways & other homes   730
The ghost of meaning 744
The ghost of the Buick 1965
Ghost wind 3474
Ghosts and grinning shadows 25
The gift to be simple 3672
Gifts of light 2168
Ginkgo 3750
Giraffe 3738
Giselle considers her future
   5215
Gists from a Presidential report
   on hardcornponeography 5054
Giving the lily back her hands
   3794
Giving up the ghost 4286
The glacier's daughters 2172
Glass 2789
A glass face in the rain 4474
Glass hat 4487
The glass houses 3321
Glass roads 1053
The glass tree 862
The glass woman 4706
The glassblower's breath 2882
Glen with one n 1251
Globe 4448
Glossary of the everyday 1752
Glowing in the dark 1862
Gnomes and occasions 3389
Goat cottage dream poems 1639
Goat dances 2835

God's body 2279
God's measurements 2772
Going 4367
Going for the rain 3540
Going on: selected poems, 1958-1980 2603
Going outside 3145
Going places 4463
Going through customs 585
Going under and Endurance: an Arctic idyll: two poems 1472
The going under of the evening land 2904
Gold 5167
Gold country 2397
Gold diggers, sex junkies, needful lovers 1265
Gold mines 5027
The golden book of words 3138
The golden calf 3766
Golden state 416
Goldbarth's book of occult phenomena 1709
The golf ball diver 505
Golgotha: letters from prison 2769
Gone sailing 27
A good journey 3541
The good message of Handsome Lake 618
Good news 2588
Good night, Willie Lee, I'll see you in the morning 4870
Good water 4380
Goodbye, yesterday 162
Goodwill, Inc. 4160
Goshawk, antelope 4361
The gospel of Celine Arnaud 1383
The gourd dancer 3275
Grace period 3260
The graces 4287
The graces of fire and other poems 2175
Grailing 3142
The grand et cet'ra 4146
Grandsire 2286
Granite lady 4139
A graph of love 4693
Graphite, BK 1 3590
The graves of Delawanna 2743
The gravity 1481

The great horned owl 140
The great kiva 2499
Great Lakes cycle 2418
The great mother and other poems 3351
The great toad hunt and other expeditions 2949
Great world circus 2554
The greater leisures 3223
The greatest show on earth 2619
Great-grandpa Nettestad was blind 1434
Greco's last book 897
Greed, parts 1-9, 11-13 4840
Green balloon 3578
Green dragons 2392
Green in the body 5101
The green kangaroo 5132
Green shaded lamps 4779
Green soldiers 341
Greenfellow 3635
Greening twig 2802
Greenwich mean time 4562
The greeting: new & selected poems 1126
Grey G. 1097
Greyhounding this America 2449
Grief; poems and versions of poems 348
Griffon 1151
Groceries 4203
Grotesca 1381
Ground fog and night 2909
Ground work 2635
Ground zero 2322
Groundwork 3303
The growing season 3628
Growth 4374
Guatemala 5036
A guide to Dungeness Spit 4812
Guilty bystander 4232
The gull wall 1377
Gumbo 264
Gunslinger 1169
Gurgle of little feet 4007
Guy's poem 2028
The gymnast of inertia 1958
Gypsies 2346
Gypsies, including animals 3413
A gypsy's history of the world 4459

Habit blue 282
Habitats 1073
A hacksaw brightness 4573
Hades in manganese 1389
Haiku revisited 1006
Hail thee who play 2932
A hairy coat near Yanwath Yat 5063
Haiti, August 13-28 285
Hakugai 2818
Half a life's history 4618
Half a loaf 1949
The half of a circle 2266
Half of the map 1161
Half-after love 3724
Half-lives 2336
Half-tones 4530
Halfway down the coast 434
Halfway from Hoxie 5067
Halfway to silence 4123
Halfway to the sun 3229
Ham operator 1855
Hanbelachia 2271
Hand to hand 692
A handful of bubbles 3110
Handfuls of us 1240
Hands (Shoemaker) 4279
Hands (Young) 5182
The hands in exile 4688
Hands in the stone 4600
The hands of time 3294
Hang me up my begging bowl 4880
The hanging at Silver Junction 277
Hangups 3407
Hannah's travel 4432
Happy deathday 1528
The happy genius 1437
The happy tree 1836
Hard acts 2388
Hard country 1179
The hard essential landscape 561
Hard facts 253
Hard freight 5145
Hard shadows 199
Harder than rain 3668
The hardness scale 3667
Harmatum 4800
Harps 3161
Hassidic exclamation on Stevie Smith's poem, "Not Waving But Drowning" 5055

The haunted computer and the android pope 514
Hawk hover 3292
The hawk's dream and other poems 215
The Hawthorne effect 4104
Hazard, the painter 3167a
Hazardous renaissance 2899
Hazel 4333
He is risen 3180
He who hunted birds in his father's village 4402
The head of the bed 2146
The head of the family 3209
Headlands, rising 2569
Health 5023
The hearkening eye 1305
The heart as ever green 3947
Heart attacks 4334
Heart in utter confusion 2559
Heart of the garfish 681
Heart of the world 2373
Heart organ part of the body 2439
Heartbreak Hotel 800
Heartland 4956
Hearts & gizzards 4917
Heart's core 2272
Hearts in space 3561
The heat bird 405
Heat death 1152
Heat simmers cold 1293
Heaven & other poems 2454
Heavy breathing 4975
Hecate the bandicoot 2819
The Heisenberg variations 548
Heirloom 1019
Hello 964
Hello: a journal, February 23-- May 3, 1976 969
Hello, darkness 4331
Hello, I'm Erica Jong 16
Hello La Jolla 1173
Hello to me with love 251
Henry's fate & other poems 402
Herbal 1927
Here 672
Here a home, there a home 4713
Here at the door 3756
Here comes and other poems 2337
Here comes everybody 1679

Here I am 231
Here in the 202
Here is no ordinary rejoicing
    3679
Heretics 5033
Hermit 3755
The hermit-woman 2331
Heroes of the Teton mythos 1877
Hesperides 1269
Hey fella, would you mind hold-
    ing this piano a moment 1930
Hickey, the days 300
Hickory and a smooth dime 3148
The hidden waterfall 5197
Hide and seek 3843
The hiding place 1861
High school confidential 4537
High there 1149
Highgate Road 114
Highlife for Caliban 2311
Hiking the crevass; poems on
    the way to divorce 1944
Hinge picture 2189
Hints to pilgrims 4661
Hiroshima flows through us
    3216
His idea 958
His many & himself 1461
History 2867
The history of the growth of
    heaven 831
A hive of souls 1978
Hives 4900
The Hobbesian apple 4437
Hobo signs 3903
The hocus-pocus of the universe
    1650
Hokum; visions of a gringa
    4438
Hold your hands to the earth
    4398
Holding patterns 3371
Hollow fix 4989
Holocaust 3886
Holy Cow: parable poems 3671
Homage to Edgar Allan Poe
    4364
Homage to Fats Navarro 1321
Home (Olson) 3509
Home (Simmerman) 4312
Home and other moments 472
The home book 4180
Home cooking 2764

Home front 4708
Home grown 1207
Home in time 1621
Home movies 1811
Homing 3664
Homing signals 2319
Honey bear on Lasqueti Island,
    B. C. 4617
Hoodoo hollerin' bebop ghosts
    3375
Hope Farm: new and selected
    poems 946
Hopi roadrunner dancing 3972
A horse of a different color 2597
Horse sacrifice 4503
Horses 393
Horses in November 2143
Hot 2309
Hot footsteps 1948
Hot knives, greasy spoons, & all
    night diners 3144
Hot weather: poems selected and
    new 3835
Hotel Nirvana; selected poems
    1953-1973 3437
Hotels 5009
Houdini 4593
Houdini, Houdini 2876
The hour between dog and wolfe
    4875
Hour, Gnats 1259
The hours of morning 700
The house 1100
House, bridge, fountain, gate
    2579
House fires 5025
House hold poems 1428
House marks 2085
The house of leaves 4653
A house of my own 1090
The house of water: early
    poems 2985
A house of words 1852
The house on marshland 1683
The house on the Saco 3400
The house party 2513
The house we lie down in 2805
House wrecking 4536
Houseboat days 195
Household tales of moon and
    water 5040
Household wounds 2408
Housework 2631

Houses (Agee) 39
Houses (Oppenheimer) 3526
How Audie Murphy died in Vietnam 2688
How could I not be among you? 4002
How I broke in/Six modern masters 797
How I escaped from the labyrinth, and other poems 1022
How I got ovah: new and selected poems 3946
How spring comes 3452
How the dead count 4270
How the Plains Indians got horses 3739
How the sky begins to fall 848
How the sow became a goddess 2070
How to 2534
How to attain lasting peace 4758
How to choose your past 1101
How to eat a fortune cookie 1534
How to eat a slug 3060
How us white folks discovered rock & roll 2144
How what? 5056
Howling at the wind 3101
Huaca 1525
Hudson 2765
Hugging the jukebox 3459
Huladance 2095
The human condition 4035
Human nature can be changed 4855
Human Songbook 4414
Human trappings 838
Human wedding 1373
Humours run deep 554
Hundreds of fireflies 2711
Hunger food 2528
The hungry lions 1083
The hunt within 1853
Hurrah!: selected poems 4526
Hush 4066
Hybrid Inoculum 3595
Hybrids of plants and of ghosts 1732
Hyde park 4240
Hymn for drum 840

Hymn to life 4177
Hymns of St. Bridget 360
Hymns to a tree 2125
Hymns to Hermes 590
Hymns to St. Geryon/Dark brown 2940
Hypogeum 4065

I am a weapon 445
I am an eagle 21
I am not a practicing angel 102
I am running home 1897
I am that we may be 1032
I am the Jefferson County Courthouse 1676
I am the sun 2446
I don't know whether to laugh or cry 'cause I lost the map to where I was going 127
I don't own you so I can't give you away 3262
I don't want to be a thunderbird anymore 2362
I dream now of the sun 3545
I knew a woman 3641
I know what the small girl knew 15
I live in the watchmakers' town 4009
I nearly died laughing 3918
I never saw 2295
I remember 523
I remember Christmas 520
I remember the room was filled with light 2007
I see America daily 3438
I suppose the darkness is ours 557
I think they'll lay my egg tomorrow 2031
I want to be a crowd 4211
I wanted to see something flying 5216
I will mean 4063
Icarus 892
Ice 3381
Ice Fishing 2345
The ice futures 2323
Icehouse Beach 4213
Icehouse lights 5119
The idol 3682
If a poet is 4523

If birds build with your hair
4396
If I could sleep deeply enough
3234
If i hold my tongue   1249
If I knew the way   4506
If I: 79 poems   984
If you are going to be famous
446
If you call this cry a song   721
If you ever get there, think of
me   2132
I'll be seeing you; poems, 1962-
1976   1424
I'll be there in the morning if
I live   2763
Illegal assembly   567
Illuminations   2551
An illustrated voice   1224
The illustrations   1214
I'm amazed that you're still
singing   3359
I'm divorced, are you listening,
Lord?   624
I'm hiding from the cat   4440
I'm in love with the Morton salt
girl echt and ersatz   3625
I'm not your laughing daughter
284
The image maker   4546
ImAges   1486
Images and other poems   2637
Images of kin   1920
Imaginary ancestors   1078
Imaginary postcards   5051
Imaginary timber   1596
Imagine a moment   3760
Imagining a unicorn   4430
Imagining the garden   2120
Imagoes   856
The immaculate conception of
the blessed virgin dyke   427
Immigrants in our land   218
Impassioned cows by moonlight
51
Imperfect correspondences
1808
Implementing standards of good
behavior   3377
Impossible buildings   4268
Impossible dreams   2090
Imprints of a heart: poems
334

In 1749
In a December Storm   525
In a dusty light   1842
In a fugitive season   1038
In a gorge with a friend   3704
In a lost world   3950
In a pig's eye   4292
In a season of birds: poems
for Maureen   2844
In a surf of strangers: poems
475
In a time between wars   2389
In a U-Haul north of Damascus
498
In a white light   645
In all this rain   4553
In America   470
In America's shoes   836
In another country; poems 1935-
1975   2639
In Baltic circles   4798
In broken country   4817
In chontales   1322
In dark, sudden with light   4360
In dressing for the part   5130
In enormous water   2577
In everything   79
In five years time   1839
In (is) out   56
In Lagos   753
In lieu of Mecca   2807
In Mediterranean air   4479
In memory of the future   2455
In my own dark way   1931
In passing   4151
In place   2149
In plain air: poems 1958-1980
4516
In pursuit of the family   156
In quire   3580
In search of Fred & Ethel Mertz
2199
In sepia   138
In solitary and other imaginations
3617
In some quiet place   3191
In the absence of horses   1987
In the aviary   936
In the basket of the blind   4339
In the boom boom room   3802
In the canyon   850
In the clock of reason   4460
In the course of the real   3097

In the dark body of metamor-
   phosis 2886
In the dead of the night 1211
In the empire of ice and other
   poems 677
In the face of descent 592
In the field at the solstice 5059
In the fourth world 1633
In the gallery 3599
In the glass of winter 2265
In the great night 2377
In the heart of our city 4036
In the house of the judge 4365
In the keeper's house 1339
In the middle way 2924
In the moment 4680
In the mood 2613
In the museum naked 3421
In the oriental forms 4970
In the presence of mothers 3256
In the red meadow 4542
In the running 1320
In the shadow of a bell 1081
In the shadowless light 3907
In the sleep of rivers 4578
In the soul's riptide 225
In the tangled grass 3908
In the temperate zone 2570
In these bodies 1911
In these rooms 2415
In touch 2980
In tranquil mood, and other
   poems 2173
In winter 4058
In winter, they 367
Incantations 501
Incarnations 3053
Incidentals in the day world
   3448
The Incognito Lounge 2306
The incompleat works of Richard
   Krech, poems 1966-1974
   2568
The Indian cheap wine seance
   2858
Indian Summer 1070
Indian territory and other poems
   4759
Indifference point 4853
Indigoes 3820
Infidelities 2996
Infinitesimals 4081
Infinity at Euclid Avenue 3337

An inhuman rival 1564
Ink, blood, semen 1704
An inland journey 4992
Inner marathons 443
Inner weather 2305
The innocent assassins 1302
Inside & out 2759
Inside my own skin 1976
Inside/outside 4004
Inside the Big O 260
Inside the bones is flesh 515
Inside the devil's mouth 828
Inside the horse 4610
Inside the piano bench 943
Inside the wind 3779
Inscripts 1981
Insights & poems 3405
Installing the bees 4876
Instances 346
Instead of an animal 4133
Instincts for the jugular 1898
Instructions to the double 1583
The insurrection of Earth in
   dragon pastures 4406
The intercourse 4884
Interesting times 1034
Interlude 4645
Intermittent release 2761
Interrupted praise 2169
Interstate 1929
The interstate poem; south on
   75 552
Intimate letters 3317
Intimate wilderness 4948
Intimations 3432
Into it 4643
Into the center of America 1768
Into the darkness we go 4982
Into the icehouse 739
The intuitive journey 1272
The intussusception of Miss Mary
   America 1916
The invasion of Italy 4323
Inventing the cats 5091
The invention of hunger 186
Investigative poetry 4094
Invincible summer 100
Invisible woman: new & selected
   poems, 1970-1982 3470
Inward a jungle 502
Irish poems 4733
Iron horse 1651
Iron man on the Hoh 345

The iron road 2845
Iron rose 1777
Irreconcilable differences 249
The is that is 57
Is that wool hat my hat? 3009
The island hunter 5024
Island of bones 4910
The island self 440
The island-maker 3105
The isle of the little god 1457
I've been a woman; new and sel-
ected poems 4089

JD. 1402
Jabbergod 1487
Jabon 1638
Jack tales 4276
Jack the Ripper 1860
Jackrabbit, North Dakota 4224
Jaguar skies 2937
Jakoba poems 2452
James Cook in search of terra
incognita 2632
Jamming with the band at the
VFW 496
The Jane poems 4450
January 2374
January thaw 1803
Jan. 31 1698
The Japanese notebook 931
Jeanne D'Arc 5030
Jesus leaving Vegas 2926
Jim and the evil 1015
The jockey poems 2524
The Joe chronicles, part 2
3566
The Joe 82 creation poems
3564
John danced 4031
Johnnie Panic and his fantastic
circus of fear 4415
The Jonestown arcane 2110
Jonquil rose: jus' one more
cowboy 4345
Journal of a hermit 3757
Journal of the sun 3268
The journals 433
Journals & dreams 4846
Journey 3111
The journey begins 4053
Journey into awareness 184
Journey into morning 1848

Journey of the medicine man
3857
A journey south 3967
Journey to the Dead Sea 4391
Journey toward the roots 2358
A journey whose bones are mine
3403
Journeying back to the world
3149
Journeys 4456
Judith's blues 4313
Judyism 564
The juggler 1535
Juicing 3873
Julia 555
The July book 1352
June 30th, June 30th 538
The juniper palace 621
Jurgis Petraskas 3689
Just friends/friends and lovers;
poems, 1959-1962 3524
Just the way I am 3601

Kabir, try to live to see this!
461
Kali yuga 477
Kansas collateral 3774
A Kansas sequence 878
Karma circuit 3436
Karma poems 3727
Kashtaninyah Segodnyah 2107
Kay Price and Stella Pajunas 14
Keeper of accounts 2492
The keeper of height 2905
Keeping 1700
Keeping company 4029
Keeping house in this forest 288
Keeping open 4329
Keeping score 1371
Keeping the night 1420
Keeping time (McCann) 2907
Keeping time (Moffett) 3271
Keeping watch 3569
The Kentucky River 396
Ketjak 4297
The keymakers 4890
Kicking the leaves 1850
Kika-da raga 3728
Kill the messenger who brings
bad news 2431
Killing floor 47
A kind of glory 4262

A kind of order, a kind of folly
   2584
A kind of psychology   3502
Kind regards   4861
The kindness of strangers, poems
   1969-1974   4972
Kindred   3960
Kinesis   4879
King of August   296
The kingdom   4085
Kingdom come   2407
The kingfisher   784
The kiss: a jambalaya   3424
Kiss the sky   1801
Kissing the murderer   5201
Kitchen   959
Kiva   656
Kneading the blood   2448
Knee: whip of occasions   2256
The knife, and other poems
   4690
Knosh 1 Cir   938
Know fish   1459
Knowledge   2006
Kodachromes in rhyme   1577
Kudzu   1159

La carreta made a u-turn   2673
La vida de la mujer   2381
Ladder of the world's joy   176
The ladder to the moon   2078
Ladidah   4883
The lady and the bailiff of time
   2710
Lady Faustus   19
The lady from the green hills
   1854
The lady in Kicking Horse
   Reservoir   2208
The lady knife-thrower   1870
The lady of   2427
Lady of the beasts   3306
The lady poems   4538
The lady who drove me to the
   airport   4838
The lady who got me to say so
   long, mom   4212
Laguna woman   4294
Lake effect country   121
A lake on the Earth   267
Lake songs and other fears
   3254

Lament   4052
Lamplights used to feed the deer
   1209
Land diving   3301
Land of little sticks   4660
The land surveyor's daughter
   1634
Landbound   4967
Landfall   4818
Landing   5115
Landler   1349
Lands   4245
Landscapes   4101
Landscapes of living & dying
   1453
Language drawn & quartered
   3791
The lark and the emperor   12
The lark, the thrush, the starling
   5044
Larry lost   3636
Last and lost poems of Delmore
   Schwartz   4186
The last days of October   1345
The last fiddler crab   4493
The last foot of shade   997
Last harvest   1743
Last house in America   3206
The last judgment   1374
Last light   1102
The last magician   906
The last poem   4832
The last ride of Wild Bill   601
Last rites (Buckley)   626
Last rites (Ransom)   3830
Last rites and other poems   781
The last stop   614
The late hour   4567
Late, passing prairie farm
   4465
Lateness   4244
Later (Barnard)   265
Later (Creeley)   970
Lauds & nightsounds   4246
Laughing past history   1605
Laws of the land   227
The lazy man comes back   3909
Lead us forth from prison   2770
The leaf path   4892
Leaf's boundary   5195
Leaning South   2790
Leap year choice   2872
Leap year; poems, 1968-1978
   3442

Leaping clear and other poems 1438

Leaping over gravestones 3055

Learn to love the haze 3971

Learning not to kill you 1028

Learning to breathe underwater 3154

Learning to count 4723

Learning to die 2013

Leave your sugar for the cold morning 709

The leaves 2833

Leaves and ashes 1837

The leaves the people 4077

Leaving Taos 3681

Leftovers 4791

Legacy 4551

The legend of John Brown 1970

Legendary acts 3568

Legerdemain 1817

Legion: civic courses 1915

Lemon center for hot buttered roll 3479

Lemurian rhapsodies 685

Less than a score, but a point 3858

The lesser light 1968

Lessons in alchemy 2113

Lessons in leaving 3803

Lessons learned 3780

Let it pass 2472

Let myself shine 2677

Let the circle be unbroken 844

Let the dance begin 2498

Letargo 4084

Lethal paper 444

Letter from an outlying province 1003

Letter to a straw hat 4615

Letter to Maxine 4947

Letter to Robert Duncan while bending the bow 3075

Letter to the ghosts 3613

Letters for my son 2133

Letters for the New England dead 275

Letters from a father, and other poems 4764

Letters from Helge 1532

Letters from the island 1531

Letters from the mines 2091

Letters from Vicksburg 1636

Letters home 146

Letters to a stranger (Goldman) 1714

Letters to a stranger (James) 2270

Letters to my daughters 3257

Letters to Pauline 1668

Letters to Proust 1628

Letters to the poetry editor 4792

Letters to Tomasito 2974

Letters to women 105

Letters to Yesenin 1932

Letters to Yesenin. Returning to Earth 1934

Leverage 2140

The levitator 4434

Li Po's sandlewood boat 701

The Liam poems 2002

Liar's dice 1562

License to kill 3655

The lich gate 1387

Licorice chronicles 1764

Lid and spoon 4724

The lie the lamb knows 1571

Lies and stories 33

The life 1760

Life among others 1872

The life beside this one 3320

Life in a gothic novel 1205

Life in the forest 2735

Life in these United States 4539

Life notes 4842

Life on the edge of the continent: selected poems 2526

Life supports; new and collected poems 580

The lifeguard in the snow 4041

Lifesavors 4619

Light (Ghiselin) 1616

Light (Weiss) 4949

The light 1681

The light at Newport 5111

Light footsteps 3978

Light from new steel 1900

Light from the furnace rising 3684

Light of paradise 1444

The light of the red horse 3401

Light years 1642

Lighter-than-night verse 4543

Lighting the furnace pilot 4040

Lighting the night sky 1905

Like a diamondback in the trunk of a witness's Buick 1818

Like any road anywhere 4090
Like ghosts of eagles 1541
Like the iris of an eye 1783
Like wings 4174
The likeness 3366
Lilith's cave 4188
A line of sight 2424
Line upon line 3558
Linear C. 1066
Lined up bulk senses 1295
Lines 3085
Lines and mounds 3492
Lines from Neuchatel 3150
A lion at a cocktail party 2138
Lion under the sun 2490
Lip service 3023
The liquid child's son 3215
Listeners at the breathing place
    3259
Lit by the Earth's dark blood
    206
A litany of friends 3818
Little America 3585
Little boat lighter than a cork
    2566
Little books/Indians 4939
Little fictions 758
Little movies 1665
Little mysteries (Mikolowski)   3211
Little mysteries (Root) 3963
Little red wagon painted blue
    2022
Little silver cloud/one bird flying
    2714
The little that is all 779
Live at the church 2895
Live free or die! 818
Lives of the poet 5194
The living and the dead 1973
Living at the movies 711
Living by the sword 1250
Living expenses 2463
Living in code 2864
Living in fear 702
Living in the boneyard 4317
Living in the open 3712
Living paradox dying 2960
Living space 4168
Living the borrowed life 479
Living together; new and selected
    poems 504
Living with it 3775
Loading mercury with a pitchfork
    537

Loading the revolver with real
    bullets 1447
Loba 1137
Loba as Eve 1141
Loba, parts 1-8 1144
Lobster & oatmeal 2795
A local habitation & a name
    2536
Local men 4990
Lock this man up 3893
Log rhythms 4886
The lone woman and others   4752
Loneliness: an outburst of
    hexasyllables 716
The loneliness factor 3490
Lonely Battle 3402
Long Division: a tribal history
    3974
Long eye, lost wind, forgive me
    1914
Long Island light 2059
Long pants 3516
A long perspective 2964
The long reach: new and uncol-
    lected poems, 1948-1984 1262
Long walks in the afternoon 1625
The long war dead 1505
Long Wolf poems 2846
A longing in the land 1775
Look for me in your dreams
    2676
Looking at Henry Moore's ele-
    phant skull etchings in Jerusa-
    lem during the war 2398
Looking at it 571
Looking at the sun 308
Looking for binoculars 3043
Looking for holes in the ceiling
    1236
Looking for minerals 526
Looking for the King of Spain
    4825
Looking ... seeing 745
Looking up 625
Looking wayward 1244
Lookout point 942
The loom 2425
The loon 462
Loony 2495
Lord Dragonfly 2051, 2064
The lost body of childhood 1068
Lost copper 3973
Lost distance 3369

The lost faces 2289
The lost heroes 1001
Lost highway 5116
Lost in the blue canyon 1087
A lost poem 4443
Lost poems 4511
The lost refrigerator 22
Lost title, & other poems 2206
The lost tribe 5029
Lost wealth 1802
Love affair 2363
Love and all the other verbs of
    life 3026
Love at the Egyptian Theatre
    1204
Love in an earthquake 3813
Love in spring 2158
Love is a dog from hell; poems,
    1974-1977 635
Love is not a consolation; it is
    a light 4069
Love is the silence; poems 1948-
    1974 3657
Love letters 4717
Love poem: the vestments of the
    dance 36
Love Poems (Cunningham) 1009
Love poems (Sanchez) 4087
Love poems for a remembered
    Black-Indian grandma 3319
Love poems to a Black junkie
    4983
Love poems to myself 2509
Love pommes 1994
A love song to Black men 517
Love touching love 5133
The love unit 5012
Love wounds & multiple fractures
    1328
Lovepoems 1942
Loveroot 2338
Lovers 1649
Lovers & agnostics 764
Loves lost and found 2329
Love's other face 2553
Lovestalk 3376
Love-tangle of roots 1495
Lovin' you 3266
Loving the days 5112
Loving you 5134
The low east 2011
Lucky life 4520
Lucky you 1474
Ludi Jr. 2496

Ludlow fugue 2440
Lullaby for sinners 542
Lumen gloriae 4082
The luminous revolver 2983
Luncheonette jealousy 5099
Lunes 1622
Lurid confessions 2560
Lust in 28 flavors 4125
Lying on the earth 1888
The lyric return 852
Lyrics for the Bride of God
    4651
Lyrics for the bride of God:
    section: the artemission 4648
Lyripol 2108

McCabe wants chimes 1121
Machineworks 1787
Mad dog black lady 855
The mad girl 2796
Made in America 1155
Madonna who shifts for herself
    2797
Maedra poems 2072
The maerchen cycle 2923
Magical Friday 4314
The magician's feastletters 4839
Magnito star mine 1885
Magnolias and such 422
Magnus annus 2520
Magpie on the gallows 1080
Magritte series 1549
Mainland 991
The Maintains 885
Maize 3555
Make me a falcon 684
The maker's name 1017
Makes sense 1761
Makeup on empty space 4851
Making 2378
Making a baby in Union Park,
    Chicago 4293
Making a sacher torte 4837
Making an angel 3237
Making faces 4774
Making hay and other poems
    3280
Making it simple 2968
Making space for our living 410
Making the house fall down 1966
Making wings 659
Malignant blues 1127

Man in the attic 2086
The man in the black chevrolet
  3289
The man in the black coat turns
  467
The man in the green chair 1253
A man in winter 4556
A man is a hook 2467
Man of moderation 2938
A man to his shadow 3244
The man twice married to fire
  748
The man who shook hands 4835
A man who writes 1417
The Manabozho poems 615
Manchester Square 1170
Man-fate; the swan song of
  Brother Antoninus 1408
Manhattan as a second language
  and other poems 1924
The Manila series: No. 4, ten
  poems 1182
The manner music 3890
Many junipers, heartbeats 3222
Many times, but then 2672
Many winters 5122
Maps & windows 895
March light 3247
The marches 4209
Mare 2039
Margaret of Cortona 698
Maria 2240
The Marisol poems 5002
The Marisol poems, II 5004
Markings 1363
Marquise 1132
The marriage of the Portuguese
  3647
Martinis 2380
The Mary caper 1107
Mary Militant 1105
A mask of motion 2004
The masks of drought 1418
Masks of the dreamer 2871
A masque of surgery 1674
Massachusetts poems 873
The master 799
Masterpiece theater 1779
The mate-flight of eagles 1411
Material goods 654
The mating reflex 1856
Matters of the heart: poems
  1279

Mattress testing 2900
Max, a sequel 1130
The Maximus poems 3498
Maxine's flattery 509
Maya 5080
The Mayan poems 4154
Maybe if I loved you more 2404
Maybe tomorrow 636
Maze/mane/wane 2315
Me, the people 4371
Me too 1435
Meadow 8--immanentist sutras
  2823
Meadows of my mind 2371
Mean rufus throw down 4356
The meantime 575
Mecanorgane 4727
The median flow; selected poems,
  1943-1973 1346
Medicine man; collected poems
  2020
The medicine woman 4592
Meditations on various grounds
  1365
Meditationsmeditationsmeditations
  2453
Medusa and others 4513
The meeting place of colors
  1620
Meetings with Conrad 3949
Memet 97
Memling's veil 4039
Memory 2294
Memory is no stranger 280
Men at table 1024
Men under fire 2523
Men with women 4362
Mentally, he's a sick man 2610
Merciful disguises 4763
Mermaid 2035
Mesopotamia 4639
A message for the recluse 2515
Message from the avocadoes 1189
The messenger 4757
Metaform 1748
Metal 3338
Metamorphosis of 741 3173
Methane 4451
Methods of birth control 4901
The microcosm 4654
The middle of the journey 4613
The middle of the world 3435
The middle passage 3192

Midnight shift in Detroit 3420
Midquest: a poem 751
Milk run 540
Milky Way poems 3911
The Milky Way: poems, 1967-1982 139
The mill of particulars 2421
Millennium dust 737
Millions of strange shadows 1991
Mind breaths; poems 1972-1977 1654
The mind-reader 5016
Miners getting off the graveyard; selected poems, 1969-1977 1864
Mining the darkness 4512
Mink coat 2129
The minutes no one owns 1593
Mirabell, books of number 3174
The miracle 1063
Miracle, miracles 882
Miracles & other poems 674
Mirages 653
Mirrors 974
Misgivings 2185
Missa defunctorum 1409
The missing Jew 2379
Mistah 2017
Mr. & Mrs. Mephistopheles and son 2849
Mistral for Daddy and Van Gogh 1896
Mobiles, the sadness of Cerberus and the bitch 2001
Mockingbird 2224
A modern bestiary 1228
A modern Dunciad 3363
Modular poems 2079
Modulations for solo voice 2734
The Mojo hands call, I must go 3743
Moments of the Italian summer 5157
Momma 103
Momma, I know why 4672
Mon autre lyre 3579
Mongo affair 70
The monocle thugs 2170
Monody 1539
Monolithos 1632
Monster 3305
The monument 4568

Moods of late 788
Moon horns/razor door 1106
The moon is always female 3714
Moonlight standing in as Cordelia 2620
The moonlit upper deckerina 2689
Moons and low times 2914
A moral proposition 3505
A more 1608
More, I remember more 521
More never again 180
More palomino, please, more fuchsia 2574
More trouble with the obvious 4773
More waters 2787
Morituri 1177
The morning after midnight 1185
Morning chores and other times remembered 3856
The morning glory 460
Morning news 4709
The morning of the poem 4183
Morning passage 3754
The morning star 3880
Morning windows 3293
The mornings 1347
Mortal acts, mortal words 2481
Mortal companions 1489
Mortal fire 1031
Moscow mansions 1804
Mostly sitting Haiku 1656
A mote in heaven's eye 1471
Motel thought in the 70's 1626
Mother is 1533
Mother, may I 4784
Mother nature is a bitch 1309
The mother's breast and the father's house 5000
Motherwriter 4509
Mountain talk 203
The mountain, the stone 2562
The mountains have come closer 3225
Mouth of the whale 4603
Movable islands 1770
Movement in Black 3592
The movie under the blindfold 1475
Moving closer 4148
Moving into the light 3693
Moving out 4871

Moving right along 1327
Moving to a new place 4169
Moving violation 1268
Much 1124
The mud actor 726
Mule Mountain dreams 1454
Mundo Ragas 937
Museum 1184
Music from home: selected
    poems 2966
Music from the middle passage
    631
Music in the winepress, parrots
    in the flames 2575
The music of what happens 3539
The music variety 1288
Musical comedy 3279
The musics 1776
The mutabilities 1051
Muted war drums 2859
My daddy is a cool dude, and
    other poems 1567
My experiences in Parnassus
    3809
My father photographed with
    friends 576
My flashlight was attacked by
    bats 774
My God the proverbial 1286
My grandfather's house 824
My grandparents were married
    for sixty-five years 4167
My hat flies on again 977
My life with the Tsar & other
    poems 1476
My pleasure 770
My Quaker-atheist friend 5057
My regrets 144
My summer vacation 4881
Myrtle Whimpler's sampler
    4978
Myself 967
The mysteries 3838
The mystic writing pad 1565
The myth of a woman's fist
    1046
The mythology of dark and light
    719
Myths, dreams and dances 212

Nailing up the home sweet home
    4872

Nails 1635
Naked 4984
Naked as my bones in transit
    2122
Naked charm 2793
The name 3165
The name encanyoned river 1384
The nameless garden 3771
Names 877
Names, dates, and places 3523
The names of a hare in English
    5181
The names of the lost 2746
The names of the survivors 76
The names you gave it 1156
Naming the creeks 3281
Nappy edges 4236
Narcissa Notebook 1201
Narrative of this fall 4652
Narratives from America 3962
Narrowgauge to Riobamba 527
The narrows 3361
Nations and peoples 979
Native land 1762
Natives 3718
Natural affinities 1572
Natural birth 1104
Natural histories 4731
The natural lean 2682
Natural world 1936
Near the bone 1493
Near the fire 2282
Near misses 338
Nearing land 3703
Necessary lies 1552
The necessities 3197
Necrocorrida (bullfight with the
    dead) 835
The need for chocolate and other
    poems 761
The need to hold still 3342
Needlepoint 4607
Negative space 1614
Neither late nor sensitive 4857
Neither of us can break the
    other's hold 4320
Nervous houses 1986
Nettles 35
Never stop dancing 5213
New and collected poems, 1961-
    1983 1227
New and selected poems (Berto-
    lino) 412

New and selected poems (Carroll) 712
New & selected poems (Church) 777
New and selected poems (Feldman) 1439
New and selected poems (Scarbrough) 4136
New and selected poems (Wild) 5019
New & selected things taking place 4622
The new body 3285
New days; poems of exile and return 2342
New green over old green 2436
A new house 2385
New laugh poems 1109
New letters from Hiroshima and other poems 2586
The new life 4054
New listings 173
The new physics 5220
New poems (Mitchell) 3264
New Poems (Rexroth) 3877
New poems from the bell-branch 1974
New season 2745
New shoes 1550
A new way 4111
New Words 262
New work 522
New York head shop and museum 2852
News from Niman farm 2894
News from the glacier; selected poems 1960-1980 1843
Next to nothing 506
Nicole 3663
Nictitating membrane 319
A niggered amen 5221
Night blindness 3923
Night blooming 1431
Night blooming cactus 4911
Night conversations with none other 3854
Night cries 320
Night fishing 2587
Night herding song 1959
A night in the Hard Rock Cafe 5185
Night light 2368
Night lights 94

Night Music 1785
Night of the broken glass: poems of the Holocaust 490
Night rained her 3924
Night road 3245
Night shift 1666
Night shift at the poetry factory 3035
The night still in your kiss 3025
The night sun 4285
Night talk and other poems 3692
The night train & The golden bird 3151
The night watches 3198
The night we stood up for our rights; poems, 1969-1975 4338
The night won't save anyone 4428
Nightblind 1055
Nightfire 3141
Night-fishing on Irish Buffalo Creek 2500
Nightlatch 766
Nightmare begins responsibility 1919
Nightmare of mouse 4574
Nightmare township 1266
Night's dead letters 2634
Nights we put the rock together 1388
Nightseasons 884
Nigredo 4945
Nijole's house 4940
Nine mysteries (four joyful, four sorrowful, one glorious) 3781
Nine poems for Cesar Vallejo 3049
Nine songs 802
The nine songs 4867
19, in celebration 1825
1933 [Nineteen thirty-three] 2744
Ninety notes towards partial images & lovers' prints 3282
Ninth life 4635
No apologies 4127
No bread without the dance 4043
No capital crime 2814
No chance encounter 620
No dogs in heaven 3113

No harm done   5006
No hiding place   5117
No matter where you travel, you
   still be black   229
No metaphysics   3788
No moving parts   1074
No name stalks the land   2096
No one took a country from me
   1544
No ordinary world   2903
No place fast   3394
No radio   1284
No running on the boardwalk
   3814
No time for good reasons   1592
No title yet   3103
The no traveling journal   3560
No vacancies in hell   1369
No warning   4968
No witness but ourselves   1728
No witnesses   3278
Nobody laughs, nobody cries
   3696
Nocturnes   2730
Noise in the trees   2034
Nolo contendere   980
Non sequitur O'Connor   2487
None, river   646
Nonesuch Creek   3109
The nonny poems   2464
Nonrequiem   2533
The noose; retrospective of 3
   decades   982
The normal heart   1694
North   2444
North Beach poems   5095
North of Athens   2356
North of Manhattan: collected
   poems, ballads and songs,
   1954-1975   3207
North poems   2783
North Sea   2276
Northbook: poems   3300
A northern calendar   4062
Northern lights (Ludvigson)
   2874
Northern lights (McNally)   3015
Northern spy   4726
Northwest ecolog   1452
Nostalgia of the fortune teller
   2458
Not coming to be barked at
   2538

Not just any death   4907
Not native   3331
Not seeing is believing   3685
Not so much love of flowers   174
Not such a bad place to be   2497
Not that far   3227
A note for the flowers I didn't
   send   3618
A note on apprenticeship   1386
The notebooks   4018
Notes from Custer   2069
Notes from the castle   3334
Notes from the exile   283
Notes of a daughter from the old
   country   3654
Notes of the siege year   2112
Notes on space/time   581
Notes toward a family   3662
Nothing breaks off at the edge
   3777
Nothing for you   385
Nothing is lost   1967
Notice the star   703
Noticing   4150
November burning   941
November woman   2953
Now and then; poems 1976-1978
   4895
Now is always the miraculous
   time   4115
Now let us eat of this pollen
   and place some on our heads,
   for we are to talk of it   2892
Now, swim   5107
Now there's a morning, hulk of
   the sky   1298
Nox   4295
Nuestra Señora de los Dolores
   4277
Numbers and letters   4023
Numerous avalanches at the point
   of intersection   2578
Nursery rhymes for the dead
   3562

O Africa, where I baked my
   bread   2285
O, and other poems   4131
O/I,   910
O mountaineers!   4965
O my generation, and other
   poems   4120

Reasons for the sky 1902
Reasons why I am not perfect 2357
Recent visitors 358
The reckless sleeper 1229
Reckless wedding 1504
Recollections of Gran Apacheria 1167
The record of a green planet 2360
Records of a chance meeting 211
Recoveries: a poem 4953
The red coal 4521
Red deer 69
The red dreams 1612
The red house 3537
Red leaves in the air 2888
Red lettuce 4
Red light with blue sky 303
Red Mountain, Agatha Christie & love 3108
Red pine, black ash 65
Red River blues 4793
Red wagon 383
The red, white, & blue bus 3031
The red white & blue poem 4142
Reeds 4028
Reflections 1042
Reflections of Samson 2816
Reflections on espionage: the question of cupcake 2148
Refractions 4388
Refusal to break 2804
Regardless of title 901
Reggae or not! 256
Regions with no proper names 78
Rejoicings; selected poems, 1966-1972 4519
Relativity 765
The re-learning 2221
Release the breathless 1722
Relics 2123
Remembering the movies 4769
Repairs 3349
Requiem 1883
Research 890
Reservations 3904
Resident alien 2098
Residue of song 315
Resort and other poems 1893
The rest 4118
Rest in love 3155

Resultances 3068
Resuming green: selected poems, 1965-1982 1503
The resurrection of the snails 3913
The resurrection on Friday night 4591
Retaining wall 4222
The retrieval system 2580
Return from the desert 3072
Return of the shaman 1523
Return; poems collected and new 110
Return to a place lit by a glass of milk 4303
Returning to Earth 1933
Returning to Oregon 1196
Returning to the body 5090
Returning what we owed 5143
Returning your call 3367
Reunion 157
A reunion 3095
Re-up 3708
Revenge 3037
The revisionist 955
Revolutionary at home 4137
Revolutionary petunias 4868
The rhymes and runes of the toad 4140
Rhymes of a jerk 1422
Ride the shadow 2717
Riding bike in the 'fifties 1191
Riding the dog 2251
Riding the Earthboy 40 4959
Riding to Greylock 4106
Riding with the fireworks! 1048
The rift zone 1857
Riggwords 2437
The right madness on Skye 2215
Ring of bone; collected poems 1950-1971 4960
Ring piece 2012
Ripening 1832
Rippling rhymes and fairy tales 1010
Rising and falling 3126
A risk of green 2703
Risky business 2136
Rite for the beautification of all beings 534
Rites of strangers 2273
Rituals and gargoyles 352
Rituals of our time 2021
Riven doggeries 4659

River 747
River dogs 2283
The river is always straight
   ahead 3852
The river menace 4502
The river painter 1792
River through Rivertown 1643
River-root 1410
Riverside 4337
Riversongs 125
Road ends at Tahola 2213
The road is everywhere or stop
   this body 4863
The road to Deadman Cove 166
Roadsalt 1197
The robber's cook 2115
Rock and chairs 2023
Rocks 3927
Rocky dies yellow 2611
Rocky Mountain man 3768
The Roman sonnets of G. G.
   Belli 3439
A romance 4925
The romantic muse 2821
Rome in Rome 2510
A roof with some clouds behind
   it 1271
Room for error 3090
A room full of walls 3195
Room rented by a single woman
   5139
Room to breathe 811
The room where summer ends
   883
Roosevelt tracks the last buffalo
   4439
Root, route & range 3356
Roots 4612
Rose, a color of darkness 2811
Rosebud 3054
A Roseliep retrospective 3989
Roses in lyric light 3194
The roses of Portland 1013
The rote walker 2277
Rotwang, or the delirious pre-
   cision of dreams 2088
Roughened roundnesses 3242
Round and round 4587
Rounding the horn 4349
Routes from the onion's dark
   2353
Routine risks 1835
Roving across fields 4475
Rowing across the dark 1181

Rubbing torsos 2638
Ruby for grief 647
Rue and grace 3798
Rufus 1426
The ruined motel 1619
The ruins of Providence 4859
A rumor of inhabitants 4347
Rumor verified 4897
Rumors of ecstasy, rumors of
   death 668
Runaway Pond 904
Runaways 987
The runner (Gildner) 1637
The runner (Hausman) 1960
Running 4994
Running around 1294
Running backwards 2142
Running in place 2774
Running lights 695
Running on empty 3701
Rural route 4381
Russell, the man, the teacher,
   the Indian 4051
Rust (Hilberry) 2084
Rust (Hogan) 2137
Rusty Jack 1738

'S 916
Sacco & Vanzetti: a narrative
   longpoem 1576
A sack full of old quarrels
   4924
The sacrifice 418
The sacrifice consenting 1123
Sacrifice, exile, and night 428
A sacrifice of dogs 4452
The sacrifice poems 2625
Sad advice 975
Sad days of light 235
Sad dust glories 1653
Sad-faced men 2842
Sadness and happiness 3722
Sadness at the private university
   28
Safe passage 3038
Safety 3942
Sail away, silvery moon 3017
Sailing bones 3985
Sailing too far 2456
Saint Venus Eve 1712
The St. Vlas Elegies 4529
The salamander migration and
   other poems 4902

Salt 1553
Salt air 622
The salt ecstasies 4981
Salt fever 3642
The salt lesson 1561
Sam Hamill's Triada 1881
The Samisdat poems of W. D.
  Ehrhart 1278
Sam's world 927
San Quentin's strangers 4887
Sandpainting 2259
The sandpipers; selected poems,
  1965-1975 3764
Santiago poems 4206
Santorini: stopping the leak
  3177
Sanza mezzo 4083
The Sargentville notebook 4565
Sarah Bernhardt's leg 2485
Sarah's gorilla 787
Satan says 3487
Saturday town 4686
A savaging of roots 1338
Sax's songs 875
Say it 1502
Saycred Laydy 4605
Saying things 4683
Sayings & doings 394
Scaling the walls 1753
Scarlet 634
Scars 3749
Scatter: selected poems 2257
Scattered brains 1739
Scattered on 3998
The scenery for a play & other
  poems 3868
Scenes from another life 2921
Scenes from a marriage 261
Scenes from a second adoles-
  cence 2831
SCENE/s in bk & wh 3643
The scent of apples 4906
Scissors, paper, rock 4375
A scoundrel breeze 4663
Scrap book 4208
Scrawny sonnets 220
Scripts for the pageant 3175
Scrut 3932
School for dark thoughts 4307
The science of goodbyes 4342
Sea air in a grave ground hog
  turns toward 3844
Sea lanes out 2217
Searching the drowned man 2691

Searching for someone 5135
Searching for the ox 4324
Seasonal rights 1873
Seasons 241
Seasons and seasoning 4921
Season's edge 2119
The seasons of Vermont 1336
Seaward 891
Second chance 4086
Second grace 3426
Second growth 2116
Second sight (Aaron) 3
Second sight (Jennings) 2291
Second thoughts 2636
Second wind 687
Secret history of the dividing
  line 2191
The secret lover 1315
Secretary to the spirits 3861
Section: the artemission 4650
See Rock City 3717
Seed leaves: homage to R. F.
  5015
Seed of milkweed, spun of steel
  182
Seeds 3507
Seeds & chairs 1874
Seeds to the wind 80
Seeing for you 77
Selected and collected poems
  2511
Selected and new poems (Berri-
  gan) 378
Selected and new poems (Dubie)
  1219
Selected & new poems (Harrison)
  1935
Selected and new poems (Miller)
  3236
The selected code poems 4938
Selected founds 3762
Selected longer poems 118
Selected poems (Anderson) 136
Selected poems (Creeley) 966
Selected poems (Crews) 981
Selected poems (Di Prima) 1142
Selected poems (Dorn) 1172
Selected poems (Ferrini) 1458
Selected poems (Hugo) 2214
Selected poems (Ignatow) 2230
Selected poems (Jong) 2339
Selected poems (Justice) 2367
Selected poems (Kinnell) 2482
Selected poems (Lowell) 2868,
  2870

Selected poems (MacLeod) 2999
Selected poems (Mayo) 3139
Selected poems (Nims) 3425
Selected poems (Owens) 3565
Selected poems (Rosten) 4008
Selected poems (Strand) 4569
Selected poems (Stryk) 4581
Selected poems (Watson) 4909
Selected poems (Welch) 4961
Selected poems (Wills) 5079
Selected poems and ballads 24
Selected poems in five sets
    3906
Selected poems, 1958-1980
    4421
The selected poems, 1951-1977
    115
Selected poems, 1970-1980 837
Selected poems, 1960-1975 3078
Selected poems, 1969-1981 4263
Selected poems 1923-1975 4894
The selected poems of Edwin
    Honig, 1955-1976 2167
The selected poems of Frank
    O'Hara 3481
The selected poems of Gwendolen
    Haste 1954
The selected poems of Howard
    McCord; 1955-1971 2947
Selected poems of Linda Pastan
    3606
Selected poems of May Sarton
    4122
Selected poetry 3042
Selected poetry of Amiri Baraka
    255
Selected shorter poems 5046
Selected shorter poems, 1950-
    1970 5048
The selection of heaven 436
Self-portrait in a convex mirror
    192
Self-portrait with hand micro-
    scope 1067
Semblances, 1962-1971 3783
A Seneca journal 4020
Sensing 3021
Sensually yours 643
Sentence 2432
Sentences 3392
A sentimental education 4552
Separate creatures 3531
Separations 1822
September blackberries 2935

September inventory 342
Sequence 1226
Serenade 4962
A serious morning 832
The serpent of the white rose
    4685
The serum of the water 3695
A set for Edwin Honig 2694
Set/sorts 124
Setting the table 3608
Settling down 4060
Seven dead fleas 2925
7 Mendocino songs 3968
7 on style 4889
Seven poems 1423
7 poems for Pilar Crespi 3050
Seven robins 1734
7 years from somewhere 2749
XVII machines 2043
17 Sonnets 3735
Seventh heaven 4379
76 Sexuality 2723
Severing the cause 510
Sex object 2525
A sexual tour of the Deep South
    1040
Shade 373
The shade-seller; new and sel-
    ected poems 2260
Shadow train 198
Shadows of remembered ances-
    tors 3238
Shagbark 3629
Shake a spear with me, John
    Berryman 2165
Shaker House poems 2784
Shaker light 3673
Shaker poems 2779
Shaman 4847
Shaman deer 5085
A shaman's songbook 3328
Shanghai Creek 3232
Shanghai Creek fire 3231
Shankum Naggum 5065
The shape of waters 4609
Shape, shadow, elements move
    1281
Shaping: new poems in traditional
    prosodies 2280
Shatterhouse 874
She; a sequence of poems 4000
She had some horses 1913
She said yes 181
She wears him fancy in her

night braid 2471
A sheath of dreams, and other
    games 3921
Sheltered at the edge 3790
Shemuel 3567
Sherds 3806
The shingle weaver's journal
    3882
Shinto suite 4637
The shit-storm poems 3092
Shoes 3454
Shooting a farmhouse 2537
Shooting at shadows, killing
    crows 3937
Shooting rats at the Bibb County
    dump 497
Shop posh 4728
The shoplifter's handbook 4202
The shore 4067
Short circuits 3347
A short guide to the high plains
    801
Short-lived phenomena 1573
Shoshoni River witching hour
    3694
Should anyone listen? 3193
Shoulder the sky 1256
Shouting at no one 2348
Showing my age 4336
Shrift, a winter sequence 4572
Shrine, shelter, cave 2898
Shrunken planets 2863
Sidetracks 2950
Signal-noise 1719
Signals from the safety coffin
    1333
Signatures 4579
Signs and wonders 1092
Signs of life 1627
Silence and metaphor 572
Silence as a method of birth
    control 2019
Silence, love, and kids I know
    4376
Silent partner 2815
Sileutia lunae 4532
Silhouettes of women 4238
Silks 4433
The silver swan 3879
A simple progression 3272
Simple truths 4632
Since 1964; new and selected
    poems 4158
Singing arrows 3240

Singing happy sad 2757
The singing knives 4483
The singing man my father gave
    me 3357
Sings 1624
The sinister pinafore 44
Sister to the sun 421
Sister Vayda's song 2956
Sisters and other selves 2942
Sit in: what is it like 3872
Sitio 1340
The sitting duck 4435
Sitting here 960
Sitting in our tree house waiting
    for the apocalypse 4668
Sitting up, standing, taking steps
    4296
Six 3163
Six buildings 3441
Six Dutch hearts 1891
Six elegies 2349
Six hundred acres 1128
Six minnesinger songs 4397
Six poems (Palmer) 3582
Six poems (Towner) 4703
Six troubadour songs 4395
Six-piece suite 117
Sixteen odes 2426
Sixteen poems and a story 2044
Sixteen poems of V.S. 4223
Size queen and other poems 2420
Skin deep 2990
Skin of doubt 1791
Skins on the earth 4068
Skull of Adam 3335
Sky heart 1313
Sky hourse 531
Sky in my legs 3987
Sky sea birds trees earth house
    beasts flowers 3876
The sleeping beauty 720
Sleeping in Damascus 4231
Sleeping in the woods 4811
Sleeping obsessions 478
Sleeping on doors 3530
Sleeping on fists 3916
Sleeping over 4216
The sleeping porch 680
Sleeping with an elephant 201
Sliding down the wind 214
Slow juggling 565
Slow train to Cincinnati 457
Slow transparency 1829
Slowly, out of stones 5222

Small bones, little eyes 3445
Small change 3235
The small emptiness in our bodies 3665
Small mercies 4918
A small quirk in the fuselage 2029
Small song 3205
Smile 1766
Smoke the burning body makes 4176
Smoke's way: poems from limited editions, 1968-1981 4476
The smuggler's handbook 1706
Snake blossoms 312
Snake in the strawberries 1990
Snake's tooth 4316
Snapshots from Europe 3309
Snoring in New York 1088
Snout to snout 2383
Snow 2326
Snow country 1995
The snow falls upward 3396
The snow hen 2060
Snow on snow 4488
The snow poems 116
The snow prince 5110
The snow queen 2247
Snow quiet 2370
A snow salmon reached the Andes lake 274
The snowcat poems 3646
So 919
So far 909
So going around in circles; new and selected poems, 1958-1979 387
So this is the map 4108
Soft light falling quickly 5186
Soft lightenings 826
Soft rock 408
Soft where, inc. 3070
Soie sauvage 595
The solera poems 650
Soli 1131
Solitary confinement 4006
Solstice (Di Piero) 1136
Solstice (Sanders) 4096
Solstice (Payack) 3619
Solstice II 3620
Solstice III 3624
Solstice blossom 2936
Somapoetics 3793
Some early poems 3497

Some lamb 3894
Some madonna poems 2785
Some nerve 2708
Some of my best friends are trees 4809
Some one sweet angel chile 5074
Some particulars 790
Some pastorals 1348
Some psalms 3993
Some recent fiction 5176
Some recent snowflakes (and other things) 2082
Some special times 4005
Some trees 196
Some want for saving 2675
Somebody talks a lot 2171
Someday, maybe 4461
Someone else to love 4175
Something further 1429
Something more than force: poems for Guatemala, 1971-1982 161
Something tugging on the line 2288
Sometimes (Cornish) 925
Sometimes (Yau) 5173
Sometimes a poet will hijack the moon 4822
Sometimes I think of Maryland 543
Sometimes like a legend 4473
Somewhere is such a kingdom 2089
Son dream/daughter dream 2052
Song 4179
A song, a chant 354
Song cycle 661
Song for Anninho 2330
Song in a strange land 2411
Song made out of pale smoke 3871
Song of the blood 4372
Song of the godbody 589
Song, poetry, language 3543
Songs 1742
Songs for Gaia 4403
Songs for the harvester of dreams 3412
Songs for the unborn second baby 3451
Songs from ragged streets 623
Songs of bloody Harlan 3638
Songs of freedom 3863

Songs of ourselves 1746
Songs of the gypsy women 2287
Songs of the pine-wife 3415
Songs to a handsome woman 597
The sonnets 388
Sonnets for an analyst 4159
Sonnets for women 4500
Sonnets from the interior life
     and other autobiographical
     verse 500
Sonnets in a new form 3112
Sonnets (memento mori) 154
Soon it will be morning 2135
Soothsayers and omens 5163
Sorting it out 3659
Sorting metaphors 3615
Soul claiming 74
A sound of one hand 2973
Sounds of the River Naranjana &
     The tablets I-XXIV 4199
Sounds of silence 4453
Soundscape with humans 3651
The South Dakota guidebook 295
South moccasin 935
The Southern Cross 5151
The space I occupy 2332
The space my body fills 455
Space of 2267
The space of half an hour 4860
Spacks Street: new & selected
     poems 4431
The spade in the sensorium 129
Spare poems 4985
Sparks from your hoofs 2508
Speaking in sign 143
Speaking poems 3114
Spearmint & rosemary 3496
Special effects 1984
Species of intoxication 1672
Spectral emanations 2150
The spell of Hungry Wolf 746
Spellbound, and other poems
     3346
Spells & blessing 569
Spelunking & other poems 560
Spend sad Sundays singing songs
     to sassy sisters 1568
Spending Christmas with the man
     from receiving at Sears 4834
Sphere: the form of a motion
     112
Spik in glyph? 109
Spiked flower 1695
Spirals 2959

Spirit beast chant 4076
Spirit hand 4522
Spirit run 230
Spiritual exercises 2434
Spiritual rodeo 3039
Splendite-Hotel 4417
Splinters of bone 323
Splinters of the light 205
Split ends 2988
Splurge 4801
The spoils of August 1750
Spoken in sleep 903
A spool of blue 4545
Spoon River on campus 3627
Spring clay 2302
Spring of violets 3640
Spy Wednesday's kind 4598
The stain of circumstances;
     selected poems 1547
Stained glass 3251
Stamping ground 3910
The stance 573
Standard-4 3508
Standing on my head 3102
Standing watch 658
Star child 85
Starless & Bible black 2622
Stars 1906
Stars in my eyes 1465
Stars which see, stars which
     do not see 316
Starting from bloodroot 3867
Starting from Troy 1828
Starting with coquille 1498
State lounge 371
Statues of the grass 177
Staves 3416
Staves calends legends 3201
Stealing the children 5142
Steeplejacks in Babel 727
Step carefully in night grass
     278
Step on the rain 3980
Stepping outside 1582
Steps to break the circle 3742
Stereoscopic 2994
The stick; poems 1969-73 4485
Stickball on 88th Street 273
Sticks and stones 3124
Stigma 376
Stiletto 171
Still another pelican in the bread-
     box 3612
Still at the edge 2889

Still life (Bailey) 223
Still life (Bennett) 337
The still point 3988
Still-life and other poems 3721
Stills 2731
Stinking and full of eels 2799
Stone 4735
Stone Mountain escape 2141
Stone, paper, knife 3716
Stone roses 5088
Stone run: tidings 1780
Stone soup 2030
Stone-Crazy 4524
Stones (Aldan) 60
Stones (Zimmerman) 5214
The stop book 4275
The stories in the light 4908
Stories that could be true 4467
The story of our lives 4566
The story they told us of light
    2333
Stoutes Creek Road 3688
Straight poems 1557
A strange affinity 335
The strange animal 325
Strange coast 1404
Strange days ahead 607
Strange family 3912
Strange meat; poems, 1968-1974
    492
Strangers (Etter) 1395
Strangers (Ferry) 1460
Straws of sanity 5092
Stray prayers 3702
Stream 2027
Street feet 4786
Street fire 1871
Street pieces 4787
Streets 926
Streets after rain 2501
Streets of San Miguel 5086
The strength of fields 1114
Stretching fence 1162
Stretching the agape bra 10
Striations 1110
Strictly personal 476
Striking the air for music 3964
Striking the earth 5127
String 4161
Struggle for the dawn 426
The students of snow 1496
Studies for an actress 1602
Studying the ground for holes
    145

Studying hunger 3136
Stumbling 2861
Subject to change 3751
Subpoemas 610
Substituting memories 1845
Succession 4608
Sudden around the bend 4112
Sudden Ripples 2993
Suddenly it gets light and dark
    in the street: poems 1961-
    74 1287
Suggestions from the border
    2304
A suitable church 2071
Suite 793
The summer anniversaries 2369
Summer celestial 3741
Summer morn ... winter weather
    1647
A summer of the heart 2161
Summer sleeper 381
Summerbook 2258
The summit of sun & poems that
    dream peace 2310
Summits move with the tide 403
Summoned 3483
The sun and the moon 2157
Sun exercises 604
The sun fetcher 605
The sun in cancer 2177
Sun in his belly 3981
The sun on your shoulder 1840
Sun the blond out 4845
Sunbelly 1468
Sunday 2883
The Sunday naturalist 4405
The sunflower 1014
Sunlight and shadows 4777
Sunlight on the wall 3202
Sunrise (Seidel) 4219
Sunrise (Tarachow) 4642
Sunshine days and foggy nights
    2401
Sunspots 978
Superbounce 45
Sure, really I is surrealist
    poems 2300
Sure signs 2540
The surgeon general's collection
    2010
Surprised by others at Fort Cronk-
    hite 5108
Surreal songs 2354
Survival Kit 4346

Survival song 4302
Susanna Martin 415
Suspended sentences 4163
Swallowing dust 4560
The swamp fox 1341
Swampfire 420
Swan research 732
The swastika poems 2049
Swath 3653
Sweet ass'd angels, pilgrims &
  boogie woogies 4344
Sweet dreams 2457
Sweet Gwendolyn and the coun-
  tess 1466
Sweet tomorrow 2670
Sweethearts 3699
Sweets for the dancing bears
  2860
Swerving straight: poems, sel-
  ected & new 2324
Swiftly now 4544
A swim off the rocks 3333
Swish of cow tail 3990
Sympathetic magic 456
Synthesis 1-24 1350

A table with people 2386
Tables of the meridian 4944
The tablets, xvi-xviii 4194
Taffeta and lace 4969
Tailings 1357
Take it with you 5184
Take me like a photograph
  4904
Take one blood red rose 854
Taking chances, taking chances,
  taking chances 724
Taking notice 1823
Taking on the local color 1606
Taking possession 91
Taking up the serpent 640
The tale of sunlight 4423
The tale of the amazing tramp
  3785
A tale whose time has come
  4291
Tales of crazy John: or, beating
  Brautigan at his own game
  5093
Tales of virtue and transforma-
  tion 1813
Tales told of the fathers 2147
Talfulano 3826

Talkin' B.A. blues 4491
Talking at the boundaries 168
Talking cure: poems 5202
Talks & selected poems 3529
The tall poets 4392
Tamsen Donner 4996
The tangerine birds 849
Taos Pueblo 3408
Tap dancing on a tightrope 3040
Tapestry, a finespun grace &
  mercy 432
Tar 5045
Tarantulas on the lifebuoy 2884
The tarot of Cornelius Agrippa
  3298
Tarot poems 2541
The taste of rope 430
A taste of the knife 4882
Taxidermy lessons 3041
Tea 4729
Teach me, dear sister 1440
Teaching the penguins to fly
  4429
Teachings 1479
The teachings of Grandfather Fox
  3368
Teak 3864
Tear Down the walls 3398
The tears of Edmund Burke 2422
Tell it like it is 384
Tell me how willing slaves be
  52
Telling it 4599
Temper 3461
The temperate voluptuaries 3182
The temple 1875
The temple in Nimes 5160
Ten poems 1183
10,000 corpses 2556
10,000 rpm and diggin it, yeah!
  4888
The ten thousandth night 1985
Ten years after 3051
The tenderness of the wolves
  893
Tendril in the mesh 1407
Tens; selected poems 1961-1971
  3159
Terminal placebos 411
Terra Incognita 4230
Terrorism 5140
The testament of Israel Potter
  1160
Testimony: The United States
  (1885-1915) 3891

Texas liveoak 1513
The text's boyfriend 1483
Thank a bored angel: selected poems 1983
Thank you call again 3210
Thantog 5083
That back road in 535
That beauty still 578
That certain x 3538
That crow that visited was flying backwards 532
That Dada strain 4026
That house in Venice 4710
That other alone 4462
That Salome she sure cd dance 2557
Thaw 3778
Thawing out 2281
Theatre 1011
Theme & variations (Alta) 104
Themes & variations (Cage) 678
Theories of rain and other poems 5198
There is a country 842
There is no balm in Birmingham 1072
There is singing around me 397
There's nothing I wouldn't do if you would be my POSSLQ 3549
These green-going-to-yellow 317
These people 4192
These rooms 357
Thieves' afternoon 4590
A thin volume of hate 499
The thing king 1255
Things I do in the dark 2343
Things I meant to say to you when we were old 3059
Things stirring together or far away 1285
Things that happen where there aren't any people 4472
Thinking of offerings: poems 2505
Thinking of you 5136
Thirsty day 41
13 poems 2686
Thirteen ways of deranging an angel 2461
Thirteen ways of looking at a Model A 1193
35 [Thirty-five] 796
35 Sundays 2792

31 letters and 13 dreams 2212
36th light poem; in memoriam Buster Keaton 3002
Thirty things 961
33 [Thirty-three] 1500
Thirty years of poetry, 1949-1979 2298
Thirty years on the force 5128
This attic where the meadow greens 513
This Bag 1098
This body is made of camphor and gopherwood 463
This breast gothic 2565
This day's madness 4218
This earth is a drum 617
This eating and walking 4134
This gathering season 3283
This journey 5161
This once; new and selected poems, 1965-1978 1664
This paradox shadow 3315
This practice; tablet XIX and other poems 4195
This slave dreads her work as if she were a lamb commanded to be a musician 4995
This stubborn quantum 2239
This tree will be here for a thousand years 464
This will kill that 3058
Thoreau stalks the land disguised as a father 4647
Thor's home 3386
Those who ride the night winds 1661
Though silence: the Ling Wei texts 2196
A thought is the bride of what thinking 2003
Thoughtful roads 666
The thoughts of giants 4204
A thousand little things, and other poems 1216
Thread 189
A threat to Genesis, and other poems 5113
Threats instead of trees 4057
Three 4932
Three & one 3510
Three halves are whole 2920
3 light poems for 3 women 3003
Three memorial poems 399
Three musicians 4704

THREE

Three poems (Kinnell) 2478
Three poems (Merwin) 3186
Three songs for my father 2179
Three Zen poems, after Shinkichi
    Takahashi 4582
Threshold 2545
The threshold of the year 2483
Thrice chosen 3951
Throne falcon eye: poems 4221
Thrones and dominions 3776
Through a coal cellar darkly 4547
Through the eyes of man 665
Throwing spitballs at the nuns
    2725
Thumbprint 4916
Tickets for a prayer wheel 1125
Tidewater salt & other poems
    1368
Tiger lilies 1064
Tight corners and what's around
    them 570
Tight lines 3084
Tightening the circle over eel
    country 3920
The tightrope walker 3840
Tilamook Burn 1198
Time 2695
Time and other birds 4284
Time and trouble 4789
Time, details of a tree 1296
Time of the king and queen 4144
Time payment 4697
Time to close the cottage 3323
Time to destroy/to discover
    1492
A time to mend 3104
Time, pieces 190
Time, wait 2372
The times between 3787
Timespace Huracan 107
Timing devices 3079
Tiny fingers 4191
Title 1546
Tjanting 4298
To a blossoming pear tree 5159
To a dark moon 3473
To a student dying young 4426
To a young poet 4848
To all appearances 3212
To be a pilgrim 4554
To be of use 3711
To burn California 1886
To catch the sun 786
To creature 1640

To frighten a storm 690
To go on 4378
To her hand 4927
To keep the blood from drown-
    ing 1494
To keep the house from falling
    in 1021
To know we are living 2742
To leave the standing grain 929
To lesbians everywhere 1759
To open 3166
To other beings 1730
To Paris 1982
To read to read: new & selected
    poems 710
To the far side of somewhere
    3862
To the man reporter from the
    Denver Post 4903
To the waters and the wild 3414
To touch the water 1280
To Utah 1939
To what listens 395
Toad's Europe 2834
Toccata of the disturbed child
    4575
Today we are brother and sis-
    ter 38
Toddler 4322
Tokyo annex 297
The Tokyo-Montana express
    539
Told by the weather 4667
Tollbridge 2955
Tolle lege 880
Tongue and thunder 825
Tongues 4999
Tonight is the night of the poem
    2275
Too bright to see 1772
The torches 4658
Tornado watch 1788
The tortured stem 1518
Tossing and turning 4749
Totemic 239
The touch code 2865
Touch earth 1581
Touch me if you love me 4623
Touch of the marvelous 2615
The touched life 3851
Touching 2476
Toujours l'amour 3574
Toward new weather 3929
Toward spring bank 289

Toward sunset, at a great height 3249
Toward the liberation of the left hand 134
Town and country matters 2145
The town at dusk: poems 2327
The town of Hill 1851
The town scold 4269
Track made good 3831
Tracking (Steele) 4495
Tracking (Terris) 4669
Tracks 3046
The tracks run together 2531
Trader 3143
The trail beside the River Platte 2033
The trail that turns on itself 1691
Trailing the raven 4589
Trails through the Northwoods 3374
Train ride 386
Train windows 1401
Trained bears on hoops 4558
The trains 2065
The tramp's cup 3849
The transcripts 4505
Transfiguration 2929
The transformation poems: January to March, 1981 2841
Transitions 4128
Translation of light 2219
Translations of the Gospel back into tongues 5141
Transmigration solo 736
Transmuting gold 9
Transparencies 4271
Transplants (Macdonald) 2957
Transplants (Pagoulatou) 3577
The Trans-Siberian railway 4778
The trash dragon of Shensi 1675
The trashing of America 3746
The traveler who repeats his cry 468
The traveler's tree 4389
Traveling 2475
Traveling in the castle 3795
Traveling light 4700
Traveling mind 2400
A traveller's alphabet 841
Travelling light 4814
The travels of Ben Sira 3387
Travis and other poems of the Swannanoa Valley 4976

Tread the dark 2232
A tree grown straight 983
The tree of bones and other poems 3252
Tree taking root 5035
The tree witch 4782
The trench 2045
Trespassing stoplights and attitudes 2971
Trial impressions 3117
The triangle fire 1442
Triangles in the afternoon 3576
The trick 4561
A trick of resilience 1507
Trickster tabs 1757
Trilogy: Coins & coffins; Discrepancies and apparitions; The George Washington poems 4826
Trinity 4368
Trip out and fall back 2599
Triumph of the will 4196
Trolling 2678
Trompe l'ame 221
Trophies 4836
Tropicalism 1324
Tropicalization 992
Tropicana 4915
Troublante 1876
Truck/9:15 1641
Truckstop dance 1522
Trunk & thicket 3302
Trying to leave 4633
Trying to surprise God 3153
Tryptych 1037
Tsalagi 188
Tu 921
Tucky the hunter 1113
Tuft by puff 4469
Tulsa kid 3575
Tumacacori 5021
Tunes for bears to dance to 4878
Tuning 224
Turfs, fields, pitches, arenas 2552
The Turler losses 1806
Turn 4756
Turn again to me, and other poems 26
Turner 827
Turning inward, reaching out 4377
Turning out the stones 1938

The turning point 4646
Turning the wood 3134
Turns 3129
Turtle Island 4401
TV poems 639
Twelve losses found 577
Twelve moon 3493
12 photographs of Yellowstone
  2523a
Twelve poems for Cezanne's black
  clock 2628
The twelve-spoked wheel flashing
  3713
Twenty love poems 3551
Twenty poems 2535
24 [Twenty-four] 4987
Twenty-one love poems 3899
21 matched asymmetries 3005
20,000 A.D. 4095
22 [Twenty-two] 3052
Twist of lemon 3905
Two 2462
Two about music 4470
Two bodies dark/velvet 2756
2x2 4770
Two citizens 5155
Two continents 1678
Two for the seesaw/One for the
  road 2830
Two hundred push-ups at the
  YMCA 3033
Two owls 2681
Two poems 2480
Two summer sequences 2828
Two views of pears 1050
Two-headed woman 815
Two-part inventions 2183
Tycoon boy 1799

UHFO 1485
The ugliest woman in the world
  and other histories 4625
Uintah blue 1878
The ultimate dare 2335
The ultimate double play 5192
Uncertain the final run to win-
  ter 2493
Uncertain health 1555
Uncertainties and rest 4497
Uncle time 4200
The uncorrected world 1903
Under cover 1697

Under many a star 3146
Under red skies 1810
Under sealed orders 3680
Under stars 1586
Under the fortune palms 803
Under the weight of the sky 3938
Under words 2435
The unexpected 353
Unexpected manna 2162
Unfinished poems 1039
Unfree associations 908
Unhooked 951
The unicorn captured 2313
The unicorn's choice 1890
An unknown woman: a journey
  to self-discovery 2530
Unless 915
Untinears & antennae for Maur-
  ice Ravel 5062
Up in bed 1554
Up my coast 2602
Up north 4810
Upstate Madonna 2782
US 651
Us: women 1499
Use no hooks 1765
Uses 4930
Uses and other selected poems
  4936
Utopia TV store 763

Vacancies 2543
A valentine for Noel 5047
The valley of minor animals
  5129
Valley of the anointers 759
Vanish 2074
Vanishing species 4596
The vanishings 1735
Vari-ari-ations 3217
Variations on a theme 1603
Variety is 1731
The various light 924
Various poems 3265
Varmit Q 473
The veil poem 990
The Venetian vespers 1992
Venice in the fog 4390
The Venice poem 1234
The ventriloquist 2205
The ventriloquist 2204
The veritable years: poems
  1949-1966 1416

The Vermont notebook 193
The Vermont suicides 4943
Verses for the zodiac 61
Very close and very slow 2008
Vessels 4189
Vestiges 1863
Vibes of the saints 1790
Victoria Mundi 1515
Video ranger 1789
Vienna blood & other poems
  4024
A view from the ark 4920
View from Mount Paugus, and
  other poems 804
Views & spectacles 4952
The village and other poems
  2296
Village journal 2594
Violence 429
Viper jazz 4657
Virtuoso literature for two and
  four hands 4830
A vision of the chariot in heaven
  4019
Visions of the fathers of Lascaux
  1391
A visit from St. Alphabet 3311
A visit from St. Nicholas (to a
  liberated household) 4802
Visiting rites 2274
Visitor 2758
Vital provisions 3782
Vital signs; new and selected
  poems 4348
Vivaldi in early fall 1335
Vivisection 1519
Vivisections 4289
A voice in the mountain 1062
Voice of the beech oracle: a
  shaman song 2244
Voices from beyond the wall
  2972
Voices from the forest 3341
Voo doo/love magic 2253
Vowels 151
The voyage 5049
The voyeur of our time 4185
A vulgar elegance 1306

W. Tungsten 4241
The wacking of the fruit trees
  1589

Waiting for my life 3609
Waiting for the King of Spain
  4833
Waiting for water 1235
Waiting in the bone and other
  poems 4454
Waiting out the rain 3686
Waiting to be fed 5190
Waiting to disappear 697
Wake to the bell 3982
Wakefulness 3870
The wakers in the tongue 2245
Waking 952
Waking at the bottom of the
  dark 808
Waking to my name 3570
Walk easy on the earth 2403
Walk in love 3983
Walking along the Missouri River
  2987
Walking away 945
Walking four ways in the wind
  89
Walking home dead 1241
Walking home from the icehouse
  4056
Walking on Dante 2153
Walking out 34
Walking the boundaries: poems,
  1957-1974 1061
Walking with Deirdre 4207
Wall writing 207
Wallflowers and wayfarers 3100
Waltzing Matilda 3453
Wanderer's daysong 2737
Wandering on the outside 66
The wandering tattler 4827
War cry on a prayer feather
  5123
War story, Vietnam War poems
  2910
Warm rooms and cold 1816
Warm spell 4265
Warm-blooded animals 1490
Warm-bloods, cold-bloods 1084
Warmed by love 3423
Watch for the fox 3250
Watching how or why 1289
Water 2760
Water and stone 4803
Water astonishing 4594
Water before and water after
  4109

The water circle 586
Water colors 757
The water in the pearl 950
The water inside the water 3267
Water tables 4214
The Watergate elegy 1036
Watering places 3083
Watermark 769
Waters, places, a time 1299
The waters reborn 762
Waterweed 3179
Waterworks 4799
Waves 4644
Waves & license 484
Waving arms at the blind 3829
Wax lips 3427
The way all rivers run 1058
The way it happens to you 481
A way through for the damned 2246
Ways of light 1260
We 3824
We are all children searching for love 3422
We are love 4730
We come around the years 131
We do what we can 1599
We drive through Tyndall's theory of sight 3353
We have lost our fathers 3914
We shall curse the dead 829
We will wear white roses 1154
Weather 2474
The weather book 2395
Weather forecast for utopia and vicinity 4311
Weather-fear: new and selected poems, 1958-1982 1337
Weathering (Ackerson) 20
Weathering (Smith) 4386
The wedding at Touisset 3362
The weed garden 4718
The week the dirigible came 3147
Weighing the penalties 559
The weird kid 4796
Welcome, brothers: poems of a changing man's consciousness 4507
Welcome to the medicine show 1600
We'll come when it rains 3388

We'll see who's a peasant 1758
Well water and daisies 4807
Well, you needn't 1396
The Wellfleet whale and companion poems 2585
The wellsprings; poems, 1975-1980 2766
The werewolf sequence 3996
West Battery 4369
West of Chicago 1399
West of New England 1056
West of the American dream; poems to be read aloud 785
The Western approaches 3390
The western borders 2190
The whale in the web 3478
Whaler frigate clippership 2423
Whales 2092
The whale's scars 4611
What are birds worth 4942
What color are your eyes? 756
What Dillinger meant to me 3677
What friends are for 2590
What happened when the Hopi hit New York 3975
What happens next 2241
What I don't know for sure 1086
What I own 4514
What I want 1548
What manner of beast: poems 1473
What moon drove me to this 1912
What she means 1385
What the bird sees 3286
What the diamond does is hold it all in 1961
What the fox agreed to do 465
What the trees go into 4427
What the wind forgets 2227
What the worms ignore, the birds are wild about 2
What thou lovest well, remains American 2210
What use are moose? 1432
What we women know 3133
What you know with no name for it 5
Whatever happens 2718
What's for dinner? 4181
Wheat among bones 276
The wheel 401
Wheels of light 3048

When all the wild summer 1108
When elephants last in the door-
yard bloomed 512
When I know the power of my
Black hand 2284
When I walk I change the earth
2567
When sky lets go 1079
When the creature is silent
2391
When they have senses 4866
When things get tough on easy
street; selected poems 1963-
1978 798
Where sparrows work hard
4425
Where the warm wind blows
2995
While dancing feet shatter the
earth 5087
Whiplash on the couch 329
Whisper 1403
Whisper to the earth 2235
Whispering leaves 2713
Whispering to fool the wind
3917
White: a new version 4309
White Center 2216
White corn sister 454
The white coverlet 1867
White flowers in the snow 1943
The white line 3623
White monkeys 3812
White noise 283a
White River poems 4515
White sail 4419
White screen 328
White smoke 2026
White spaces 209
The white words 5131
Whiteboy 3895
Whitlathe walrus 3406
Who are we now? 1451
Who gathered and whispered
behind me 1707
Who I am 2727
Who is Little Enis? 5053
Who knows some of this might be
real 2873
Who shall be the sun? 4816
Who will love me in my madness?
2405
Whole hog 4815

(W)holes 2958
Who's listening out there 169
Who's that pushy bitch? 1923
Why did I laugh tonight? 291
Why God permits evil 5068
Why I cannot take a lover 731
Why I live in the forest 3428
Why shouldn't I 2195
The Wichita poems 4771
The Wichita poems 4772
Wide-ons 775
The widow's taboo; poems after
Catawba 3770
Wife of light 18
Wild angels 2707
Wild craft 3731
Wild Indians 2097
Wild night irises 3233
The wild olive tree 3203
Wild onions 2878
A wild patience has taken me
this far; poems, 1978-1981
3902
The wild piano 2704
The wild white rose 64
Wild-craft 3730
Wilderness 5032
A wilderness of monkeys 1957
Wildflower, poems for Joy 3639
The wind is rising 4964
Wind over ashes: selected poems
3825
Wind songs 5193
Windfall losses 4858
The window 562
Windowpane 350
Windows and mirrors 3284
Windowsills 3204
Windrose: poems, 1929-1979
1617
Winds of imagination 243
Windy place 441
Wines & roses 5100
Winesburg by the sea 5109
Winter constellations 450
Winter contracts 494
Winter count 3066
Winter dreams 947
Winter has lasted too long 2402
Winter in the rex 1319
Winter journey 2308
Winter man 2982
Winter morning in Charlottes-
ville 1952

Winter news (rev. ed.) 1844
Winter of the fortune teller 2459
Winter of the salamander: the
 keeper of importance 5191
Winter Oysters 1595
The winter rooms 3869
Winter sequences 4823
Winter tunes 3736
Winter weeds 2218
Wintering 2680
Wintering with the abominable
 snowman 2629
Winters without snow 2967
Wit or without 3915
Witch-hazel 4501
With Akhmatova at the black
 gates 349
With ignorance 5043
With light reflected 1342
With no answer 3246
With our hands 3822
With sincerest regrets 1274
With Wanda; town and country
 poems 5206, 5210
Within the rose 4804
Without music 3584
Without roof 1607
Without wishing 3364
Witness (Beausoleil) 302
Witness (Heyen) 2053
Witnessing 3045
Wits end 55
Wit's end 1145
The wolf last seen 3797
Wolf Moon 3632
Wolf stone, wolf stone, and
 other poems 3378
Woman and nature 1784
Woman before an aquarium 1892
A woman from Memphis 4116
Woman in search of herself 5211
The woman on the bridge over the
 Chicago River 1796
The woman poems 3521
A woman under the surface
 3554
The woman who could read the
 minds of dogs 4132
The woman who saw through
 paradise 1379
Women and children first 1071
Women & horses 1059
The women and the men 1659

Women chopping 489
The women in the mirror 707
Women of the revolution 4215
The women poem 3883
Women talk 4027
Women, the children, the men
 3200
The women who hate me 88
Women whose lives are food,
 men whose lives are money
 3469
The women's house 4549
The wonderful focus of you 2601
Wonders 4399
The wood path 3934
Woodworking and places near by
 949
Wordings like love 3314
Wordrows 1964
Words on paper 691
Words touching ground under
 1282
Work & love 1239
Work, for the night is coming
 723
Work lights 5180
The work of a common woman
 1736
Work songs 4165
The work, the joy, and the
 triumph of the will 4198
Working against time 2963
Works 332
Workweek 566
The world & its streets, places
 1290
The world does not belong to old
 ladies 1480
The world has a familiar face
 1591
A world of difference 2979
The world was a bubble 1462
Worldly hopes 120
Wrecked hearts 11
Wrecks and other poems 3261
The wrestlers & other poems
 3503
Wright: a profile 5149
Writings to an unfinished ac-
 companiment 3184
Wry wine 4966

Yankee shoes 2573
Yannina 3170
Yarbrough Mountain 2542
The year of our birth 3020
Year of the fires 3456
Year of the hare poems 2880
The yearnings 3196
Years that answer 141
Yellow dog journal 3255
Yellow flowers 5168
Yellow for peril, black for
beautiful 728
Yellow light 2163
Yellow Lola 1175
The yellow pages; 59 poems
3171
Yellow pears, smooth as silk
2160
Yellow squash woman 3067
Yellow stars and ice 4533
Yerba buena 1393
Yet 912
Yo Yo poems 1526
You 4484

You and me against the world
5072
You are this nation 3434
You bet! 1763
You can't have everything 4260
You don't love magic 2254
You keep waiting for geese 4963
You know me 3954
You; poems 1957-67 4486
Young dogs in the moonlight
4873
Young lust & others 2263
Younger anger 2724
Your father 4928
Your name is you 1574

ZZ 1323
Zenryu and other works, 1974
3729
The Zimmer poems 5205
The zodiac 1111
Zuleika's book 536
Zuni Butte 5028